# The Law Commission
(LAW COM No 327)

This it
You n

# MAKING LAND WORK: EASEMENTS, COVENANTS AND PROFITS À PRENDRE

*Presented to Parliament pursuant to section 3(2) of the Law Commissions Act 1965*

Ordered by the House of Commons to be printed on 7 June 2011

HC 1067          London: The Stationery Office          £37.00

Any enquiries regarding this publication should be sent to us at The Law Commission, Steel House, 11 Tothill Street, London SW1H 9LJ.

This publication is also available on www.official-documents.gov.uk

ISBN: 9780102972504

Printed in the UK for The Stationery Office Limited
on behalf of the Controller of Her Majesty's Stationery Office

ID 2434185                    06/11

Printed on paper containing 75% recycled fibre content minimum.

# THE LAW COMMISSION

The Law Commission was set up by the Law Commissions Act 1965 for the purpose of promoting the reform of the law.

The Law Commissioners are:

> The Right Honourable Lord Justice Munby, *Chairman*
> Professor Elizabeth Cooke
> Mr David Hertzell
> Professor David Ormerod
> Miss Frances Patterson QC

The Chief Executive of the Law Commission is Mr Mark Ormerod CB.

The Law Commission is located at Steel House, 11 Tothill Street, London SW1H 9LJ.

The terms of this report were agreed on 20 May 2011.

**The text of this report is available on the Easements project page of the Law Commission's website at www.lawcom.gov.uk.**

# MAKING LAND WORK: EASEMENTS, COVENANTS AND PROFITS À PRENDRE

## CONTENTS

|  | Paragraph | Page |
|---|---|---|
| **PART 1: EASEMENTS, COVENANTS AND PROFITS À PRENDRE: INTRODUCTION** |  | **1** |
| The scope and impact of the project | 1.1 | 1 |
| The background to the project | 1.6 | 2 |
| A summary of this Report and of our recommendations | 1.13 | 4 |
| Impact Assessment | 1.26 | 7 |
| Human rights | 1.32 | 8 |
| Acknowledgements | 1.34 | 8 |
| **PART 2: ESTATES AND INTERESTS IN LAND: THE CURRENT LAW** |  | **9** |
| Introduction | 2.1 | 9 |
| The foundations of land law | 2.3 | 9 |
| Estates and interests in land | 2.3 | 9 |
| Legal and equitable rights | 2.6 | 10 |
| The modern structure of legal and equitable estates and interests | 2.10 | 11 |
| Easements, covenants and profits à prendre | 2.16 | 13 |
| Easements | 2.18 | 13 |
| Profits | 2.31 | 17 |
| Covenants | 2.37 | 18 |
| Estate rentcharges | 2.44 | 20 |
| The creation and registration of easements, profits and covenants | 2.50 | 21 |
| Title registration | 2.55 | 22 |
| Land Charges registration | 2.64 | 24 |
| The extinguishment of easements, profits and covenants | 2.65 | 24 |

|  | Paragraph | Page |
|---|---|---|
| Conclusion | 2.72 | 26 |
| **PART 3: REFORM OF THE LAW OF EASEMENTS AND PROFITS** |  | **27** |
| Introduction | 3.1 | 27 |
| (1) The creation of profits | 3.3 | 27 |
| (2) The implication of easements | 3.11 | 29 |
| The current law | 3.11 | 29 |
| Codification or reform? | 3.25 | 32 |
| Implied grant and implied reservation | 3.28 | 32 |
| The options for reform | 3.31 | 33 |
| (3) Section 62 of the Law of Property Act 1925 | 3.52 | 37 |
| The current law | 3.52 | 37 |
| Reform of section 62 of the Law of Property Act 1925 | 3.59 | 39 |
| (4) The acquisition of easements by prescription | 3.71 | 41 |
| Introduction | 3.71 | 41 |
| Abolition? | 3.74 | 42 |
| The current law | 3.86 | 44 |
| Conclusions on the current law | 3.110 | 50 |
| A new statutory scheme for prescription | 3.115 | 51 |
| Prescription and the Crown | 3.175 | 63 |
| Transitional provisions | 3.179 | 63 |
| (5) Easements that confer the right to extensive use | 3.188 | 64 |
| The legal principles | 3.188 | 64 |
| Extensive or exclusive use | 3.199 | 67 |
| Reform | 3.205 | 69 |
| (6) The extinguishment of easements and profits by abandonment | 3.212 | 70 |
| The current law | 3.212 | 70 |
| The proposals in the Consultation Paper | 3.220 | 72 |

| | Paragraph | Page |
|---|---|---|
| (7) The termination of the estate to which an interest is appurtenant | 3.232 | 74 |
| The decision in *Wall v Collins* | 3.232 | 74 |
| Reactions to *Wall v Collins* | 3.242 | 77 |
| Responses to our consultation | 3.244 | 77 |
| Our recommendation | 3.251 | 79 |
| **PART 4: REFORMS FOR REGISTERED TITLES** | | **83** |
| Introduction | 4.1 | 83 |
| Section 58 of the Land Registration Act 2002: a clarification | 4.11 | 84 |
| The "unity of seisin" rule | 4.19 | 85 |
| Land Registry practice and development plans | 4.25 | 87 |
| Mortgages of part | 4.34 | 89 |
| Land that falls into common ownership | 4.39 | 89 |
| Consultees' responses | 4.41 | 90 |
| Our recommendation | 4.44 | 90 |
| The express release of registered interests | 4.52 | 92 |
| The use of short-forms for the creation of easements | 4.59 | 93 |
| **PART 5: COVENANTS: THE CASE FOR REFORM** | | **95** |
| Introduction | 5.1 | 95 |
| Problems in the law relating to covenants | 5.4 | 96 |
| Positive obligations: the case for reform | 5.21 | 100 |
| The practical problems connected with positive obligations | 5.21 | 100 |
| The arguments for and against reform | 5.29 | 102 |
| Safeguards to accompany positive obligations | 5.44 | 106 |
| Recommendations for the reform of freehold covenants | 5.63 | 111 |
| Additional details | 5.77 | 114 |
| Land obligations in unregistered land | 5.78 | 114 |

|  | Paragraph | Page |
|---|---|---|
| The future for the rule in *Tulk v Moxhay* and the current law of restrictive covenants | 5.82 | 115 |
| Land obligations and commonhold | 5.90 | 117 |
| Land obligations, negative easements and easements of fencing | 5.92 | 117 |
| **PART 6: A NEW LEGAL INTEREST IN LAND** |  | **120** |
| Introduction | 6.1 | 120 |
| Land obligations in the draft Bill | 6.7 | 121 |
| A new power for estate owners | 6.7 | 121 |
| The exercise of the power: creating an appurtenant right | 6.14 | 122 |
| The nature of a land obligation | 6.22 | 124 |
| Ancillary rights | 6.33 | 126 |
| Future freehold covenants | 6.37 | 126 |
| The creation and registration of land obligations | 6.46 | 129 |
| The requirements for the creation of legal and equitable interests in land | 6.46 | 129 |
| Land obligations in unregistered land | 6.54 | 131 |
| Land obligations to be created only expressly | 6.59 | 132 |
| Further provisions for registered title | 6.63 | 133 |
| Consequential provisions about registration | 6.64 | 133 |
| Recommendations derived from Part 4 above | 6.75 | 135 |
| The enforceability of land obligations | 6.90 | 138 |
| Transmission of the benefit of a land obligation | 6.92 | 138 |
| Transmission of the burden of a land obligation | 6.101 | 140 |
| Transmission of part of the burdened land | 6.118 | 143 |
| Adverse possession | 6.134 | 147 |
| Liability and remedies for breach of land obligations | 6.146 | 149 |
| The cause of action | 6.147 | 149 |
| Liability for breach | 6.150 | 149 |

|  | Paragraph | Page |
|---|---|---|
| Remedies for breach of a land obligation | 6.159 | 151 |
| Land obligations and the Crown | 6.179 | 154 |

## PART 7: THE JURISDICTION OF THE LANDS CHAMBER OF THE UPPER TRIBUNAL

|  | Paragraph | Page |
|---|---|---|
| **PART 7: THE JURISDICTION OF THE LANDS CHAMBER OF THE UPPER TRIBUNAL** |  | **157** |
| Introduction | 7.1 | 157 |
| The background to section 84 | 7.3 | 157 |
| The proposals in the Consultation Paper | 7.6 | 158 |
| Consultees' responses | 7.12 | 159 |
| Our recommendations and the draft Bill | 7.24 | 162 |
| Extending the jurisdiction of the Lands Chamber by bringing more interests within its scope | 7.27 | 162 |
| Extending the jurisdiction of the Lands Chamber to enable it to make declarations | 7.39 | 165 |
| The grounds for the discharge and modification of interests in land | 7.52 | 167 |
| **PART 8: LIST OF RECOMMENDATIONS** |  | **175** |
| **APPENDIX A: DRAFT BILL AND EXPLANATORY NOTES** |  | **185** |
| **APPENDIX B: ADVISORY GROUP MEMBERS** |  | **237** |
| **APPENDIX C: SAMPLE REGISTERS** |  | **238** |
| **APPENDIX D: A NOTE ON ENFORCEMENT** |  | **245** |
| **APPENDIX E: SECTION 84 OF THE LAW OF PROPERTY ACT 1925** |  | **250** |
| **APPENDIX F: LIST OF CONSULTEES** |  | **254** |

# THE LAW COMMISSION

# MAKING LAND WORK: EASEMENTS, COVENANTS AND PROFITS À PRENDRE

*To the Right Honourable Kenneth Clarke QC, MP, Lord Chancellor and Secretary of State for Justice*

# PART 1
# EASEMENTS, COVENANTS AND PROFITS À PRENDRE: INTRODUCTION

## THE SCOPE AND IMPACT OF THE PROJECT

1.1 We live on a small island. Land is in great demand; it provides homes and places of business, security for debt, space for recreation, a source of food and minerals; the list is endless. Ownership of land is important and valuable. In this project we are concerned not with the ownership of land, but with the complex web of rights and obligations that link different parcels of land, and their owners, together. Some are security rights – principally mortgages – and those are not part of this project. This project is about easements, profits à prendre and covenants.

1.2 These three types of rights can be shortly described, but the law that relates to them is vast. Easements are, in general, rights to do something on someone else's land; private rights of way are the most obvious examples.[1] Profits à prendre – which from here onwards we call simply "profits" – are rights to take something from someone else's land, such as grass for grazing, or fish. Freehold covenants[2] are a type of contractual promise which, as we shall explain in more detail later, behave like property rights because some of them can be enforced against future owners of the land, rather than just against the person who made the contractual promise.

1.3 An easement, profit or covenant can be thought of as, on the one hand, imposing a burden on a piece of land. Anyone who buys land that is subject to a drainage easement, say, in favour of a neighbour, has to accept the burden of that easement; land lawyers say that the right binds the land and that the purchaser cannot take the land free from it. On the other hand, the right gives a benefit to the right-holder, who will in most cases be another landowner.

1.4 Over three quarters of freehold properties are affected by one or more of these rights.[3] They can be very valuable. Land that is burdened with a restrictive

---

[1] Public rights of way are not easements and fall outside the scope of this project.

[2] The covenants with which the project is concerned are freehold, not leasehold; leasehold covenants operate under a wholly different legal regime. See, para 5.3 n 4 below.

[3] Easements, Covenants and Profits à Prendre (2008) Law Commission Consultation Paper No 186 (we refer to this document as the "Consultation Paper" in this Report), para 1.3.

covenant not to build upon it, for example, may be safeguarded as a precious green space; or the covenant may be released for a considerable sum if the person who has the benefit of that promise not to build decides that he or she would prefer to be bought out. Easements may be convenient facilities, as are most rights of way, or they may be vitally necessary: if the benefit of an easement of support is lost, a building may collapse. They may add considerable value to a property; a particularly valuable example is an easement to park a car.[4] Easements and covenants together may ensure that the boundaries and roadways of a group of properties in one development are properly maintained, that drains can be shared, and that the design, character and the communal parts of the estate are not compromised.

1.5 The law relating to these three types of right is ancient. It has been reviewed and reformed periodically over the centuries, but little has been done in recent years because the efforts of Parliament have been focused on the legal structures for land ownership and registration of title to land. The time is ripe for a comprehensive review and reform of this group of rights.

## THE BACKGROUND TO THE PROJECT

1.6 This project is a natural development of earlier Law Commission work. We examined the law of easements and covenants in our 1971 Working Paper on Appurtenant Rights,[5] and made quite far-reaching provisional proposals for the amalgamation and re-classification of easements, covenants and profits. In 1984, we published the Report on *Transfer of Land: The Law of Positive and Restrictive Covenants*,[6] which included a draft Bill. That Report took into consideration the 1971 Working Paper and responses to it, but the 1971 plan was considered in retrospect to be "too ambitious" and reform of easements and other analogous rights were therefore excluded.[7]

1.7 The 1984 Report recommended the replacement of the current law of freehold covenants with a scheme of land obligations. Land obligations would have been legal interests in land, embodying positive and negative obligations, segregated by type (positive or negative) and context ("development" obligations for large developments and "neighbour" obligations in all other cases). In 1998 the Lord Chancellor announced that the Government had decided not to implement the recommendations in the Report, and that he would ask the Law Commission to consider "how future developments in property law might affect the recommendations in [the 1984] Report".[8] It was understood that the Lord Chancellor was mainly referring to the introduction of commonhold.[9]

---

[4] See Nationwide Building Society, *What adds value to your home?* (May 2006) http://www.nationwide.co.uk/hpi/historical/What_Adds_Value_06.pdf (last visited 13 May 2011), which suggests that a parking space adds 6.5% to the value of a property.

[5] Transfer of Land: Appurtenant Rights (1971) Law Commission Working Paper No 36 (we refer to this as the "1971 Working Paper").

[6] (1984) Law Com No 127 (we refer to this as "the 1984 Report").

[7] The 1984 Report, para 1.6.

[8] Written Answer, *Hansard* (HL), 19 March 1998, vol 587, col 213.

[9] See para 1.9 below.

1.8 Two major developments led to the inclusion of our current project in the Law Commission's Ninth Programme of Law Reform. One was the enactment of the Land Registration Act 2002, implementing the recommendations of the Report: *Land Registration for the Twenty-First Century: A Conveyancing Revolution.*[10] In that Report, produced jointly by the Law Commission and HM Land Registry,[11] detailed consideration of the reform of the law of prescription was expressly postponed pending a comprehensive review of the law of easements and covenants.[12]

1.9 The other was the enactment of the Commonhold and Leasehold Reform Act 2002. One major feature of the current law of freehold covenants is that a covenant which imposes a positive obligation does not run with land, meaning that obligations cannot be passed to successive owners; it is often said that this is the reason why freehold flats cannot be marketed. The commonhold system was devised as an answer to that problem. Physically interdependent properties ranging from flats, sharing both structure and servicing arrangements, to separate houses, sharing responsibility for an estate road, can now be marketed as commonhold. Their community obligations can be managed by the commonhold association, without the imposition of a landlord to which so many objected on both practical and principled grounds.

1.10 Accordingly, a major lacuna in the law has been filled: positive obligations can run with land in the context of groups of properties that satisfy the requirements of the commonhold regime. It remains for this project to repair the existing problems in the law of easements and profits, and to look at what remains to be achieved in the law relating to covenants. In particular, the problem of positive covenants has been resolved only in the context of commonhold developments, which is suitable only for truly interdependent properties which share some common parts. There is still no simple and effective mechanism in the law to enable the imposition of more straightforward obligations, for example to allocate responsibility for mending a fence between two adjoining properties.

1.11 The Consultation Paper was published in 2008.[13] It was a wide-ranging exploration of the law relating to easements, profits and covenants. It focused on some important and well-known problems such as the complexity of the rules concerning the acquisition of easements, the ambiguous status of certain parking rights, and the range of obligations needed to link and manage the plots of land involved in a freehold development, to name but a few. It also explored a range of less notorious problems, so as to enable us to hear from consultees what scale of reform could most usefully be recommended. It focused on the general law and did not address problems with specific rights, such as rights to light.

1.12 In reporting now on our recommendations at the close of this general project, we note that there is scope for a further review of the law relating to rights to light.

---

[10] (2001) Law Com No 271 (we refer to this document as "the 2001 Report").

[11] We refer to HM Land Registry in this Report as "Land Registry".

[12] The 2001 Report, para 1.19.

[13] We received a total of 89 responses to the Consultation Paper. A list of consultees is annexed to this Report as Appendix F (the list excludes the three consultees who asked for their response to remain confidential).

This is an important area with significant financial implications; the general work that we have done lays a foundation for future work in this specific area.

**A SUMMARY OF THIS REPORT AND OF OUR RECOMMENDATIONS**

1.13    Following this introductory Part, Part 2 is an account of the current law, including both the background law relating to land ownership and the rules specific to the three interests with which we are here concerned.

1.14    Part 3 deals with easements and profits, and with a group of reforms designed to modernise and simplify some very long-established law which is causing difficulty – and unnecessary cost – by its complexity and antiquity. Much of this Part is taken up with the reform of the law of implication and prescription. There is currently a multitude of different ways in which an easement or a profit may be granted (to a buyer) or reserved (by a seller) by implication, rather than express grant, in a conveyance; there are also several ways in which an easement or a profit can be acquired by long use (known as prescription). We recommend that it should cease to be possible to acquire profits in this way, and we recommend a simplification and rationalisation of implication and prescription for easements. We also look at the way in which easements may be lost through abandonment, and at the current legal confusion surrounding easements to park. Finally we examine some of the ways in which interests in land can be brought to an end in the light of the Court of Appeal's decision in *Wall v Collins*.[14]

1.15    In Part 4 we make recommendations for three reforms that relate only to registered land. One is the amendment of a rule in the current law. We recommend that where title to all the land involved is registered, it should be possible in future to create easements or profits that benefit and burden defined areas of land even though they are owned by the same person. This will mean that where, say, a developer's land is to be sold off in plots, the rights and obligations required between the plots of land will be able to be defined and created before the individual plots are sold. This will greatly simplify the Land Registry procedure for the formation of new developments, and will therefore simplify matters for developers, as well as facilitating mortgages of part of the land in a title. The second reform that we recommend in Part 4 relates to the express variation and release (that is, bringing to an end) of interests in land; our reform ensures that legal interests cannot be expressly released unless they are also removed from the register of title, so eliminating the situation in which the register can become out of step with dealings between the landowners. Thirdly, we recommend an amendment to the Land Registration Act 2002 to clarify the scope of Land Registry's guarantee of title to interests in land; and finally we address to Land Registry a recommendation about the creation of short-forms for easements and profits.

---

[14]    [2007] EWCA Civ 444, [2007] Ch 390. See our discussion of *Wall v Collins* in Part 3; para 3.232 and following below.

1.16 In Part 5 we consider the law relating to freehold covenants.[15] We explore the problems in the law relating to both negative and positive covenants, and particularly the fact that as things stand the burden of a positive obligation cannot run with land. We examine the arguments for and against reversing that position, putting positive covenants on the same footing as negative covenants while transforming both into legal interests in land. We conclude by recommending that reform.

1.17 In Part 6 we set out a scheme to effect that reform. We recommend the introduction of a new legal interest in land, called a "land obligation", and we recommend that for the future covenants both positive and negative should take effect as land obligations. The draft Bill defines them functionally, as obligations to do something on one's land or on a boundary structure or to make a payment in return for the performance of another obligation. There would be no requirement that they be drafted as covenants or that particular words be used in their creation. They would be able to bind successors in title, but would also be registrable, so as to make publicly available the details of the land that they burden and benefit. We discuss the enforceability of positive obligations, and the remedies available for breach.

1.18 Two important features will be obvious within Part 6: first, we have moved away from some of the detail proposed in the Consultation Paper. We do recommend the creation of a new legal interest, but we have aimed to make that interest structurally as close as possible to other legal interests in land. So far as creation and enforceability are concerned, land obligations would behave very much as an easement does, rather than having new and purpose-built requirements and formalities. But it would not be possible for land obligations to arise by prescription or implication. Secondly, existing restrictive covenants, and the law that relates to them, remain exactly as they are. We have made it a high priority not to disturb existing rights and obligations.

1.19 The reforms that we recommend in Part 4, with reference to easements and profits in registered land, are equally recommended for land obligations.

1.20 In Part 7 we examine the powers of the Lands Chamber of the Upper Tribunal[16] (formerly the Lands Tribunal) to discharge and modify interests in land. It is important that land should not be burdened with obsolete adverse interests, so as not to render it unsaleable or unusable. Currently it is possible for the Lands Chamber to make orders discharging or modifying restrictive covenants.[17] In Part

---

[15] The covenants studied in this project are commonly referred to as freehold covenants. The contrast is with leasehold covenants, but to spell that out precisely we have to say that the class of covenants addressed in this Report is all except those made between landlord and tenant that relate only to the demised premises. Covenants within that exception, to which we refer as leasehold covenants, have developed along very different lines, and we make no recommendations about these. Covenants outside that exception, and therefore within our project, are called freehold covenants by way of shorthand, but we have to bear in mind that they may be entered into between leaseholders (that is, the lessee of Blackacre may covenant with the lessee of Redacre to mend the boundary fence between them).

[16] We refer to the Lands Chamber of the Upper Tribunal in this Report as the "Lands Chamber".

[17] Under the Law of Property Act 1925, s 84.

7 we recommend that that jurisdiction be extended to land obligations (both positive and negative), and to easements and profits created after implementation of reform.

1.21 Our Report concludes with a draft Bill and Explanatory Notes, as Appendix A; we make reference to the Bill's provisions throughout the discussion of our recommendations. We have included some further Appendices to illustrate some of the material we discuss in the Report; in particular Appendix C contains two sample registers of title; Appendix D is a note on the enforceability of positive land obligations, and Appendix E reproduces section 84 of the Law of Property Act 1925.

1.22 Of the many possible reforms mooted in the Consultation Paper, this Report and the draft Bill focuses on those that we think have the greatest potential to improve the lives of those whose properties are affected by them. We recommend the simplification of some over-complex law by the remedying of certain defects and by introducing some new legal tools.

1.23 One of our objectives throughout this project has been to make our recommendations as clear, straightforward and as uncontroversial as possible; we have also endeavoured to keep this Report to a manageable size. However, this has been an extremely wide-ranging project addressing a whole system of law, and conciseness inevitably involves some omissions. In particular, we have not been able to do justice in this Report to the very detailed and helpful consultation responses that we received. Moreover, we have given very little space in this Report to possible reforms that were canvassed in the Consultation Paper but which we have decided not to recommend.[18] In some cases this was because they were not sufficiently supported on consultation but in others it was because they were not, in the end, seen to be significant enough priorities to warrant the expense of reform.

1.24 However, alongside this Report we have also published an Analysis of Responses. In it we summarise what consultees said in response to each of the 100 questions in the Consultation Paper. We quote at some length from those responses and give a more detailed account of our reactions to many of the points of detail that consultees raised. We have also explained those cases where we made provisional proposals in the Consultation Paper but did not proceed to recommend reform in this Report. The Analysis is available on our website, where it can be downloaded free of charge.[19]

1.25 Other publications issued together with this Report and draft Bill are an Executive Summary and an Impact Assessment.[20]

---

[18] For example, the discussion in Part 13 of the Consultation Paper about the potential for the conversion of existing covenants to Land Obligations and the treatment of obsolete covenants.

[19] See http://www.justice.gov.uk/lawcommission/easements.htm (last visited 13 May 2011).

[20] All of the publications referred to in this paragraph are available on our website: http://www.justice.gov.uk/lawcommission/easements.htm (last visited 13 May 2011).

**IMPACT ASSESSMENT**

1.26 Since its formation in 1965 the Law Commission's recommendations have been framed in the light of our assessment of their impact on those affected by them. Our founding statute requires us to recommend simplification of the law and the removal of anomalies.[21] It is a matter of common sense that the law is improved if it is as simple as is consistent with the achievement of its objectives. Sometimes, however, fairness and efficiency require detailed provisions; over-simplification can produce bad law.

1.27 At paragraph 1.34 of the Consultation Paper we asked consultees to give us information and views about the likely impact of our provisional proposals, and we received some very helpful comments that have informed our eventual recommendations. In this very wide-ranging project we have endeavoured to simplify the law as much as we can, to reduce anomalies, and to ensure that where we recommend the introduction of new material it fits within the existing grammar of land law. We have endeavoured to weed out complexity from the current law – the reduction of the methods of prescription from three to one is an obvious example – without removing important material. Our recommendations on the implication of easements, for example, bring together the useful elements of the current law, but make them clear and accessible.

1.28 We have been particularly concerned in this project to work with Land Registry to ensure that impacts are positive for Land Registry itself and for its customers, and also to make recommendations that will have a beneficial impact upon the public and upon developers and mortgagees. We have also worked with the President and staff of the Lands Chamber in framing recommendations for the development of the Lands Chamber's jurisdiction.

1.29 In the Impact Assessment we have endeavoured to quantify the financial impact of our recommendations, and we are indebted to those who have assisted us in its preparation.

1.30 Our Impact Assessment formally identifies two options for implementation of our recommendations. Option 1 is to implement them all together. That would enable Government to adopt our draft Bill in its entirety, and would bring into effect an integrated package which would modernise this whole area of law and bring about the greatest benefits. This is by far our preferred option.

1.31 However, we recognise that implementation has costs, and that in a time when resources are under particular scrutiny and pressure, the implementation of the whole package of reform might prove difficult. We have therefore identified an option 2, which would put into effect our recommendations for easements and profits without introducing land obligations. That would bring about important and necessary reforms whilst postponing the initial cost and complication of more fundamental reforms. It would also be a missed opportunity, because the benefits of introducing land obligations – and thereby moving away from the archaic and problematic law of freehold covenants – would not be realised. But we put it forward as a pragmatic solution to what we hope is a short-term difficulty in the implementation of valuable law reform.

---

[21] Law Commissions Act 1965, s 3.

**HUMAN RIGHTS**

1.32 In a project concerned with property law, it is essential that we have in mind the need to respect the rights of everyone to peaceful enjoyment of their possessions, in view of the provisions of Article 1 of the First Protocol to the European Convention on Human Rights and Fundamental Freedoms, which reads:

> Every natural or legal person is entitled to the peaceful enjoyment of his possessions. No one shall be deprived of his possessions except in the public interest and subject to the conditions provided for by law and by the general principles of international law.
>
> The preceding provisions shall not, however, in any way impair the right of a State to enforce such laws as it deems necessary to control the use of property in accordance with the general interest or to secure the payment of taxes or other contributions or penalties.

1.33 At paragraph 1.29 of the Consultation Paper we asked consultees for their views on the human rights implications of our provisional proposals. The responses we received to that question were very positive; they are summarised at paragraphs 1.1 to 1.11 of the Analysis of Responses. We have taken care to avoid making any recommendation that disturbs existing property rights; we have taken particular care to ensure that none of our recommendations would compromise either the value or the usefulness of existing restrictive covenants.

**ACKNOWLEDGEMENTS**

1.34 We have held a number of meetings with individuals and organisations during the course of this long-running project; Law Commission Reports are always the outcome of a collaborative process, and we are extremely grateful for all the help we have received. We are thankful to all those who responded to the Consultation Paper, helping us to shape our ideas and the recommendations contained in this Report.

1.35 Three groups deserve particular mention. We are particularly indebted to Land Registry for its time, assistance and support. We have spent many hours with a Land Registry working group comprising Jill Cousins, Michael Croker, Pascal Lalande, Alasdair Lewis, Patrick Milne and Francis Twambley; we are deeply grateful for that group's time and expertise. Although this Report has not been produced jointly with Land Registry, its text has been approved by Land Registry prior to publication.

1.36 We are also extremely grateful to George Bartlett QC, President of the Lands Chamber of the Upper Tribunal, and Registrar Stella Rozanski, who gave us a great deal of assistance with our thinking in relation to Part 7.

1.37 Finally, we extend our warm thanks to our Advisory Board, whose members are listed at Appendix B.

# PART 2
# ESTATES AND INTERESTS IN LAND: THE CURRENT LAW

## INTRODUCTION

2.1 This project involves concepts at the heart of land law. We have written this Part as an introduction to the relevant law as it stands at the moment. Many of our readers will be familiar with this background; those for whom it is new material may want to go beyond the introduction we give here, and are referred to the standard texts.[1] We take the opportunity within this Part to mention a number of points that we raised in the Consultation Paper but have decided not to pursue; they are discussed in more detail in the Analysis of Responses.

2.2 In this Part we discuss the current law in four sections:

    (1)    we look at the foundations of land law, and discuss the nature of legal and equitable estates and interests in land;

    (2)    we look at the nature of easements, covenants and profits and at some of their characteristics, and we also look briefly at estate rentcharges;

    (3)    we sketch the requirements for the creation and registration of these interests; and

    (4)    we discuss briefly the ways in which these interests may come to an end.

## THE FOUNDATIONS OF LAND LAW

### Estates and interests in land

2.3 The land law of England and Wales is founded upon the idea of rights in land. The most significant of the available rights are the fee simple (or freehold) and the lease. These are rights to possession of land, and are colloquially regarded as ownership rights.[2] If X is the freeholder of a house, it belongs to X, subject to the Crown's eventual rights if X dies and there is no-one to inherit the land. If X has a lease, long or short (the shorter leases are known as tenancies), X has the exclusive right to possession of it for the duration of the lease, at which point it reverts to the landlord. These ownership rights are known as estates. There are numerous less extensive rights known as interests, and we have already discussed a number of them in Part 1. There are the security rights – mortgages and the like – and there are also rights to make use of land, or to control its use – in particular easements, covenants and profits. The latter are the subject-matter

---

[1] Suggested texts are S Gardner, *An Introduction to Land Law* (2nd ed 2009); K Gray and S F Gray, *Elements of Land Law* (5th ed 2009) (to which we refer as "*Gray and Gray*") and C Harpum, S Bridge and M Dixon, *Megarry and Wade, The Law of Real Property* (7th ed 2008) (to which we refer as "*Megarry and Wade*"). Frequent reference will also be made throughout this Report to J R Gaunt and P Morgan, *Gale on Easements* (18th ed 2008), to which we refer as "*Gale on Easements*". See also E Cooke, *Land Law* (2006).

[2] Although a very short lease, such as a weekly tenancy, probably does not, for most people, feel like ownership.

of this Report; they do not generally give the right to possession of the land, and never to the exclusive possession of it.[3]

2.4    All these estates and interests are property rights.[4] A property right can be distinguished from a personal right in that it is alienable (it can be given away or sold), and it is enforceable against people who were not involved in creating it. So if X has an easement over Y's land and Y sells to Z, the easement is enforceable against Z. Crucially, property rights in land are protected in specific ways – the ownership rights by the law of trespass, and the rest by remedies designed to safeguard not merely their monetary value (by an award of damages when a right is infringed) but also, where practicable, their true function and purpose as rights in land. So the obstruction of an easement can be prevented by an order of the court, as can the infringement of a restrictive covenant.

2.5    Only certain rights are regarded by the law as suitable to be property rights. It is reasonably intuitive to say that while a right of way over X's land can be a property right, a right to receive piano lessons from X in X's house cannot because it is too personal as well as too imprecise. But what about a right to receive from X a share in the profits of the development of land sold to X, known as overage?[5] This is a distinction we shall have to pursue later.

### Legal and equitable rights

2.6    Having explained the nature of estates and interests in land, we have to introduce another technical distinction. Estates and interests in land may be legal or equitable. The distinction is ancient, and it is not particularly helpful now to say that legal estates and interests are those that the courts of law would have recognised before 1872 while equitable ones would have been enforced only by the courts of equity.[6] The practical difference, historically, has been that legal interests are enforceable against all the world (so if there is a legal easement over Blackacre, all future owners of Blackacre are bound by it) while equitable interests bind all except a purchaser of the legal estate who has given value for it and knows nothing about the right (traditionally referred to as the *bona fide* purchaser of the legal estate for value without notice).

---

[3]    In other words, they never enable the right-holder to exclude all others from the land at all times. Only the estates in land give exclusive possession.

[4]    There is of course extensive learning on the meaning of "property". Although for the purposes of this project we have to draw a bright line between personal rights and property rights, ultimately the distinction is a matter of degree. See for example *Gray and Gray*, para 1.5.1 and following.

[5]    See para 5.52 below.

[6]    For a further explanation of the historical relationship between the common law and equity, see S Worthington, *Equity* (2nd ed 2006) ch 1.

2.7 That historical distinction has become very nearly irrelevant because of the advent of two systems of registration. As a general rule, the enforceability of legal and equitable interests in land depends now upon their being protected, either by a notice on the register of title at Land Registry (if the ownership of the land burdened by the interest is registered),[7] or on the Land Charges Register (a survivor from the days when title was not registered, which remains the route to registration for interests in land where title has remained unregistered).[8]

2.8 It is important to appreciate that when a right in land can be protected within the title registration system,[9] or as a Land Charge, its enforceability depends not upon its legal or equitable status but upon the rules of the registration system.

2.9 Where the legal/equitable distinction remains crucial, however, is in relation to the guarantee of validity given by the register of title; only legal estates and interests can have their validity guaranteed as a result of registration.[10] We discuss this at paragraph 2.60 below. Accordingly the distinction does still have considerable importance.

**The modern structure of legal and equitable estates and interests**

2.10 The land law of England and Wales underwent major reform in 1925. Section 1 of the Law of Property Act 1925[11] sets out the modern grammar of estates and interests as follows:

> 1 Legal estates and equitable interests
>
> (1) The only estates in land which are capable of subsisting or of being conveyed or created at law are—
>
> > (a) An estate in fee simple absolute in possession;
> >
> > (b) A term of years absolute.
>
> (2) The only interests or charges in or over land which are capable of subsisting or of being conveyed or created at law are—
>
> > (a) An easement, right, or privilege in or over land for an interest equivalent to an estate in fee simple absolute in possession or a term of years absolute;

---

[7] See Land Registration Act 2002, s 32 (referred to as "the LRA 2002" in the footnotes of this Report); some legal easements are overriding interests (see schedules 1 and 3 to the LRA 2002) and so their priority is protected even though they do not appear on the register (see para 2.61 below).

[8] For further detail about the way in which these two forms of protection work, see paras 2.55 to 2.64 below.

[9] Whether by notice on the register or as an overriding interest; see para 2.61 below.

[10] LRA 2002, s 58(1).

[11] We refer to this legislation as the "LPA 1925" in the footnotes of this Report.

(b)    A rentcharge in possession issuing out of or charged on land being either perpetual or for a term of years absolute;

(c)    A charge by way of legal mortgage;

(d)    . . . and any other similar charge on land which is not created by an instrument;

(e)    Rights of entry exercisable over or in respect of a legal term of years absolute, or annexed, for any purpose, to a legal rentcharge.

(3)    All other estates, interests, and charges in or over land take effect as equitable interests.

2.11    So rights in land now fall into three groups:

(1)    the fee simple and the term of years absolute (known as the lease) – the ownership rights discussed above – are the legal estates;

(2)    the legal interests in land listed in subsection (2); these are the rights that fall short of absolute ownership. They are rights that one person may hold over someone else's land; and

(3)    everything else: all other property rights in land are equitable interests.[12]

2.12    This is obviously a hierarchy; legal estates and interests are more secure than equitable interests – in particular, as mentioned above, their validity can be guaranteed by Land Registry.

2.13    All the estates and interests listed as legal in subsections (1) and (2) of section 1 of the Law of Property Act 1925 may alternatively exist as equitable interests. Equitable versions of these interests may be created deliberately (as when A declares that he holds land on trust for B; B now has an equitable fee simple in A's land, the legal fee simple remains with A). Equally they may happen accidentally, when the formalities required for a legal interest have not been complied with (for example, if the interest has not been created by deed, or has not been registered). A four-year lease created in writing but not by deed takes effect as an equitable lease, provided that the requirements for the formation of a valid contract are complied with.[13] An easement granted by deed for the benefit of registered land but not completed by registration[14] remains an equitable

---

[12]    For example restrictive covenants. See paras 2.14 and 2.37 and following below.

[13]    *Lysaght v Edwards* (1875-76) LR 2 Ch D 499. The requirements for a valid contract to create or transfer an interest in land are contained in the Law of Property (Miscellaneous Provisions) Act 1989, s 2. Such a contract must be in writing, containing all the express terms of the deal, and signed by both parties; it is therefore no longer possible to create an equitable interest in land without compliance with those formalities.

[14]    LRA 2002, s 27.

easement until it is registered.[15] An equitable interest may also arise where the grantor of the interest had only an equitable estate; so someone who has only an equitable fee simple, such as B above, can only grant an equitable lease.

2.14 However, some interests can only ever be equitable. While an easement may be legal or equitable, depending on its characteristics and the way it was created, a restrictive covenant cannot exist as a legal interest in land; it will always be an equitable interest.

2.15 Such, then, are the building blocks of land law: the legal and equitable estates and interests. Next we look at the characteristics of the interests that form the subject matter of this project.

## EASEMENTS, COVENANTS AND PROFITS A PRENDRE

2.16 Easements, covenants and profits are all rights that one person may hold in someone else's land. They are linked by a functional similarity in that they are all rights either to do something on someone else's land or to control the way that the land is used by its owner. They are sometimes described as "third party rights"; the civil law systems label them *iures in re aliena*.[16] It would be helpful if we had one word to describe the three, but English law has not provided one; it would be difficult to follow American usage and refer to them all as servitudes, since Scotland, and civil law countries generally, use that term to describe rights that correspond to easements and not to covenants. We can give a cumbersome description and say that they are non-possessory, non-security rights in land.

2.17 In this section of this Part we look at the essential characteristics of these three rights, by way of background to the reforms we propose later in this Report. We mention some proposals made in the Consultation Paper which we have decided not to take further, giving reasons briefly here and in more detail in the Analysis of Responses. Finally as a postscript to this section we explain the nature of estate rentcharges, and explain why they are relevant to our project.

### Easements

2.18 Easements are nowhere defined in English law. Most types of easement can be described functionally, as rights to do something on another's land. *Megarry and Wade* introduces them by saying:

> The common law recognised a limited number of rights which one landowner could acquire over the land of another; and these rights were called easements and profits. Examples of easements are rights of way, rights of light and rights of water.[17]

---

[15] It is possible, but very unlikely, that such an equitable easement might itself be protected by notice on the register of the burdened land, so that it will be enforceable against a purchaser of that land; see paras 2.61 and 2.62 below.

[16] Roughly translated as "rights in the property of others".

[17] *Megarry and Wade*, para 27-001.

Many further examples could be given; and we might note that rights of way can exist in various forms – rights of way on foot or on horseback, vehicular rights and rights of way by bicycle – as can other easements, for example rights of drainage. There is no closed list of easements, as there is of servitudes in some civil law jurisdictions. But the requirements for the validity of easements do themselves restrict the range of rights that can exist as easements.[18]

2.19 Some easements cannot be described as rights to do something on another's land; they are the "negative easements", so called because they give one landowner a right to prevent a neighbour from doing something on the neighbour's own land. The negative easements are rights of support (enabling X to prevent Y from removing earth or a structure on Y's land that supports X's land), rights to light (enabling X to prevent Y from obstructing light through an aperture), or rights to air or water in defined channels. As we shall note when we discuss the law relating to covenants, the same effect could be achieved through the use of restrictive covenants; but historically these rights have been granted as easements, and it is clear that they can be acquired through prescription (that is, by long use).[19]

2.20 Easements can be legal interests in land, as we have seen.[20] They are generally created expressly, more often as part of a sale or lease of part of property than in a stand-alone deal; they can also be acquired by implication (where the law imports the creation of an easement into a transfer or other document)[21] and prescription.

2.21 Once validly created (and subject to registration requirements, discussed below), the easement will be "appurtenant" to the benefited land; that is, it will benefit all subsequent owners of that land without the need for it to be expressly assigned to them. Appurtenance is to an estate in land,[22] and so it is possible, for example, for the lessee of Blackacre to have an easement over adjoining land and for that easement to be appurtenant to the lease without benefiting the freeholder. We discuss in Part 3 the problems that may arise if that lease comes to an end prematurely, for example by being surrendered to the landlord.[23]

### The requirements for a valid easement

2.22 We referred above to a validly created easement, and in order to assess the validity of an easement – or of any other interest in land – we have to look both at its substantive characteristics and at the way in which it has been created. We turn to the general requirements for the creation of legal interests in land later in this Part; here we look at the characteristics that are necessary for the validity of

---

[18] As we noted in Part 1 (para 1.2 n 1), our project does not involve public rights of way; they are not easements and are subject to a very different legal regime.

[19] Easements can be acquired by prescription, whereas restrictive covenants cannot, and that may be why the law acknowledges this limited class of negative easements.

[20] See para 2.10 and following above.

[21] See further, paras 3.4 and 3.11 and following below.

[22] See para 3.232 and following below.

[23] See para 3.232 and following below.

an easement, as laid down by the decision in *Re Ellenborough Park*.[24] The Court of Appeal had to decide the status of a right for residents to use a garden in the middle of a square around which their houses were built. That case gave rise to the four well-known characteristics of easements, which the Consultation Paper took as its starting point for its discussion of easements:[25]

> (1)    there must be a dominant tenement and a servient tenement;[26]
>
> (2)    the easement must accommodate the dominant tenement;
>
> (3)    the dominant and servient tenements must be owned by different persons; and
>
> (4)    the easement must be capable of forming the subject matter of a grant.

We can look at those four requirements in turn.

2.23    First, there must be dominant and servient land:[27]

> … no person can possess an easement otherwise than in respect of and in amplification of his enjoyment of some estate or interest in a piece of land.[28]

Traditionally it has been said that there is "dominant land" and "servient land", while more modern usage (including that found in Land Registry publications) refers to benefited and burdened land. We use both sets of terms.

2.24    The alternative to the rule that there must be dominant and servient land would be for easements to be capable, generally, of existing "in gross", that is, to belong to a person without being appurtenant to land. We asked in the Consultation Paper whether the requirement for dominant land should be dispensed with, so that easements in gross would become available.[29] Most consultees regarded that as an undesirable change. We agree that such reform would not be desirable and that the introduction of easements in gross would lead to a proliferation of adverse interests in land, unlimited by the needs of the dominant land.[30] We expand on this in the Analysis of Responses at paragraphs 3.1 to 3.13.

---

[24]    [1956] Ch 131.

[25]    Consultation Paper, para 3.1.

[26]    The word "tenement" here simply means a plot of land; whether or not there is a building on the land is irrelevant.

[27]    But see our discussion of *Wall v Collins* [2007] EWCA Civ 444, [2007] Ch 390 in Part 3; para 3.232 and following below.

[28]    *Alfred F Beckett Ltd v Lyons* [1967] Ch 449, 483, by Winn LJ. The roots of the principle are much older than this – *Gray and Gray*, para 5.1.25 states that it was "rationalised" by Cresswell J in *Ackroyd v Smith* (1850) 10 CB 164, 138 ER 68. More recently, it was described as "trite law" in *London & Blenheim Estates Ltd v Ladbroke Retail Parks Ltd* [1994] 1 WLR 31, 36, by Peter Gibson LJ.

[29]    Consultation Paper, para 3.18.

[30]    Note the comments of A Lawson, "Easements" in L Tee (ed), *Land Law: Issues, Debates, Policy* (2002) p 71: "such a change would undoubtedly risk the imposition of heavy, additional burdens on servient land …".

2.25 Second, the easement must accommodate, or accommodate and serve, the dominant land. The requirement is that the right must be of some practical importance to the benefited land, rather than just to the right-holder as an individual: it must be "reasonably necessary for the better enjoyment" of that land.[31] The land can be "accommodated and served" by being made more useful; for example, by an easement entitling its owner to walk across the neighbouring field to church, or from a right of eavesdrop onto the neighbour's garden.[32] The requirement means that the two plots of land must be reasonably close to each other, even if not actually adjoining.

2.26 For example, it is difficult to say that a garden in Westminster benefits from an easement over land in Islington, 3.5 miles away, although not implausible to say that a house benefits from a right of drainage through a pipe that passes not only through the neighbour's land but also through a series of properties, some of them some distance away. We provisionally proposed in the Consultation Paper that this requirement should be retained.[33] We are convinced by the responses of consultees that this is correct. Some consultees wanted reform in response to *London & Blenheim Estates Ltd v Ladbroke Retail Parks Ltd*[34] so as to enable the creation of easements to benefit land not yet owned by a developer. As one consultee put it:

> Developers would welcome a simple and effective scheme that enables them to reserve easements for defined areas of land that they do not yet own, but which they are planning to acquire in the future.[35]

2.27 Currently the problem is managed by the use of options; the developer takes an option to require the relevant landowner to grant an easement in the future. Consideration of the practical scenarios involved, and discussion with Land Registry, led us to the view that reform to facilitate these arrangements would be a disproportionate change and would disturb well-established and relatively clear law without sufficient corresponding benefit. We discuss this in the Analysis of Responses at paragraphs 3.14 to 3.24.

2.28 The third requirement is that the dominant and servient land be in different ownership. At first sight, the rule simply states the obvious: no-one needs an easement over his or her own land. But the corollary of the rule is that no-one can create an easement between two separate plots of land, both in his or her own ownership, before selling them; and another consequence of the rule is that if the dominant and servient land in respect of an easement come into common ownership and possession, the easement is extinguished. Perhaps surprisingly, both these consequences of the rule cause significant practical problems. The solution to those problems has become a major part of the reform we are recommending, and we therefore discuss this issue separately in Part 4 below.

---

[31]  *Re Ellenborough Park* [1956] Ch 131, 170, by Lord Evershed MR.

[32]  Eavesdrop is the right for water to fall from a roof onto another property.

[33]  Consultation Paper, para 3.33.

[34]  [1994] 1 WLR 31.

[35]  The London Property Support Lawyers Group.

2.29    Finally, the easement must be "capable of forming the subject matter of a grant". This requirement encompasses a number of ideas; for example, that the easement must be clear and certain, and must not be a right merely for amusement.[36] The requirement therefore functions as a control upon the range of possible easements. Another element of it is the rule that an easement must not confer a right so extensive that it confers exclusive possession on the user[37] or deprives the servient owner of almost all use of the land. That rule has generated some pressure in the context of parking easements, and we discuss it in Part 3.

2.30    We go on in Parts 3 and 4 to recommend some changes that will make the law relating to easements more straightforward and flexible, but which will leave their fundamental nature intact.

**Profits**

2.31    Profits are, again, not defined in the law. They are generally rights to take something from someone else's land; hunting and fishing rights are obvious examples, as are grazing rights.[38]

2.32    Profits may either be "several" (also called "sole") or "in common". A several profit excludes the servient owner; so if a several fishing right is granted to X by Y over Y's land, Y can no longer fish there. Profits in common do not exclude the servient owner.

2.33    Our project is concerned mainly with several profits. Those profits that are outside its scope are rights which are "rights of common" for the purposes of the Commons Act 2006. The Consultation Paper noted that profits appendant and profits *pur cause de vicinage* (which is a customary right that allows animals to pass from one plot of land to an adjoining plot) fall outside of the scope of the project.[39] This remains the case, but no special mention is made of them in the draft Bill as profits appendant fall within "rights of common" under the Commons Act 2006. There is some debate as to whether profits *pur cause de vicinage* are properly characterised as profits.[40] If they are, then they are similarly dealt with by the Commons Act 2006 and if they are not, they are not affected by our project.

---

[36]    For example, a right to use somebody else's land for picnics. See *Gray and Gray*, para 5.1.37.

[37]    See para 2.3 above.

[38]    *Megarry and Wade*, para 27-001.

[39]    Consultation Paper, paras 6.12 and 6.13.

[40]    Contrast N Ubhi and B Denyer-Green, *Law of Commons and of Town and Village Greens* (2nd ed 2006) para 4.3.3 with *Megarry and Wade*, para 27-057.

2.34 The profits with which we are concerned are, therefore, essentially private rights rather than those profits (whether several or held in common) that can broadly be described as rights of common. One anomaly must be noted, however. Profits in common held for a term of years or from year to year do not fall within the definition of "rights in common" in the Commons Act 2006. These profits are important in the context of farm business tenancies, and so we do not want them to be excluded from both the Commons legislation and our scheme. They therefore fall within the scope of our project.[41]

2.35 Profits are not listed by name in section 1 of the Law of Property Act 1925, but fall within "an easement, right, or privilege" in subsection (2)(a). They behave very much in the same way as easements, with the important exception that they can exist "in gross"; that means that although a profit may be appurtenant to land it can, alternatively, be created and held independently, benefiting a person without benefiting land.

2.36 Profits that are appurtenant to an estate in land function in the same way as easements; in particular, the requirements in *Re Ellenborough Park*[42] apply to them. The Consultation Paper made some proposals about the ways in which profits may be created and brought to an end, which we discuss alongside the corresponding proposals made in relation to easements.[43]

**Covenants**

2.37 The third interest that is central to this project is the freehold covenant. Covenants have their origin in the law of contract. They may be positive, requiring something to be done, or negative/restrictive, preventing the covenantor from doing something.[44] The starting point of the law in this context is that only the parties to a contract are bound by it – this is the doctrine of privity of contract. Accordingly, contractual rights are not property rights: the defining feature of property rights is that they are enforceable against people who were not party to their creation.[45] If A makes a contractual promise to B not to use his land for the conduct of business, that promise can have no restraining effect upon C who was not a party to the contract, even if C buys the land.

2.38 If the covenant is made between landlord and tenant and relates to the leasehold property, then the law is very different.[46] Such covenants survive throughout the lease, even if it changes hands; later landlords and tenants of the same lease take the benefit and burden of all the leasehold covenants. That principle was established in *Spencer's Case*,[47] but it did not extend to covenants relating to

---

[41] Draft Bill, cl 42 sets out the scope of our recommendations so far as profits are concerned.

[42] [1956] Ch 131.

[43] See paras 3.7 to 3.10, 3.64, 3.69, 3.230, 4.44 and 7.35 below.

[44] Even if expressed in positive terms; a covenant always to use the land for residential purposes is a restrictive covenant. See *Gray and Gray*, para 3.3.2.

[45] See para 2.4 above.

[46] For further information on leasehold covenants, see *Gray and Gray*, paras 4.5.1 to 4.5.96 and *Megarry and Wade*, ch 20.

[47] (1583) 5 Co Rep 16a, 77 ER 72.

freehold land.[48]

2.39 The starting point for freehold covenants remains the doctrine of privity of contract. However, there have been two significant moves away from that principle. First, in limited circumstances the benefit of a freehold covenant, whether positive or negative, runs at law to a successor to the covenantee (that is, the person who buys the land from the person to whom the covenant was made). The benefit of the covenant is then said to be "annexed" to an estate in land.[49]

2.40 Second, in *Tulk v Moxhay*[50] the court determined that the burden of a restrictive covenant – that is, a covenant consisting of a promise *not* to do something on one's own land – will bind successors in title of the covenantor in certain carefully defined circumstances. One of the requirements for the burden to run is that a successor must have notice of the covenant. The effect of the Land Charges Act 1972[51] and the Land Registration Act 2002[52] is to transform this into a requirement for registration,[53] as a land charge in unregistered land and by notice on the register of the burdened land where title is registered.

2.41 As a result, restrictive covenants that meet the conditions laid down in *Tulk v Moxhay* function as property rights; the benefit of such a covenant can pass to the covenantee's successor, and the burden is enforceable against a landowner who did not make the covenant. We say that the burden runs with the land, or that the land is burdened by the covenant. But only restrictive covenants behave in this way; positive covenants do not. This is perceived to be a major weakness in English law and is the principal reason why freehold flats are inadvisable (since the physical interdependence of the property means that the owners of the flats must be required to take positive steps to maintain their property and any common parts such as the roof). On a level that affects many householders, it is the reason why there are no rules as to who should repair the fence between two properties; mostly this is managed by neighbourliness, and by mythology about the significance of markings on plans.

---

[48] *Keppell v Bailey* (1834) 2 My & K 517, 39 ER 1042; *Austerberry v Corporation of Oldham* (1885) LR 29 Ch D 750; *Rhone v Stephens* [1994] 2 AC 310. See also S Goulding, "Privity of estate and the enforcement of real covenants" (2007) 36 *Common Law World Review* 193.

[49] *Megarry and Wade*, para 32-060.

[50] (1848) 2 Ph 774, 41 ER 1143.

[51] Referred to as the "LCA 1972" in the footnotes of this Report. LCA 1972, s 4(6).

[52] LRA 2002, ss 11(4), 12(4) and 29.

[53] The requirement stated in the case was that the purchaser of land must have notice of the covenant, but the 1925 legislation effectively replaced that with a requirement for registration. The notice requirement now applies only to covenants affecting unregistered land that were created before 1 January 1926: LCA 1972, s 2(5).

2.42    A restrictive covenant is not described as an appurtenant right, because of its primarily contractual status; although it functions as a property right, it remains a contractual agreement and the original parties remain liable on it even when they have parted with the land. But it is akin to an appurtenant right in that if it "touches and concerns" the land of the covenantee, its benefit will usually pass automatically to a successor in title to the benefited land without express assignment.[54] "Touch and concern" means much the same as "accommodate and serve" and relates to the enhancement of the usefulness or amenity of land; the burden of a covenant not to use land for business can run with the land, while the burden of a covenant not to give piano lessons to a named individual cannot.

2.43    Many years of law reform work have been devoted to the problems associated with the law of freehold covenants. The problems are extensive; the major difficulty that has beset law reformers has been the wish to find an acceptable way for the burden of positive covenants to run with land, so as to bind successors in title. The Law Commission's earlier work[55] has already addressed that and other issues. In Part 4 of this Report we summarise again the problems in the current law, and present an updated solution which we believe resolves the practical difficulties and would make conveyancing simpler, without either doing violence to the current structure of land law or causing unnecessary expense.

### Estate rentcharges

2.44    Finally, we have to mention another interest in land that is peripherally relevant to this project: the estate rentcharge. A rentcharge is "any annual or other periodic sum of money charged on or issuing out of land", otherwise than under a lease or mortgage.[56] It can be used to enforce a positive obligation, because the chargor takes a right of entry:[57] a legal interest in land which enables the chargor to enter (that is, take possession of) the land in the event of default.

2.45    In practice, an estate rentcharge can be used to support a single obligation such as the maintenance of a boundary; the chargor may be the neighbouring owner, who sold the land to the chargee. Alternatively, an estate rentcharge may support a more complex system of obligations in a development of interdependent properties,[58] with the chargor being a management company. We are aware that estate rentcharges are used by a small proportion of developers who understand them, in circumstances where a leasehold or commonhold structure might have been expected.

2.46    We provisionally proposed in the Consultation Paper that, on the enactment of

---

[54]    LPA 1925, s 78, as interpreted in *Federated Homes Ltd v Mill Lodge Properties Ltd* [1980] 1 WLR 594.

[55]    See paras 1.6 to 1.12 above.

[56]    Rentcharges Act 1977, s 1. A rentcharge is defined in similar terms by the Limitation Act 1980, s 38(1) as "any annuity or periodical sum of money charged upon or payable out of land, except a rent service or interest on a mortgage on land".

[57]    LPA 1925, s 1(2)(e).

[58]    For example, a management company may covenant to provide services on a housing or industrial estate and take the benefit of rentcharges to support each unit owner's obligation to reimburse it.

provisions that would enable positive obligations to run with land, it should no longer be possible to create new estate rentcharges.[59] A majority of consultees agreed with that provisional proposal, but comments were made that convinced us that there remains a role for estate rentcharges in some specialist contexts. Trowers and Hamlins pointed out that they are:

> … essential for grant making bodies to ensure that the land in respect of which grant is made does actually get used for the purposes of the grant and in the agreed manner.

2.47   In other words, estate rentcharges can be used to enforce requirements imposed by grant-making bodies that do not hold any estate in land to which the benefit of a covenant can attach. The requirements may have a social function, for example, that the land be used for social housing, or they may ensure the retention of original or period features when a grant is made for restoration. These are important arrangements, and the estate rentcharge has proved to be an effective tool for supporting them.

2.48   We take the view that this is a valid reason for the retention of estate rentcharges for use in these special and unusual cases. We anticipate that the enactment of our recommendations for land obligations will mean that they are needed only occasionally where a positive obligation has to be imposed by a specialist body that does not hold land that can meet the "touch and concern" requirement. We explore the point in more detail at paragraphs 8.125 to 8.139 of the Analysis of Reponses.

2.49   The other legal interests listed in section 1(2) of the Law of Property Act 1925 are not relevant to this project; nor are the rest of the equitable interests referred to in section 1(3).

## THE CREATION AND REGISTRATION OF EASEMENTS, PROFITS AND COVENANTS

2.50   So how do easements, profits and covenants come into being?

2.51   Ideally, they are created expressly. We say "ideally" because a document that effects an express transaction is likely to be the most accurate way to determine what has been created. Easements and profits can, under the current law, also be created by implication and by prescription, as we have mentioned above, and we say more about that in Part 3.

2.52   A legal easement or profit can only be created expressly by deed.[60] Although restrictive covenants cannot take effect as legal interests, in fact most will be created by deed because they will have been set out in a transfer of land.

---

[59]   Consultation Paper, para 8.119.

[60]   LPA 1925, s 52.

2.53    In the Consultation Paper we made some provisional proposals about the interpretation of express grants of easements[61] and of profits,[62] in response to concerns about the decision of the Court of Appeal in *St Edmundsbury & Ipswich Diocesan Board of Finance v Clark (No 2)*.[63] We have decided, in response to what we have heard from consultees, that those concerns were not well-founded and that we should not make any recommendation about the interpretation of express grants; we explain that decision at paragraphs 4.1 to 4.13 of the Analysis of Responses.

2.54    We stated above that the enforceability of interests in land depends upon their being protected within one or other of the registration systems available today. We say more about those systems here.

**Title registration**

2.55    The register of title maintained by Land Registry acts both as the proof of an individual's title to land – instead of the traditional collection of deeds – and as a guarantee of its validity.

2.56    Most titles in England and Wales are now registered; by area, that represents about 73% of land in England and Wales.[64] The Land Registration Act 2002 lists, in section 2, the estates and interests that can be registered. These are not only the legal estates – the fee simple and the lease – but also most of the legal interests (including easements and profits).

2.57    Legal estates have their own individual register; we attach copies of two sample registered titles at Appendix C. Note that it falls into three sections: the property register, which gives details of the property itself and any rights that benefit it; the proprietorship register which says who owns the registered estate and any restrictions on their power to dispose of it; and the charges register showing the burdens attached to the land.

2.58    A legal interest, by contrast, is generally registered as a benefit appurtenant to a registered title,[65] and also appears as a burden against another title. Profits in gross and estate rentcharges are exceptions to that general rule, being legal interests that are not appurtenant to registered estates and so registered with their own title. So a legal easement is registered on the property register of the land that it benefits, and appears as a burden on another proprietor's title – rather like a credit and debit entry.

---

[61]    Consultation Paper, para 4.24.

[62]    Consultation Paper, para 6.30(2).

[63]    [1975] 1 WLR 468.

[64]    Land Registry, *Annual Report and Accounts 2009/10* (July 2010) p 12 http://www1.landregistry.gov.uk/assets/library/documents/Annual_Report_0910.pdf (last visited 13 May 2011).

[65]    LRA 2002, s 13.

2.59    Where title to an estate or interest in land is registered, any disposition of it, or any attempt to create another registrable estate out of it, has no effect at law until completed by registration.[66] So it is not possible for A to grant to B a legal lease of A's house for 10 years simply by deed; there is no legal lease until the lease is registered.[67]

2.60    Where a registrable estate or interest is registered, its validity is guaranteed by the register. The "state guarantee of title" amounts (in summary) to the principle that once title is registered, it can be relied upon, even if derived by means that would yield no title at all at common law, such as forgery.[68] Where it is found that there is a mistake on the register, it can be altered, but not so as to prejudice a proprietor in possession who has not contributed to the mistake.[69] By way of example: X forges a transfer of Y's land to Z, who was innocent of any involvement in the forgery. Z takes possession of the land. There is a mistake on the register, but Y cannot have the land back. The register will not be rectified to the prejudice of Z, but Y will be compensated out of the indemnity fund.[70] If Z was not in possession of the land, or indeed if he was involved in the forgery, the register will be rectified and Y will have the land back. Accordingly the "state guarantee" may be fulfilled in land or in money.

2.61    Registrable estates or interests that are the subject of a notice on the title to the burdened land also have their priority protected by section 29 of the Land Registration Act 2002; a purchaser of the land for valuable consideration under a registered disposition (that is, one that must be completed by registration) is bound by any interest that is the subject of a notice on the register.[71] A purchaser is also bound by registered charges and by the overriding interests listed in schedule 3 to the Act; for our purposes, the most important item in that list is paragraph 3: legal easements. Although the express grant or reservation of a legal easement affecting registered land is a registrable disposition, and therefore when created expressly cannot have legal status unless completed by registration, some express easements affecting registered land bind a purchaser despite not appearing on the register; they do so as overriding interests.[72] The same applies to easements created otherwise than expressly, by prescription and implication.

---

[66]   LRA 2002, s 27; and see para 2.13 above.

[67]   Note that not all grants of leases are registrable dispositions; generally speaking, it is only those granted for a term of more than seven years; LRA 2002, s 27(2)(b)(i).

[68]   LRA 2002, s 58.

[69]   LRA 2002, sch 4.

[70]   LRA 2002, sch 8.

[71]   Such a purchaser is protected against any interests other than those listed in LRA 2002, s 29; anyone else acquiring the land (for example, someone to whom it is given, or left by will) takes subject to the traditional priority rules, according to s 28.

[72]   This may be the case where a legal easement affecting unregistered land was, for some reason, not made the subject of a notice on first registration of the affected land.

2.62    Rights that do not qualify for registration because they are not listed among the registrable estates in section 2 of the Land Registration Act 2002 – for example, equitable easements, options to purchase and restrictive covenants – may nevertheless be recorded, or "noted", on the register by a notice on the charges register of the burdened land (but without appearing on the register of the benefited land).[73] This means that their priority is protected (by section 29 of the Land Registration Act 2002) even though their validity is not guaranteed. Thus the old contrast between legal estates that bind all the world and equitable interests that bind by notice is not relevant once title to land is registered.

2.63    Note therefore that while Land Registry's indemnity fund is engaged in respect of easements and profits appurtenant, because they are registered and are therefore covered by the guarantee, restrictive covenants are not registered and therefore their validity is not guaranteed. But they are capable of being noted and if Land Registry fails to enter a notice where one should have been entered (perhaps on first registration), or removes a notice that should not be removed, there may be a mistake in the register and an indemnity may be payable.

### Land Charges registration

2.64    Where title to land is not registered (so that proof of title is still achieved by the production of deeds), the Land Charges Register records some, but not all, equitable interests that may burden unregistered land, and a few legal interests. Where registration on the Land Charges Register is required, failure to register means that the right will be invalid against all or most[74] purchasers. Thus a legal easement does in fact bind all the world (there is no registration requirement and so the traditional rule works); but an equitable easement binds purchasers only if it is registered as a land charge.[75] A first legal mortgage binds all the world; a second or subsequent legal mortgage binds only if registered as a land charge.[76] So again the old contrast no longer holds good.

### THE EXTINGUISHMENT OF EASEMENTS, PROFITS AND COVENANTS

2.65    How do these interests come to an end?

2.66    Any of them can be released expressly, by deed in the case of legal easements and profits.[77] Express release – by contrast with various methods of implied release – is the most reliable method of bringing these interests to an end. Nevertheless where title to the land concerned is registered, express release can give rise to difficulties because the Land Registration Act 2002 does not provide that release is a registrable disposition – that is, it is not a disposition that cannot take effect at law until registered. The difficulty is that there may then be a

---

[73]    Throughout this Report we use the term "registered" to indicate that the benefit of a right is registered (and therefore its validity guaranteed) rather than merely the burden being noted.

[74]    The provision is complicated and not in issue here: LCA 1972, s 4.

[75]    LCA 1972, s 2(5)(iii).

[76]    LCA 1972, s 2(4)(i).

[77]    *Lovell v Smith* (1857) 3 CBR (NS) 120, 127; 140 ER 685, 688. See also *Gale on Easements*, para 12-18.

contradiction between the register, which still validates a registered easement, and the situation "on the ground" where the easement has indeed been expressly released. We did not raise that issue in the Consultation Paper, but after discussions with Land Registry we make a recommendation about that in Part 4.

2.67 Easements and profits can be extinguished by abandonment,[78] but this is very hard to prove, and we make a recommendation to facilitate proof of abandonment in Part 3.[79]

2.68 All three interests may, of course, also be extinguished or overridden by statute.[80]

2.69 Until recently it was the law that easements and profits were brought to an end by termination of the estate to which they were appurtenant; in Part 3 we discuss the Court of Appeal's decision in *Wall v Collins*,[81] and make a recommendation that will reinstate the law as it was before that decision, while preserving some of the important practical advantages that the Court of Appeal was concerned to secure.

2.70 We discussed in the Consultation Paper the law relating to the implied release of easements and profits as a result of excessive use.[82] We make no recommendations for reform of the law in that respect.[83] We also discussed the consequences of the use of an easement to benefit land adjoining, but not forming part of, the dominant tenement, as determined by the rule in *Harris v Flower*.[84] This is explained in full in the Analysis of Responses.[85]

2.71 Finally, restrictive covenants – alone of our three interests – can be discharged or modified by the Lands Chamber. This is an important facility for the removal of interests that are obsolete or no longer benefit anyone,[86] but it does not extend to easements or profits. We discuss this in Part 7 and make recommendations for the extension of the Lands Chamber's jurisdiction.

---

[78] See para 3.212 and following below.

[79] In the Consultation Paper, paras 6.52 and 6.54, we suggested that it should no longer be possible for profits to be brought to an end by exhaustion, that is, where the item to be taken from the land no longer exists. We have not pursued that suggestion.

[80] See para 6.13, n 6 below.

[81] [2007] EWCA Civ 444, [2007] Ch 390.

[82] Consultation Paper, paras 5.32 to 5.63; and see *Ashdale Land and Property Company Ltd v Maioriello* [2010] EWHC 3296 (Ch), [2011] NPC 1.

[83] See the Analysis of Responses, paras 5.22 to 5.41.

[84] (1904) 74 LJ Ch 127; Consultation Paper, paras 5.64 to 5.71.

[85] See the Analysis of Responses, paras 5.42 to 5.51.

[86] LPA 1925, s 84(1).

## CONCLUSION

2.72　In this Part we have sketched out some of the fundamentals of land law, as the background against which this project must be viewed. We have also looked at the characteristics of easements, profits and covenants, and at the ways in which they can be created, registered, and brought to an end. We have referred briefly to a number of proposals made in the Consultation Paper which we have not taken forward as recommendations, in the light of consultation responses and of the potential impact of reform; detail on these points has been placed in the Analysis of Responses.

2.73　In the Parts that follow we discuss the reforms that we do now recommend.

# PART 3
# REFORM OF THE LAW OF EASEMENTS AND PROFITS

## INTRODUCTION

3.1 In this Part we are concerned with reform to, and refinement of, the current law relating to easements and profits. Of the three interests with which our project is concerned, these are the ones that can at present exist as legal interests in land, title to which can be registered. They are of great antiquity, and for the most part our recommendations would simplify law which has become too complex over decades and even centuries.

3.2 This Part addresses the following topics:

(1) the creation of profits;

(2) the implication of easements;

(3) section 62 of the Law of Property Act 1925;

(4) the acquisition of easements by prescription;

(5) easements that confer the right to extensive use (in particular, parking);

(6) the extinguishment of easements and profits by abandonment; and

(7) the termination of the estate to which an interest is appurtenant.

## (1) THE CREATION OF PROFITS

3.3 As we noted in Part 2, ideally (for the sake of clarity) interests in land are created expressly. Express words are the most reliable indicator of precisely what the parties were creating. However, both easements and profits can also be created by implication and prescription.

3.4 An easement or profit may be implied in a transaction where there is no express grant or reservation, but there is some other basis – rooted in the existing use of the land, the parties' intentions, or some degree of necessity – on which it can be said that in some sense there must or should have been a grant or reservation.[1]

3.5 Prescription is the acquisition of a right by long use.[2] A claimant who behaves, over a long period, as if he or she had an easement or profit – in circumstances where the owner of the relevant land is aware of what is happening and does not take action – acquires an easement or profit, the scope of which is determined by the behaviour by which it was acquired. For example, if X walks across Y's land over a long period, and Y is aware of that behaviour and does nothing, X will acquire an easement giving him the legal right to *walk* across Y's land but nothing

---

[1] See *Gale on Easements*, para 3-17 and following.

[2] See *Gale on Easements*, ch 4.

more.

3.6 Consultees were keen to retain implication and prescription on the basis that they fulfil a useful role. Implication protects parties who failed, through inadvertence or mistake, to make express the easements that were in fact important to the success of their transaction. Prescription regularises the use of land and ensures that use that has continued uncontroversially over long periods does eventually become legitimate and secure. We say more below about the reasons why we support the continued existence of implication and prescription so far as easements are concerned.

3.7 Profits, on the other hand, are a different matter. They can arise by prescription and implication, but arguably this is particularly oppressive to servient owners and far less appropriate than is the prescriptive acquisition of easements, because it involves something being taken from the land; that sort of arrangement is far more naturally regarded as something to be made commercially and expressly. Even in the agricultural context, where they are probably most used, it is difficult to imagine circumstances in which the grant or reservation of a profit is essential to make land usable. The Law Reform Committee in 1966 took the view that:

> The acquisition of a profit is normally a transaction of a more commercial character than is the acquisition of an easement and it is not unreasonable that the purchaser should be required to prove the bargain upon which he relies.[3]

3.8 We agree; we proposed in the Consultation Paper that for the future it should only be possible for profits to be created by express grant or reservation and by operation of statute, thus abolishing the rules of implication and prescription for both profits appurtenant and profits in gross.[4] Such a reform would promote certainty by making it easier to discover the existence of profits; and it would be consistent with the approach taken by the Commons Act 2006 whereby rights of common can no longer be acquired by prescription.[5] The proposal was supported by most consultees.[6]

3.9 **We recommend that profits should, for the future, be able to be created only by express grant or reservation or by statute.**

---

[3] Acquisition of Easements and Profits by Prescription: Fourteenth Report (1966) Law Reform Committee, Cmnd 3100, para 98.

[4] Consultation Paper, para 6.30(1).

[5] Commons Act 2006, s 6(1).

[6] See the Analysis of Responses, paras 6.1 to 6.10.

3.10 That recommendation is effected by clauses 18 and 19 of the draft Bill. It would of course have no effect where profits have been acquired by prescription or created by implication before the implementation of reform.[7]

## (2) THE IMPLICATION OF EASEMENTS

### The current law

3.11 Implication operates on the basis that, on a sale or other disposition of part of an estate, the full extent of the rights benefiting or burdening the estates involved have not been expressly set out in the transfer or lease. An easement can be implied by virtue of a number of separate rules, each of which is set out in detail in the Consultation Paper.[8] We summarise them briefly here. In doing so, we omit discussion of section 62 of the Law of Property Act 1925, which is better regarded as an aspect of the express creation of easements rather than as a form of implication and which we consider separately.[9]

### *Easements of necessity*[10]

3.12 These are implied in a transaction where the right is essential for the use of the land. Easements of necessity arise from the common law maxim that a person who grants some thing to another person or reserves some thing from a grant is "understood to grant [or reserve] that without which the thing [that is, the land granted or reserved] cannot be or exist".[11]

3.13 Whether the right claimed is essential for the use of the land granted or retained is a question of whether the land can be used at all without the implied grant or reservation. Claims are only successful where the land is "absolutely inaccessible or useless" without the easement.[12] So, for example, land will have to be truly landlocked for an easement of necessity to be implied so as to create an access; it will not be implied merely because it makes it more convenient to use the land. A right of way over land will not be deemed necessary where it can be accessed by water.[13] In one case where the land could be accessed, albeit by climbing a 20 foot cutting, an easement of necessity to give an alternative access was not

---

[7] Where, say, ten years' prescriptive use has been completed prior to the implementation of reform, that use will never give rise to a profit; the former potential claimant has lost nothing, since he or she had at that point only the possibility of a right in the future. So no transitional provisions are needed, with one exception: the case where 19 years' use or more has been achieved towards completion of a claim under the Prescription Act 1832; see paras 3.183 to 3.186 below.

[8] Consultation Paper, para 4.54 and following. *Waterman v Boyle* [2009] EWCA Civ 115, [2009] 21 EG 104, decided since the publication of the Consultation Paper, established no new principle but illustrates the difficulties in this area of law.

[9] See para 3.52 and following below.

[10] See *Gale on Easements*, paras 3-115 to 3-125 and *Megarry and Wade*, paras 28-009 to 28-012.

[11] J W Simonton, "Ways by Necessity" (1925) 25 *Columbia Law Review* 571, 572. Claims to the reservation of an easement of necessity are rather more difficult to establish than are claims to the grant of such an easement; see *Gale on Easements*, para 3-117.

[12] *Gale on Easements*, para 3-119, citing *Union Lighterage Co v London Graving Dock Co* [1902] 2 Ch 557.

[13] *Manjang v Drammeh* (1990) 61 P & CR 194.

implied.[14]

3.14 The necessity must exist at the time of the disposition, subject to an exception where, at the time of the grant, the owner of the servient land knew that a necessity would arise at a later date.[15] It is unclear what happens where the facts that gave rise to the necessity cease. There is some authority which suggests that, in such circumstances, the easement of necessity should also cease;[16] against this is considerable authority to the effect that where a grant of an easement is implied, it should not be "affected by the chance subsequent acquisition of other property".[17]

### Easements of intended use[18]

3.15 Easements of intended use arise where they are necessary to give effect to the manner in which the land retained or demised was intended by both parties to be used. As explained by Lord Parker in *Pwllbach Colliery Co Ltd v Woodman*:

> The law will readily imply the grant or reservation of such easements as may be necessary to give effect to the common intention of the parties to a grant of real property, with reference to the manner or purposes in and for which the land granted or some land retained by the grantor is to be used.[19]

3.16 Both parties must, at the time of the grant, have shared an intention, either express or implied, that the land demised or retained would be used for a particular purpose.[20] A well-known example concerned a cellar let to a tenant for use as a restaurant subject to a covenant to control and eliminate all smells and odours caused by such use. On that basis, there was implied an easement allowing the tenant to fix a ventilation shaft to the wall of the upper floors, in the landlord's ownership, because without that he could not have used the kitchens.[21]

3.17 In deciding whether or not to find an easement implied by common intention, the court will have regard to "the terms of the conveyance, the position on the ground, and the communications passing between the parties before the execution of the conveyance".[22] However, as explained in the Consultation

---

[14] *Titchmarsh v Royston Water Co Ltd* (1899) 81 LT 673.

[15] *St Edmundsbury and Ipswich Diocesan Board of Finance v Clark (No 2)* [1975] 1 WLR 468.

[16] *Holmes v Goring* (1824) 2 Bing 76, 130 ER 233; *Donaldson v Smith* [2006] All ER (D) 293.

[17] *Maude v Thornton* [1929] IR 454, 458, by Meredith J. Also see *Proctor v Hodgson* (1855) 10 Exch 824, 156 ER 674; *Barkshire v Grubb* (1880-81) LR 18 Ch D 616; *Huckvale v Aegean Hotels Ltd* (1989) 58 P & CR 163, 168 to 169, by Nourse LJ.

[18] See *Gale on Easements*, paras 3-26 to 3-31 and *Megarry and Wade*, paras 28-011 and 28-013.

[19] [1915] AC 634, 646.

[20] Although, as stated in *Megarry and Wade*, para 28-012, "easements are implied much more readily in favour of a grantee, on the principle that a grant must be construed in the amplest rather than in the narrowest way".

[21] *Wong v Beaumont Property Trust Ltd* [1965] 1 QB 173.

[22] *Adam v Shrewsbury* [2005] EWCA Civ 1006, [2006] 1 P & CR 27 at [28], by Neuberger LJ.

Paper,[23] this does not sit easily with the principle of interpretation set out by Lord Hoffman in *Investors Compensation Scheme Ltd v West Bromwich Building Society*,[24] where previous negotiations and declarations of subjective intent were described as being inadmissible in claims other than for rectification.

3.18 The principle can found both the grant and the reservation of an easement; like the rule in *Wheeldon v Burrows* the doctrine has its roots in the principle of non-derogation from grant.[25]

### *The rule in* Wheeldon v Burrows[26]

3.19 On a disposition of part of a property, quasi-easements used by the seller may be transformed into easements in favour of the buyer. A quasi-easement is when a landowner uses one part of his or her land for the convenience or other advantage of another part, provided that that use could have been an easement if the two areas were in different ownership.

3.20 The diagram below shows a typical *Wheeldon v Burrows*-type situation, where X formerly owned both fields, and accessed the highway from a house on field 1 by walking along the path over field 2. This is known as a quasi-easement: it would be an easement if the two fields were in separate ownership and the right had been granted expressly or acquired by implication or prescription. When field 1 is sold, an easement will be implied into the disposition for the benefit of field 1.

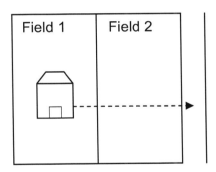

3.21 Easements may be implied by the rule in *Wheeldon v Burrows* in favour of the disponee if they are continuous and apparent, necessary for the reasonable enjoyment of the property granted, and used at the time of the grant by the common owner for the benefit of the part granted. The estate disposed of can be legal or equitable and the easements created will assume the same status. The transfer of the land from the common owner does not have to be for value. The parties can, by express provision or by implication, exclude the effect of the rule.

---

[23] Consultation Paper, para 4.89.

[24] [1998] 1 WLR 896.

[25] For a summary of the principle of non-derogation from grant, see *Gale on Easements*, para 3-52.

[26] (1879) LR 12 Ch D 31; see *Gale on Easements*, paras 3-53 to 3-114 and *Megarry and Wade*, paras 28-014 to 28-018.

### *Further bases for implication*

3.22 It is not easy to specify exactly how many methods of implication there are. The principle of non-derogation from grant, for example, may be listed as a method of implication; the doctrine was explained succinctly by Bowen LJ:

> ... a grantor having given a thing with one hand is not to take away the means of enjoying it with the other ... .[27]

3.23 There is little evidence of easements being implied solely on the basis of the rule.[28] The principal importance of the doctrine is to provide a justification for the implication of easements[29] pursuant to other rules such as that arising from *Wheeldon v Burrows* and easements of intended use.

3.24 *Gale on Easements* discusses a further possibility for the implication of easements from the description of the land in the conveyance,[30] but it seems likely that such implication can be explained by the other principles discussed above.

### Codification or reform?

3.25 In the Consultation Paper we put forward a number of options. We did not raise the possibility of abolishing the law of implication; it is generally agreed that implication is a useful safeguard, enabling the creation of rights that would have been created expressly but for inadvertence or ignorance and thereby preventing land from falling into disuse or becoming unmarketable.

3.26 The options we presented embodied a range of alternative principles on which a reformed law of implication might operate; we discuss these below. As a further alternative, we asked for consultees' views on the option of codifying the current law, with minor amendments.[31] That would involve setting out in statute the various separate methods of implication currently found in the law, with their different principles of operation and overlapping effects.

3.27 Very few consultees favoured this option, and those that did were not satisfied with the formulation we essayed.[32] We take on board these comments and we do not think that codification of the current law would improve it.

### Implied grant and implied reservation

3.28 A further preliminary suggestion made in the Consultation Paper was that there should no longer be a distinction between implied grant and implied reservation. As has been seen, while the principles of intention and necessity can support the

---

[27] *Birmingham, Dudley and District Banking Co v Ross* (1888) LR 38 Ch D 295, 313.

[28] Colin Sara refers to the case of *Cable v Bryant* [1908] 1 Ch 259: see C Sara, *Boundaries and Easements* (4th ed 2008) para 13.25. See also A Lawson, "Easements" in L Tee (ed), *Land Law: Issues, Debates, Policy* (2002) p 75.

[29] *Megarry and Wade* discusses the potential of the doctrine at para 27-035.

[30] *Gale on Easements*, paras 3-20 to 3-25.

[31] Consultation Paper, para 4.150.

[32] See the Analysis of Responses, para 4.89 and following.

implied grant or reservation of easements, and so can benefit either party to a disposition, *Wheeldon v Burrows* assists only those acquiring an estate in land. More generally, we can say that the law is readier to imply a grant than a reservation.

3.29    The Consultation Paper suggested that, in determining whether an easement should be implied, it should not be material whether the easement would take effect by grant or by reservation.[33] The vast majority of consultees were in favour of this change.[34] Implication serves a useful purpose where there has been inadvertence or mistake, and such things befall disponors as much as disponees.

**3.30    We recommend that in determining whether an easement should be implied, it should not be material whether the easement would take effect by grant or by reservation.**

**The options for reform**

3.31    The obvious problem with the rules of implication is their complexity: as we have said, there are at least three methods,[35] which operate differently but may overlap (claims are commonly litigated under different heads in the alternative).

3.32    We take the view that a single statutory test for implication is required, to replace the existing group of methods. The Consultation Paper set out alternative tests, derived from the current law, which could be employed to determine whether an easement is to be implied. It offered consultees the option of an approach based upon ascertaining the actual intentions of the parties; or an approach based upon a set of presumptions which would apply in each transaction. The idea behind the latter option was that it would be presumed that the parties intended certain easements, which would then take effect unless either party could show that intention was absent; for example, it could be presumed that the parties intended that the land should be accessible, and should have services and other rights needed for its intended use. A third option offered to consultees was a single rule based on what is necessary for the reasonable use of the land – by which, we explained, we meant a more generous test than the current law of easements of necessity.[36] Finally, we discussed a test based upon the contractual rules of implication.

3.33    While there was almost unanimous consensus among consultees that reform was appropriate, there was a divergence of opinion as to how best to achieve this.[37] Some wanted the potential for implication to be reduced while others were unsure that that would help. One consultee said that "the reduction of the bases

---

[33]    Consultation Paper, para 4.53. We also suggested, in para 4.53, that "in either case, the person alleging that there is an easement should be required to establish it"; that is clearly the case – he or she who alleges must prove – and we do not discuss it further.

[34]    See the Analysis of Responses, paras 4.33 to 4.41.

[35]    Identified at paras 3.11 to 3.24 above; it is unclear whether the principle of non-derogation from grant can by itself effect the implication of an easement. For a recent consideration of the doctrine see *William Old International Ltd v Arya* [2009] EWHC 599 (Ch), [2009] 2 P & CR 20.

[36]    Consultation Paper, paras 4.140 and 4.141.

[37]    See the Analysis of Responses, paras 4.62 to 4.94.

to a single general principle ... is academically attractive, but is unlikely to serve the purpose of the reforms well".[38]

3.34 We have profited from a discussion of this issue with our Advisory Board. From that discussion, and from consultees' responses, we concluded that what is desired by practitioners is a test for implication that will replicate all the useful instances of implication in the current law.

3.35 We have also concluded that a contractual test would be unacceptable, being alien to the context of a property right. Terms may be implied into a contract on the basis of a group of alternative tests, generally described as necessity,[39] business efficacy[40] and the "officious bystander" test.[41] Our Advisory Board members in particular felt that the introduction of an unfamiliar test in this context would add to uncertainty.[42] The test we are minded to recommend picks up elements of the contractual test but adapts them specifically to land contracts by directing attention to the purpose of the implied easement and its link with the use of land.

3.36 Reform of the law of implication of easements will not, of course, have any impact upon the contractual rules for implication. There may be occasions when the contractual rules will be successfully pleaded so as to imply a term into a land contract, to the effect that a particular easement would be granted; specific performance could then be sought to enforce that term. We are not aware of cases where this has been attempted, but it would always remain a possibility, perhaps in unusual circumstances.

3.37 There was some support for an intention-based test. But more consultees expressed concern about the evidential difficulties to which such a test would give rise – a view which we think has merit.[43] The difficulties would be considerable, and would become more pronounced over time and with changes of ownership. The test would be impracticable where the disposition was by will.

3.38 The difficulty with a test based on actual intention is that in most cases there is no actual intention to grant rights that do not appear on the face of the documentation. The fact that a right is reasonable or necessary does not mean that anyone intended to grant it. The test is simply unrealistic and would quickly lead the courts into inference and thence into fiction, as we have seen so vividly in the jurisprudence of the common intention constructive trust.[44]

3.39 We therefore do not support a test for implication based upon the actual

---

[38] HHJ Ian Leeming QC.

[39] *Liverpool City Council v Irwin* [1977] AC 239.

[40] *The Moorcock* (1889) LR 14 PD 64, 68.

[41] *Shirlaw v Southern Foundries (1926) Ltd* [1939] 2 KB 206, 227.

[42] Consultees who commented on the contractual test for implication noted that it is designed only to affect the parties to a contract, and not for easements which will bind future owners of the servient land: see the Analysis of Responses, paras 4.80 to 4.83.

[43] See the Analysis of Responses, para 4.77.

[44] See in particular *Stack v Dowden* [2007] UKHL 17, [2007] 2 AC 432.

intentions of the parties. The only role we see for actual intention lies in the ordinary contractual remedies available to the parties to the disposition, in particular rectification; we make no recommendation to change the availability of rectification in the very limited circumstances in which it is available.

3.40 We also reject an approach based on the presumption that certain rights were intended. We see no merit in presuming an intention that can then be rebutted – so that what is eventually implied, or not implied, may bear no relationship to what is actually needed to make the land viable. And while consultees did, on the whole, prefer an approach based upon presumptions to one based upon the parties' actual intentions, the responses highlighted the difficulty in settling a list of presumptions.

3.41 For example, while a presumption of access to services is likely to be seen as sensible, should such a presumption include a reciprocal payment obligation? Should it include a presumption that the dominant land should not overload services? What of the presumption of the right of way? Should there be time limits on its use, or a restriction on the number of vehicle movements? A list of presumptions appropriate for all dispositions of part is unlikely to be sufficiently comprehensive, certain and universally applicable, and is unlikely to stand the test of time. So we do not wish to pursue that model; as will be seen, we think that the test we now recommend picks up the useful elements within it.

3.42 A test of what is necessary for the reasonable use of the land attracted significant support from consultees, and we have come to the conclusion that this is the most appropriate principle upon which to base the implication of easements. It is an objective test, which does not depend upon the state of mind of the parties nor upon factual details such as whether or not a quasi-easement is visible. It is likely to encompass all those cases where the implication of an easement is of practical importance.

3.43 The wording "necessary for the reasonable use of the land" derives from the American Restatement,[45] which provides some useful commentary. In order to assist parties and the courts in determining whether that test has been passed, we have also concluded that it would be useful for the test to be accompanied by a non-exclusive list of factors that a court is to bear in mind in assessing what is necessary for the reasonable use of land. In formulating that list of factors we have had in mind the current law and the elements within it that consultees regard as important, and also the sort of practical problems that tend to arise on the ground.[46]

3.44 One point on which a number of consultees laid some stress is the fact that implication involves reading a term into a specific transaction, and that therefore

---

[45] American Law Institute, *Restatement (Third) of Property: Servitudes: Volume 1* (2000) p 202. The American Restatement, in §2.15, uses the words "necessary to [the] reasonable enjoyment of the land".

[46] During consultation we were informed of a recent deal where a shop had been sold without a drainage easement; certainly such an easement would be necessary for any use of the land, but a test for implication should enable the owner to connect up to the existing drain, running through the vendor's retained land, rather than laying a fresh one. This sort of point is reflected at paras 3.45 and 3.48 below

any test for implication must be applied as at the date of the transaction itself. That is beyond dispute; the fact that an easement becomes necessary some time after land was bought, for reasons that were not contemplated by the seller or the buyer, cannot be a ground for implication of that easement as a term of the acquisition of the land. Any suggestion to the contrary would mean that one can force one's neighbour to be bound by an easement at any time if one needs it, which is clearly not acceptable.

**3.45** **We recommend that an easement shall be implied as a term of a disposition where it is necessary for the reasonable use of the land at that date, bearing in mind:**

> **(1)** **the use of the land at the time of the grant;**
>
> **(2)** **the presence on the servient land of any relevant physical features;**
>
> **(3)** **any intention for the future use of the land, known to both parties at the time of the grant;**
>
> **(4)** **so far as relevant, the available routes for the easement sought; and**
>
> **(5)** **the potential interference with the servient land or inconvenience to the servient owner.**

3.46   Our recommendation is embodied in clause 20 of the draft Bill, and would have effect for transactions entered into on or after the date of enactment save where the transaction is made pursuant to a contract or court order made before that date.

3.47   Our recommended test would replace all the other methods of implication in the current law.

3.48   The factors we have listed can be seen to replicate the most useful and practical features of the current law, particularly in their focus on the physical characteristics of land and the intentions of the parties for future use. So far as that latter aspect is concerned, it is important to note that the intention referred to in point (3) must be known to both parties; an intention locked in the mind of the claimant is not enough. We have earlier argued against a test of intention as the primary test for implication; the difference here is that what has to be proved is much simpler. The question "did one of the parties, to the knowledge of the other, intend the land to be used as a residential property?" is very different from, and simpler than, "did they both intend it to have an easement to lay sewerage pipes with a right to connect into existing infrastructure?".

3.49   Should it be possible for the parties to a transaction expressly to exclude the implication of easements? It is certainly possible, and widely done, at the moment. Any well-drafted sale of part will include terms that expressly exclude or modify some or all of the rules of implication. Consultees did not dispute this; and there is no evidence of land being rendered sterile by such provisions. What is important is that the original parties, and their successors, are in no doubt as to whether implication has been excluded. We can envisage circumstances where, if the parties cannot exclude the implication of easements, a transaction would not proceed. So we do not make any recommendation to change the current position, that implication can be expressly excluded.

3.50 Our recommendation involves no mention of, and no change to, the doctrine of non-derogation from grant. It remains a useful and important doctrine; it can be seen as a historical foundation for the law of implication,[47] and has wider effect within the general law.

3.51 We conclude our discussion of implication by noting that our proposals would not impact upon ancillary easements. These are the rights that are necessary in order to exercise an easement itself – for example a right of access to a pipe to repair it, ancillary to an easement to use the pipe.[48] We do not believe that it is possible expressly to exclude these under the current law, as they arise from the construction of the grant,[49] and our recommendations would not change that. Ancillary easements do not survive the extinguishment of their parent easement and are best analysed as a matter of interpreting the scope of the parent easement itself.

## (3) SECTION 62 OF THE LAW OF PROPERTY ACT 1925

### The current law

3.52 Section 62 of the Law of Property Act 1925 is a word-saving provision, derived from section 6 of the Conveyancing Act 1881. The provision was intended to avoid any question as to whether a particular easement or right would or would not pass with a conveyance.[50] However, it can also create new easements and profits.[51]

3.53 This curious effect is best understood by starting from the opening words of the section:

---

[47] We mooted in the Consultation Paper explicit reform of the doctrine to ensure that it could not by itself give rise to implied easements: Consultation Paper, para 4.106. The form of our recommendation at para 3.45 above means that a separate recommendation to this effect is unnecessary; and see the Analysis of Responses, paras 4.54 to 4.61.

[48] *Pomfret v Ricroft* (1669) 1 Wms Saund 321, 85 ER 454; *Liford's Case* 11 Co Rep 46b, 52a; 77 ER 1206, 1218, *Pwllbach Colliery Co Ltd v Woodman* [1915] AC 634, 646.

[49] As they arise from the construction of the grant, the mechanism by which ancillary easements are "excluded" is by tighter drafting of an easement to preclude the potential for ancillary rights to emerge (for example, a right of way with, expressly, no right to park). See E Slessenger, "Car Parking Rules OK" [2008] *Conveyancer and Property Lawyer* 188 and K Reid, "Accessory Rights in Servitudes" [2008] *Edinburgh Law Review* 455.

[50] J T Farrand, *Wolstenholme and Cherry's Conveyancing Statutes: Volume 1 Law of Property Part I* (13th ed 1972) p 139. See also *Gale on Easements*, para 3-126 and *Megarry and Wade*, para 28-019.

[51] See N Hopkins, *The Informal Acquisition of Rights in Land* (2000) pp 213 to 214. For a recent discussion see *Campbell v Banks* [2011] EWCA Civ 61, [2011] NPC 13.

(1) A conveyance of land shall be deemed to include and shall by virtue of this Act operate to convey, with the land, all buildings, erections, fixtures, commons, hedges, ditches, fences, ways, waters, watercourses, liberties, privileges, easements, rights, and advantages whatsoever, appertaining or reputed to appertain to the land, or any part thereof, or, at the time of conveyance, demised, occupied, or enjoyed with or reputed or known as part or parcel of or appurtenant to the land or any part thereof.

3.54 The section in effect writes terms into a conveyance of a legal estate, deeming it to have set out among its terms certain facilities ("all … liberties, privileges, … rights, and advantages whatsoever") enjoyed with the land[52] at the time of the conveyance.[53] So as well as conveying along with a freehold any easements appurtenant to it, the section has been held to have two further effects.

3.55 First, on the conveyance to a tenant of the freehold in the land that was subject to the lease, any property rights which are annexed to the leasehold estate are "upgraded". By being written into the conveyance of the freehold, they become freehold easements or profits appurtenant to it. Second, other arrangements (to use a broad term) which are not easements or profits, but could be,[54] are transformed by their incorporation into the conveyance into interests appurtenant to the estate sold.

3.56 So section 62 can upgrade interests (from leasehold to freehold); and it can create them by transforming less formal arrangements. An example of the latter effect is illustrated in the diagram below.[55] X owns the freehold, and Y holds a lease of the shaded area. While Y held the lease, Y had X's permission, but no legal right of way, to walk across the yard to the road. Y then buys the freehold of the shaded area. Section 62 writes into the conveyance all the rights, privileges and advantages that were enjoyed with the land, including the right to pass on foot across the yard; that right is now incorporated into the deed, and so it becomes an easement.

---

[52] "Enjoyed with" is defined by reference to the factual user of the land: *International Tea Stores Co v Hobbs* [1903] 2 Ch 165.

[53] This refers to the date of the completion of the conveyance, not the date of exchange of contracts, nor the date of commencement of the lease; *Goldberg v Edwards* [1950] Ch 247.

[54] *Regis Property Co Ltd v Redman* [1956] 2 QB 612. In other words, the *Re Ellenborough Park* conditions must be met: see para 2.22 above. As an example of this, the tenant in *International Tea Stores Co v Hobbs* [1903] 2 Ch 165 had permission to cross a yard. An easement could have been granted for this purpose and the permission is therefore capable of being transformed into an easement.

[55] Based on *International Tea Stores Co v Hobbs* [1903] 2 Ch 165.

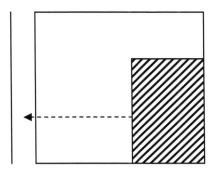

3.57 Section 62 overlaps to some extent with the rule in *Wheeldon v Burrows* because it can transform into an easement a quasi-easement such as the one represented in the diagram above.[56] The quasi-easement was an advantage enjoyed with the property. The section writes into the conveyance something like "the right to pass on foot over the path across field 2", and the deed therefore grants a legal easement.[57] The overlap is not complete; while section 62 operates only where there is a conveyance, *Wheeldon v Burrows* will operate where there is only a contract, or where the quasi-easement was being enjoyed at the time of the contract but not of the conveyance.

3.58 Section 62 is discussed in some texts as part of the law of implication, because it creates easements where the parties to a transaction did not draft wording in order to do so, and indeed overlaps with one form of implication. However, it is not implication, because it deems a conveyance to have included a right among its express terms;[58] and it differs from implication in that it operates neutrally, without regard to intention or necessity.

**Reform of section 62 of the Law of Property Act 1925**

3.59 In the Consultation Paper we noted that section 62 is a trap for the unwary, as well as being uncertain in its effect and in the extent to which it overlaps with *Wheeldon v Burrows*.[59] There have been numerous expressions of dissatisfaction with the section's transformation of precarious rights into legal interests.[60] It may prevent important rights from being lost; but it does so only when the facts fit a particular pattern, and it may equally preserve unimportant arrangements, converting a friendly permission into a valuable property right, contrary to the

[56] See para 3.20 above.

[57] In these circumstances the position seems to be that the quasi-easement will have to be shown to have been continuous and apparent, unless there was diversity of ownership and occupation prior to the conveyance: *Long v Gowlett* [1923] 2 Ch 177; *Sovmots Investments Ltd v Secretary of State for the Environment* [1979] AC 144; C Harpum, "Easements and Centre Point: Old Problems Resolved in a Novel Setting" [1977] *Conveyancer and Property Lawyer* 415.

[58] The authors of both *Gale on Easements* and *Megarry and Wade* distinguish rights created by implication and those arising from operation of the LPA 1925, s 62. *Gray and Gray*, para 5.2.40, n 1, discusses section 62 as part of its treatment of implication, but concedes that it may be more accurate to describe its operation as "by way of express grant".

[59] Consultation Paper, paras 4.74 to 4.77.

[60] See, for example, *Hair v Gillman* (2000) 80 P & CR 108, 116, by Chadwick LJ; *Commission for the New Towns v JJ Gallagher Ltd* [2002] EWHC 2668, (2003) 2 P & CR 3 at [61] by Neuberger J. See also L Tee, "Metamorphoses and Section 62 of the Law of Property Act 1925" [1998] *Conveyancer and Property Lawyer* 115.

intention of the "grantor". Because it operates subject to expressed contrary intention, well-drafted contracts provide for its exclusion, either in whole or as regards certain rights such as light.

3.60 We therefore provisionally proposed that section 62 should no longer operate to transform precarious benefits (that is, those enjoyed by permission) into legal easements.

3.61 Consultees generally supported our proposal.[61] The potentially unexpected effects of section 62 were regarded as unwelcome; particular dangers were highlighted in the context of rights to light. The Chancery Bar Association said:

> [The creative effect] of section 62 is capricious and has led to pernicious results where the creation of a legal easement was clearly not intended, but was not properly excluded.

3.62 There was some disagreement, on the basis that section 62 may operate as a protection against the inadvertent omission of rights. We agree that it may; but the difficulty with section 62 is that it is a blunt instrument operating only on a very specific fact-pattern. The enactment of a single statutory rule of implication, supported by guidelines that replicate the practical focus of the current law, will mean that the random operation of section 62 will no longer need to be continued for the sake of those instances where it is important, for example in preserving drainage easements or other vital facilities where they have formerly been used by permission.

3.63 Moreover, those who feel that the effect of section 62 is needed for a particular transaction can draft a term of their contract and transfer to that effect (although, as we noted above, the usual practice of conveyancers is to exclude section 62). Our attention has also been drawn to "reverse section 62" clauses, emulating the effect of the section but for the benefit of the seller, not of the buyer.[62] Again, it will remain open to parties to include such provisions.

**3.64 We recommend that section 62 of the Law of Property Act 1925 shall no longer operate to transform precarious benefits into legal easements or profits on a conveyance of land.**

3.65 That recommendation is embodied in clause 21(1) of the draft Bill. It will have no effect, of course, upon easements already created by virtue of the section's operation.

3.66 Nor will it have any effect upon the potential of section 62 to upgrade leasehold easements into freehold ones; we take the view that in this context section 62 is fulfilling a useful and necessary function. Where the transfer of a reversionary interest to a tenant is consensual, and the transferor is to retain some adjoining land, then the parties may agree in the transfer to grant new rights to benefit the land transferred. Equally, they may provide expressly, by excluding section 62, that those rights which previously benefited the leasehold estate do not survive,

---

[61] See the Analysis of Responses, paras 4.42 to 4.52.

[62] See the Analysis of Responses, para 4.53.

or become upgraded. But the parties may give no thought to the matter, and we think that in this context in particular the section may be a helpful protection against inadvertence.

3.67    It is even more useful where a transaction is not consensual, in particular leasehold enfranchisement. A group of statutory provisions provide, in similar words, that conveyances or leases that effect such transactions "shall not exclude or restrict the general words implied under section 62 of the Law of Property Act 1925".[63] The objective of these sections is to ensure that in these cases where the transferor or lessor has had the transaction forced upon him or her, the transferee or lessee takes with the new estate the ancillary rights formerly appurtenant to the lesser interest, made as durable as the estate now acquired. Without the compulsion of these provisions, an unwilling seller might well refuse to grant as freehold easements the rights that were formerly enjoyed by the tenant as leasehold easements.

3.68    So the upgrading effect of section 62 remains, so far as easements are concerned; but we do not think that the section should continue to operate to upgrade leasehold profits to freehold profits. Such cases are likely to be extremely rare, and we take the view that profits should be created expressly, by deliberately drafted wording, or not at all.

**3.69    We recommend that section 62 of the Law of Property Act 1925 should continue to be able to convert easements, but not profits, from leasehold to freehold interests.**

3.70    That recommendation is put into effect by clause 21(1)(b) of the draft Bill.

## (4) THE ACQUISITION OF EASEMENTS BY PRESCRIPTION

### Introduction

3.71    Prescription is another way in which an easement or profit can come into existence even though there has been no express grant. If a landowner makes use of a neighbour's land for a long period without permission, openly and peaceably, in a way that *could* amount to an easement, the law of prescription may create an easement, appurtenant to the user's freehold estate in land. A profit may currently be created in the same way, but we have recommended that that should not be the case for the future.[64]

3.72    The law of prescription is ancient, with roots in the medieval period and analogies with Roman law.[65] Like the law relating to adverse possession, it legitimises trespass, although its legal foundations are not the same.[66] It is complex and consists of a number of different sets of rules, some statutory and some arising

---

[63]    The provisions we have identified are: Leasehold Reform Act 1967, s 10(1); Housing Act 1985, sch 6, para 1; and Leasehold Reform, Housing and Urban Development Act 1993, sch 7, para 2 and sch 9, para 9.

[64]    See para 3.9 above.

[65]    See J Getzler, "Roman and English Prescription for Incorporeal Property" in J Getzler (ed), *Rationalising Property, Equity and Trusts: Essays in Honour of Edward Burn* (2003) p 281.

[66]    See *Megarry and Wade*, para 28-034.

from the case law; a claimant may choose the rules that suit his or her situation. In *Housden v Conservators of Wimbledon and Putney Commons* Mummery LJ said:

> The rapid expansion of home ownership, the increasing pressures on land available for development and the almost universal reliance on cars for travel outside the city all mean that the need for a simpler law of prescription has become of more rather than less concern.[67]

3.73 In what follows we ask, first, whether the law of prescription should be retained. We look at the merits of having such a system in principle, and at the responses of consultees to the question we asked about it. Having reached the conclusion that the law of prescription for easements should not be abolished, we look at the current sets of rules of prescription. We conclude that if prescription is to be retained then the law must be much more straightforward. We then explain the design of the new statutory scheme for prescription set out in the draft Bill.

## Abolition?

3.74 In *R v Oxfordshire County Council, ex parte Sunningwell Parish Council* Lord Hoffmann said that:

> Any legal system must have rules of prescription which prevent the disturbance of long-established de facto enjoyment.[68]

Many agree with his view. But the usefulness of a law of prescription has to be assessed on its own merits, and we make no assumption that abolition is unthinkable or impossible. Indeed, the Law Reform Committee recommended its abolition 40 years ago, albeit by a narrow majority.[69] Some common law jurisdictions have abolished it.[70]

3.75 The arguments in favour of retention are that prescription has proved invaluable over centuries as a way of regularising long use, bringing the legal position into line with practical reality. More specifically, it is valued as a way of ensuring the continuation of facilities that are essential for the use and marketability of land, and of making good omissions in conveyancing.

3.76 However, the other side of the coin is that prescription penalises neighbourliness and generosity. A landowner who has made no objection to a neighbour's walking across his or her land may regard it as very unfair if that tolerance eventually leads to the land being burdened with a legal easement.

---

[67] [2008] EWCA Civ 200, [2008] 1 WLR 1172 at [72].

[68] *R v Oxfordshire County Council, ex parte Sunningwell Parish Council* [2000] 1 AC 335, 349.

[69] Acquisition of Easements and Profits by Prescription: Fourteenth Report (1966) Law Reform Committee, Cmnd 3100, para 32 and following.

[70] The position is different, for example, between different Australian states; prescription is not possible in New South Wales and Queensland, but remains available in other states. See L Griggs, "Possession, Indefeasibility and Human Rights" (2008) *Queensland University of Technology Law and Justice Journal* 286, 292.

3.77    Prescription may also give rise to practical problems. As there is no express grant involved, it is unlikely that there will be documentary evidence of the existence of an easement acquired by prescription. The prescription period may have been completed in the distant past, and there may be no recent evidence of enjoyment of the right,[71] so that even the most careful of purchasers can be taken by surprise. The lack of written form or evidence also makes it more difficult to determine the precise nature and extent of an easement acquired by prescription. The provisions of paragraph 3 of schedule 3 to the Land Registration Act 2002 have to some extent addressed that problem, by ensuring that an unregistered easement that is not known to, or readily discoverable by, a purchaser and has not been used in the last year will not override a registered disposition; but a purchaser may still be caught unawares, and easements that had overriding status before 2003 will always retain that status.

3.78    So there are competing views about the value of a system of prescriptive acquisition. It is important to note that abolition would not disturb already vested rights acquired by prescription. And it is not clear that modern conveyancing practice is as careless about the express creation of easements, whether by grant or reservation, as may have been the case in the past.

3.79    However, consultees strongly favoured the retention of prescription. We asked in the Consultation Paper whether the current law of prescription should be abolished without replacement, and most consultees said no.[72] They believed that it still serves a useful purpose. We also note that abolition may lead to unforeseen problems; a number of jurisdictions that have abolished both prescription and implication have had to introduce new statutory methods for providing important easements that have been inadvertently omitted from land transfers.[73]

3.80    So we do not recommend the abolition of prescription.

3.81    We asked in the Consultation Paper if prescription might be abolished for negative easements only, on the basis that such easements are in any event an anomaly in the law, and that prescription for such rights (particularly light) gives rise to disproportionate practical problems.[74] The views of consultees varied widely on that question, but again there was no consensus in favour of abolition. Caution was urged particularly about rights to light, which of course are a very important factor in the context of urban development.[75] We do not therefore recommend the abolition of prescription for negative easements.

---

[71]   Clearly there is a related problem here: the difficulty of establishing that an easement has been extinguished by abandonment, which we discuss below at para 3.212 and following below.

[72]   Consultation Paper, paras 4.174 and 4.193(1). We address these two questions together in the Analysis of Responses at paras 4.95 to 4.109.

[73]   See F Burns, "Easements and Servitudes Created by Implied Grant, Implied Reservation or Prescription and Title-by-Registration Systems" in M Dixon (ed), *Modern Studies in Property Law: Volume 5* (2009) ch 3.

[74]   Consultation Paper, para 4.193(2); see the Analysis of Responses, paras 4.110 to 4.118.

[75]   See the Analysis of Responses, para 4.115.

3.82 We have heard calls throughout this project for additional work to be carried out, focused on the reform of rights to light. That would be a major piece of work, as the relevant property law would have to be examined alongside the relevant planning issues. As explained in the Consultation Paper,[76] this project is concerned only with the general law and not specific rights – although we do consider the effect of prescription in respect of rights to light. So we do not wish to recommend special measures for rights to light in the course of this project.

3.83 We asked in the Consultation Paper[77] whether proprietary estoppel could fulfil the role of prescription, and consultees were almost unanimous that it could not. We agree; we said in the Consultation Paper that proprietary estoppel is ill-suited to serve the function of prescription. The specific requirements for representation and detrimental reliance needed to establish estoppel[78] would make it very difficult for the doctrine to function in circumstances where prescription operates.[79] Moreover, the discretionary nature of the courts' response to estoppel means that the doctrine cannot reliably be used as a means of acquiring easements.

3.84 So if the law of prescription is to be retained, what form should it take? It is widely acknowledged that the current law is unsatisfactory, and we summarise briefly the reasons for that before going on to describe the scheme that we recommend.

3.85 It is worth emphasising at the outset that the reform we recommend will have no effect at all upon the law relating to the acquisition of village greens by long use. This is governed by the Commons Act 2006, which will remain untouched by our reform. The Commons Act 2006 uses the same concepts as does the current law of prescription of easements; important case law on those concepts has arisen in the context of the acquisition of village greens,[80] and has been equally authoritative as to the meaning of those concepts in the context of the prescription of easements. In amending the law relating to the latter, we leave untouched the law relating to village greens.[81]

**The current law**

3.86 There are currently three alternative methods of prescriptive acquisition. Although each is a discrete ground on which to base a claim for an easement, it is common practice for claimants to rely on more than one of these simultaneously. The three methods have in common two things. One is the legal fiction that prescriptive use is evidence that an easement was, at some point, expressly granted; the other, which flows from that, is the requirement that the claimed right must have been exercised in a particular way.

[76] Consultation Paper, para 1.24.

[77] Consultation Paper, para 4.193(3); see the Analysis of Responses, paras 4.119 to 4.126.

[78] *Megarry and Wade*, ch 16.

[79] Consultation Paper, para 4.189.

[80] In particular *R v Oxfordshire County Council, ex parte Sunningwell Parish Council* [2000] 1 AC 335; *R (Beresford) v Sunderland City Council* [2003] UKHL 60, [2004] 1 AC 889; *R (Lewis) v Redcar and Cleveland Borough Council (No 2)* [2010] UKSC 11, [2010] 2 AC 70.

[81] See R Meager, "Deference and user as of right: an unholy alliance" [2009] *Rights of Way Law Review* 147.

### The fiction of grant

3.87 The fiction of grant is a powerful and troubling idea. It determines the shape of the law of prescription; many of its features stem from it. One of those is the rule that a landowner without the capacity to grant an easement cannot suffer prescription.[82] Another is the rule that prescription can be claimed only by a fee simple owner against a fee simple owner.[83] The idea is that only a freeholder has the ability to grant an easement for the equivalent of a fee simple. Accordingly, a leaseholder cannot prescribe for the benefit of his or her lease. Long use by a leaseholder may found a claim for an easement appurtenant not to his or her lease but to the freehold of the land. Similarly, use made of the putative servient land while it is let may – subject to conditions that we discuss below – give rise to a prescriptive easement that burdens the freehold.[84]

3.88 The fiction of grant is troubling because it need bear no relation to the truth of what has happened, and a court may find that a grant was made even in the face of clear evidence that it was not.[85]

### The requirements for prescriptive use

3.89 The fiction of grant determines the quality of use required in order to found a claim to a prescriptive easement. The claimant's use of the neighbouring land must have been "as of right"[86] or, more helpfully, "as if of right";[87] in other words, the claimant must have used the land as if he or she was entitled to do so by virtue of an easement already granted to him or her.[88] The English courts have taken their definition of use as of right from Roman law and so have taken it to mean that the use must not be by force, nor by stealth, nor by permission.[89] We describe those characteristics here, since they form an important part of the scheme that we go on to recommend; the reader is referred to the standard texts for the details.[90]

3.90 First, the use must not be by force; breaking through a locked gate cannot amount to prescriptive use. Use by force also includes use in the face of the

---

[82] *Gale on Easements,* paras 4-71 to 4-75; see para 3.165 and following below. The leading case is *Housden v Conservators of Wimbledon and Putney Commons* [2008] EWCA Civ 200, [2008] 1 WLR 1172, although in that case it was held that the conservators of the common did have the necessary power.

[83] Consultation Paper, para 4.238.

[84] But see paras 3.107 and 3.108 below on rights to light under the Prescription Act 1832.

[85] See para 3.101, n 104 below.

[86] *Gale on Easements,* paras 4-77 and 4-78.

[87] *R (Beresford) v Sunderland City Council* [2003] UKHL 60, [2004] 1 AC 889 at [72] by Lord Walker.

[88] "That is to say, openly and in the manner that a person rightfully entitled would have used it": *R (Lewis) v Redcar and Cleveland Borough Council (No 2)* [2010] UKSC 11, [2010] 2 AC 70 at [67] by Lord Hope. The Supreme Court held in that case that the fact that the claimant's use of the land was courteous, deferring to the use that others made of the same land, did not prevent it being "as of right".

[89] Because of the Roman origins of this idea, it is often expressed in Latin: "*nec vi, nec clam, nec precario*".

[90] See para 2.1, n 1 above.

landowner's objections or protests.[91]

3.91 Secondly, the use must not be secret;[92] walking across the land in daylight is acceptable, doing it only under cover of darkness is, generally, not. The use must be such that an ordinary diligent owner, acting in the protection of his or her interests, would have had a reasonable opportunity to become aware of the use.[93]

3.92 Thirdly, the use cannot be by permission; use as of right is inconsistent with the permission of the servient owner since someone who has a right does not need permission. Permission may be express or may be inferred from "overt and contemporaneous acts of the owner".[94] Permission is thus different from acquiescence, which amounts to a deliberate but passive acceptance and is therefore consistent with (and evidence of) use as of right.

3.93 It is not clear whether the law also imposes separate requirements, first that the servient owner must have acquiesced in the claimant's actions, and, second, that the servient owner must have known or have had the opportunity to find out about the use. Are these two additional elements that the claimant must prove, or are they encapsulated in the requirements that the use be not by force, nor by stealth nor by permission?

3.94 We take the view that acquiescence is a way of describing what is required for prescription. It is not the same as permission (which of course must be absent), but is rather a state of tolerance, where the use is carried out openly, and the servient owner does not object, but does not actively permit. The idea of knowledge, or of opportunity for knowledge, is built into the idea that the use is not secret, and acquiescence is part of our understanding of the requirements for prescription.[95] Neither has to be proved as a separate element in the claim.[96] Lord Hoffmann, in *R v Oxfordshire County Council, ex parte Sunningwell* stated:

---

[91] *Dalton v Henry Angus & Co* (1880-81) LR 6 App Cas 740, 786; *Newnham v Willison* (1988) 56 P & CR 8, 19. In *Smith v Brudenell-Bruce* [2002] 2 P & CR 4, two strongly worded letters sent by the servient owner objecting to the use was held to mean that use made by the claimant after that point was contentious and therefore by force. For further discussion on this topic see *Gale on Easements*, para 4-84 and following; *Megarry and Wade*, para 28-036 and *Gray and Gray*, para 5.2.67.

[92] See *Liverpool Corporation v H Coghill & Son Ltd* [1918] 1 Ch 307, which concerned the secret discharge of waste fluid from a factory into the public sewer, and *Dalton v Henry Angus & Co* (1881) 6 App Cas 740.

[93] *Union Lighterage Co v London Graving Dock Co* [1902] 2 Ch 557, 571, by Romer LJ. See also *Gale on Easements*, para 4-90 and following; *Megarry and Wade*, para 28-037 and *Gray and Gray*, para 5.2.68.

[94] *Gale on Easements*, para 4-95, citing *R (Beresford) v Sunderland City Council* [2001] EWCA Civ 1218, [2002] QB 874 at [13] by Dyson LJ. See *Gale on Easements*, para 4-94 and following. See also *Megarry and Wade*, para 28-038 and *Gray and Gray*, para 5.2.69.

[95] *Dalton v Henry Angus & Co* (1880-81) LR 6 App Cas 740, 773 to 774, by Fry J.

[96] We mention one small exception at para 3.170 below.

There is in my view an unbroken line of descent from the common law concept of *nec vi, nec clam, nec precario* to the term "as of right" in the Acts of 1832, 1932 and 1965.[97]

3.95   Finally, what the claimant does, although tortious, must not have been a criminal offence, except in circumstances where the use would *not* have been criminal if an easement had been granted.

3.96   In *Bakewell Management Ltd v Brandwood*,[98] the claimant sought to establish an easement to drive over common land in order to access his home by car – as he and other home owners had been doing for many years. Section 193 of the Law of Property Act 1925 provides that it is an offence, punishable by a fine, to drive a vehicle over common land without lawful authority. The claim therefore failed at first instance and in the Court of Appeal, because the use was unlawful. However, it succeeded in the House of Lords, on the basis that the use of the access was not "unlawful" because a prior grant of a right of way (which, as we have seen, forms the basis of a prescriptive claim) would have been "lawful authority" for the purposes of section 193(4) of the Law of Property Act 1925.

3.97   So much for the quality of the use. For how long must the use have gone on, continuously, in order to found a prescriptive claim? The answer differs under the three different methods of prescription.

### Prescription at common law

3.98   This is the oldest of the three methods of prescription and probably the least satisfactory. The principle behind common law prescription is that where a right has been enjoyed since time immemorial it is presumed to have a lawful basis; "since time immemorial" is defined by statute as since 1189.[99] The evidential difficulty in proving this is obvious. The current common law rule is that if use as of right for a period of 20 years can be shown then it is presumed that this has been the case since 1189.[100] However, where it can be shown that the enjoyment of the right commenced since 1189, or that it could not have existed at that date or subsequently, this will rebut the presumption.[101]

### Prescription by lost modern grant

3.99   As time marched on and the limit of legal memory slipped further into the past, the vulnerability of a claim based on prescription at common law increased. The courts responded by introducing a new form of prescription, namely, prescription

---

[97]  [2000] 1 AC 335, 355 to 356, referring to the Prescription Act 1832, the Rights of Way Act 1932 and the Commons Registration Act 1965.

[98]  [2004] UKHL 14, [2004] 2 AC 519.

[99]  This date (the date of the accession of Richard I to the throne) was fixed by statute in 1275. See *Gale on Easements*, paras 4-05 to 4-07 for a fuller explanation of the historical origins of the presumption. See also *Megarry and Wade*, paras 28-044 to 28-046.

[100]  *Megarry and Wade*, para 28-045.

[101]  *Hulbert v Dale* [1909] 2 Ch 570, 577; *Megarry and Wade*, para 28-044 notes that "a claimant to prescription at common law must therefore have the boldness to assert that he and his predecessors have enjoyed the right since 1189", meaning that evidence that the right had not been enjoyed during that period would destroy the claim.

by lost modern grant. The introduction of the doctrine, which recognises that use dating back to 1189 can rarely be proved, was not without controversy, but was finally established by the House of Lords in *Dalton v Henry Angus & Co.*[102]

3.100 Lost modern grant was explained by the Court of Appeal in *Tehidy Minerals Ltd v Norman* thus:

> Where there has been upwards of 20 years' uninterrupted enjoyment of an easement, such enjoyment having the necessary qualities to fulfil the requirements of prescription, then unless, for some reason such as incapacity on the part of the person or persons who might at some time before the commencement of the 20-year period have made a grant, the existence of such a grant is impossible, the law will adopt a legal fiction that such a grant was made, in spite of any direct evidence that no such grant was made.[103]

3.101 The presumption that arises from 20 years' use as of right cannot be rebutted even by proof that no grant was made.[104] However, it is a good defence to a claim based on the doctrine that during the entire period when the grant could have been made, there was nobody who could lawfully have made it.[105]

### Prescription under the Prescription Act 1832

3.102 The Prescription Act 1832 did not supplant prescription at common law or by lost modern grant, and it is not unusual to plead all three methods alternatively. The statute introduced two periods for prescription, of 20 and 40 years.[106] Twenty years' use prevents the servient owner from resisting a prescriptive claim on the basis that the right claimed could not have existed in 1189. Forty years' use can give rise to an easement even if the use was enjoyed with the oral permission of the owner of the land over which the use was exercised.

3.103 The use must have been continuous, as of right, and have been enjoyed for the requisite period immediately prior to the proceedings to which the claimant of the right is a party.[107] The requirement that the use continues right up to the issue of

---

[102] (1880-81) LR 6 App Cas 740. The earliest case in the reports is said to be *Lewis v Price* (1761), noted in 2 Wms Saund 175, 85 ER 926.

[103] [1971] 2 QB 528, 552, by Buckley LJ.

[104] *Bridle v Ruby* [1989] QB 169. In this case the claimant had used his neighbour's driveway for access to his garage for 22 years in the mistaken belief that the right to do so had been reserved in an earlier conveyance. In fact the reservation had been deleted from the conveyance and the deleted clause had been initialled by his predecessor in title. The Court of Appeal held that the presumption of lost modern grant was not rebutted by evidence that the grant had not in fact been made.

[105] *Tehidy Minerals Ltd v Norman* [1971] 2 QB 528, 552, by Buckley LJ. See also *Gale on Easements*, para 4-08 and following, *Megarry and Wade*, para 28-047 and following, and *Gray and Gray*, para 5.2.75.

[106] Prescription Act 1832, s 2. Section 1 of the Act also introduced periods of 30 or 60 years for profits. As we recommend that it should no longer be possible to prescribe for profits, we make no further reference to profits in our discussion of prescription.

[107] Prescription Act 1832, s 4. See *Llewellyn (Deceased) v Lorey* [2011] EWCA Civ 37, [2011] NPC 14 as an example of a case that turned, in part, upon the question as to whether use was continuous.

proceedings, which is sometimes referred to as the "next before action" requirement, is a special rule unique to prescriptive acquisition under the Prescription Act 1832. The rule means that even where there has been qualifying use for the required period, or more, a claim can still be defeated if it can be shown that use ceased at some stage before proceedings were brought.[108]

3.104 The requirement in section 2 of the Prescription Act 1832 for the use to have been continuous, or "without interruption", has a technical meaning: prevention of the use (for example by obstruction) for less than a year does not stop time from running.[109] This leads to the well-known but strange result that use of, say, a neighbour's drive for 19 years and a day can almost guarantee the user an easement since the servient owner cannot now prevent it by interruption if proceedings to claim the easement are brought at exactly the right time. However, if proceedings are commenced after the 20-year anniversary, the claim will at that point fail if by then there has been a year's interruption.

3.105 Section 7 of the 1832 Act makes special provision about prescription against persons under a legal disability;[110] where the 20-year period is claimed, the period or periods during which such persons are under a disability are disregarded for the purpose of computing the prescription period.

3.106 Section 8 of the 1832 Act extends the longer period of prescription beyond 40 years in certain circumstances. It does this by excluding from the calculation of that period time during which the putative servient land has been let for a term exceeding three years. It is not clear whether the section applies to all easements[111] but it is clear that sections 7 and 8 do not apply to rights to light.[112]

3.107 There are other small but important differences in the rules that apply to the prescriptive acquisition of rights to light under the Prescription Act 1832. Section 3 provides that where a right of light has been enjoyed for 20 years, next before action and without interruption, the right shall be deemed absolute and indefeasible unless the right was enjoyed by written consent or agreement. This means that oral consent does not prevent prescription, so that 20 years' qualifying use of a purported right to light has an effect equivalent to 40 years' qualifying use of any other easement. There is no requirement that use of light be "as of right"; mere use and enjoyment of the right is sufficient and it is not necessary that the use is without force and without stealth.[113] No easement of light can be acquired over Crown land under the Act because section 3 is not expressed to bind the Crown.

[108] *Parker v Mitchell* (1840) 11 Ad & El 788, 113 ER 613. Proceedings can be brought by the owner of the servient or dominant land.

[109] Prescription Act 1832, s 4.

[110] Prescription Act 1832, s 7 lists these as "an infant, idiot, non compos mentis, feme covert, or tenant for life". This list must now be understood in the light of intervening statute law and is discussed further in *Gale on Easements*, para 4-50.

[111] There is a suggestion that there is a typographical error in section 8 of the Act, and that "watercourses" should have been the more general "easements": See *Gale on Easements*, para 4-52 and following.

[112] See *Gale on Easements,* paras 4-51 to 4-52.

[113] *Colls v Home and Colonial Stores Ltd* [1904] AC 179, 205.

3.108    Under the 1832 Act a tenant can prescribe for a right to light against his or her landlord,[114] or against another tenant of his or her landlord.[115] This is an exception to the rule that use must be by or on behalf of a fee simple owner against a fee simple owner.[116]

### The Rights of Light Act 1959

3.109    We have to conclude this sketch of the current law of prescription by mentioning the Rights of Light Act 1959, which made it possible to interrupt the enjoyment of light without the need for a physical obstruction, by introducing a form of notional interruption. The owner of land over which light passes to a building can, on obtaining a certificate from the Lands Chamber, apply to the local authority for the registration in the Local Land Charges Register of a light obstruction notice. Where successfully applied for, the notice has effect until the expiry of one year beginning with the date of registration. Once the notice is in place, then for the purposes of determining whether a person is entitled to a prescriptive right to light (under any method of prescription) the access of light to the building subject to the notice shall be treated as if it has been obstructed, to the same extent as if it had been physically obstructed.[117]

### Conclusions on the current law

3.110    In the Consultation Paper we noted that the co-existence of three methods of prescription is a major defect in the law.[118] In *Tehidy Minerals Ltd v Norman*, Buckley LJ said that the current position is:

> … anomalous and undesirable, for it results in much unnecessary complication and confusion. We hope that it may be possible for the Legislature to effect a long-overdue simplification in this branch of the law.[119]

As things stand, litigation is complicated by the need to analyse alternative claims; so is the legal analysis that has to be undertaken by Land Registry staff when an application for registration is made, since the registrar has to be satisfied that the right claimed is valid even if it is not contested. A single set of rules would have an immediate beneficial impact on the workload of all aspects of the legal system involved in the law of prescription.

3.111    We also questioned the value of the fiction of grant, which can lead to a court having to conclude that there was a grant even in circumstances where clearly

---

[114] *Foster v Lyons & Co Ltd* [1927] 1 Ch 219, 227.

[115] *Morgan v Fear* [1907] AC 425.

[116] See *Megarry and Wade*, paras 28-040 and 28-076 to 28-077; *Gale on Easements*, paras 4-68 to 4-70.

[117] For further reading see *Gale on Easements*, para 4-23 and following and *Megarry and Wade*, para 28-073 and following.

[118] Consultation Paper, para 4.168.

[119] [1971] 2 QB 528, 543, by Buckley LJ.

there was not.[120]

3.112 Accordingly, while we did not advocate abolition of the law of prescription, the Consultation Paper provisionally proposed that the three existing methods should be replaced. We maintain this view. Clearly, to have a number of different methods of prescription, as under the current law – essentially three, but with further variants (in particular for rights to light) – is untidy and unnecessarily complex. Consultees' responses were eloquent in their condemnation of the current situation.[121]

**3.113** **We recommend that the current law of prescription should be abolished, and replaced with a new statutory scheme for the prescriptive acquisition of easements.**

3.114 Clause 18(1) of the draft Bill effects that abolition,[122] and the new scheme, which we now go on to describe, is set out in clauses 16, 17 and 18(2).

## A new statutory scheme for prescription

3.115 Our provisional proposal in the Consultation Paper was for a statutory scheme based on the quality of the claimant's use of the servient land, restricted to registered land, whereby a legal easement would not be acquired until the claimed easement was registered. On further consideration, and in the light of the views expressed to us by Land Registry, we have developed and modified that proposal. The scheme we now recommend is best explained by setting out the objectives of reform and discussing the design of the new scheme by reference to those objectives.

3.116 In formulating reform, then, we have had regard to the following objectives:

(1)    simplicity;

(2)    the avoidance of litigation;

(3)    compatibility with land registration principles; and

(4)    ensuring that the scope for prescription is not extended.

3.117 We set out and explain our recommendations by reference to these objectives as follows.

### (1) Simplicity

3.118 The current methods should be abolished and replaced by a single statutory scheme that does not resort to fiction and does not have the complexity of the current methods.

3.119 The reformed scheme we recommend therefore embodies a single prescription

---

[120] Consultation Paper, para 4.171; also see *Bridle v Ruby* [1989] QB 169.

[121] See the Analysis of Responses, paras 4.95 to 4.109.

[122] Subject to transitional provisions which we explain at para 3.179 and following below.

period, and imposes exactly the same requirements for all types of easement. There are no special rules for rights to light.[123] However, the scheme employs some familiar features from the current law. Rather than inventing something entirely new, we have put together a scheme that will not be alien to practitioners, although it will be a great deal simpler than what is available at the moment.

3.120    The scheme depends upon the quality of the use of the servient land, and not upon the state of mind of the servient owner. At the heart of our recommendations for prescription is the provision that qualifying use for the requisite period should give rise to a prescriptive easement. We have avoided, so far as possible, the requirement of acquiescence.

3.121    As we noted above, we take the view that in almost all cases acquiescence is established by proof of use that was carried out without force, without stealth and without permission. If those requirements are met, there is (with an exception to which we revert below) no scope for a defence that the servient owner did not acquiesce; use of that quality proves that he or she did.[124] We take the view that it is inappropriate to introduce a requirement to prove a state of mind. The three practical elements are sufficient.

3.122    Equally, the new scheme incorporates no provisions about the claimant's state of mind, which is irrelevant under the current law[125] save in very unusual circumstances.[126]

**3.123    We recommend that:**

    **(1)    an easement will arise by prescription on completion of 20 years' continuous qualifying use;**

    **(2)    qualifying use shall be use without force, without stealth and without permission; and**

    **(3)    qualifying use shall not be use which is contrary to the criminal law, unless such use can be rendered lawful by the dispensation of the servient owner.**

The recommendation is embodied in clauses 16(1) and 17(1) of the draft Bill. The central concept here is qualifying use, a concept familiar from the current law. Clearly, "use" has a broad range of meanings in this context, and encompasses positive easements where the servient land is used as access, or for drainage, as well as the exercise of a negative easement. Where there is a right to light, for example, the unobstructed passage of light across the servient tenement enables the dominant owner to enjoy the access of light, and the

that the Rights of Light Act 1959 is retained: see para 3.109 above.

3.170 below.

*uby* [1989] QB 169.

facts of *Chamber Colliery Co v Hopwood* (1886) 32 Ch D 549 (see *Gale on* para 4-103), where use of a neighbour's land in the mistaken belief that it was der the terms of the lease was held not to be qualifying use. We have taken hese circumstances are so unusual that we should make no special licate the result in that case.

servient land is used in that sense.

3.125 The use must be continuous. That term does not carry the technical meaning that it has under the Prescription Act 1832; as in the current rules for common law prescription and lost modern grant there is no provision for interruption. This is consistent with the law of adverse possession: if a squatter is ejected, for however short a period, the period of adverse possession built up before that date will not avail the squatter in a future claim.[127]

3.126 However, the continuous use need not be by one and the same person. As in the current law, provided there is no interruption during the prescription period, that period can be made up of the total unbroken consecutive use of the servient land by the claimant and his or her predecessors in title.

3.127 The meaning of "without force, without stealth and without permission" is well-established and represents no change from the current requirements. We have chosen to use the term "permission" because it expresses the current requirement more precisely than does the word "consent" (which is perhaps rather more easily confused with acquiescence).[128]

3.128 As this is an entirely new scheme of prescription, the qualifying minimum period of long use could have been of any length. We sought, and received, suggestions on duration from consultees. There was no clear consensus although there was a general feeling that 20 years was appropriate, having the benefit of familiarity from the current law.[129]

3.129 The scheme replicates the current rule about criminal activity. This is expressed in the draft Bill by the requirement that the qualifying use must be of a kind in relation to which an easement could have been granted.[130] A purported grant of a right of way, for example, which breached the criminal law, would be unlawful "and incapable of vesting any right in the grantee"[131] – unless, as in *Bakewell Management Ltd v Brandwood*, that grant would have meant that the use was not

---

[127] Nor does the scheme incorporate any special protections to replicate sections 7 and 8 of the Prescription Act 1832. These provisions are uncertain in scope, rarely invoked, and complex, and we see no need to perpetuate them.

[128] There is authority for the use of the word "licence": in *R v Oxfordshire County Council, ex parte Sunningwell Parish Council* [2000] 1 AC 335, 350, Lord Hoffman referred to use that was "not by force, nor stealth, nor the licence of the owner". In *R (Lewis) v Redcar and Cleveland Borough Council (No 2)* [2010] UKSC 11, [2010] 2 AC 70 at [20] (by Lord Walker) and [87] (by Lord Rodger) the word "licence" was also used. We prefer, for the future, the term "permission" as being closer to ordinary language.

[129] See the Analysis of Responses, paras 4.127 to 4.136.

[130] Draft Bill, cl 17(1)(a).

[131] *Bakewell Management Ltd v Brandwood* [2004] UKHL 14, [2004] 2 AC 519 at [39] by Lord Scott.

criminal.[132]

3.130   Note that the scheme embodies no special rules for rights to light. This is a departure from the current law; although common law prescription and lost modern grant treat claims to light in the same way as any other claim, section 3 of the Prescription Act 1832 gives light a privileged status by providing – in effect – that oral consent will not prevent a claim. We saw no need to replicate this privilege. We are conscious of the sensitivity and value of claims to light and are not convinced that oral permission is compatible with the acquisition of a right to light by prescription. We also take the view that consistency within this part of the law is more important.

### (2) The avoidance of litigation

3.131   An important element of our recommendation is the absence of a "next before action" rule. Provided that the party claiming the prescriptive easement has completed a minimum of 20 years' continuous qualifying use, he or she has an easement. Prescription does not depend, as it does under the Prescription Act 1832, upon there being litigation; consultation revealed that the "next before" rule is exceptionally unpopular.[133] It is not needed for common law prescription or lost modern grant.

3.132   The "next before" requirement does, of course, encourage claimants to resolve any claim promptly, before evidence becomes stale; and that in turn may prevent the possibility of purchasers being caught unawares by rights that arose off register. We think that those risks are outweighed by the virtue of having a simple rule where litigation is not an inevitable part of the prescription process.

3.133   Where there is a dispute, and it is claimed that an easement arose some time previously, a court will naturally treat stale evidence with caution and attach less weight to it where this is appropriate. In reality, stale evidence is rarely a problem; prescription issues tend to come to light when land changes hands and the use is continuing. And the risk to purchasers is further minimised by the provisions relating to overriding interests in the Land Registration Act 2002,[134] which mean that unregistered legal easements, unprotected by notice against the servient owner's title, are vulnerable to losing their overriding status. That is particularly relevant to prescriptive easements. They do pose a threat to a purchaser; but in fact, if they are not obvious, not known to the purchaser, and infrequently used (where there is no use in the year preceding a sale)[135] they will cease to burden

---

[132]   Draft Bill, cl 17(1)(a). Clause 17(2) of the draft Bill also provides that it is not possible for anyone to prescribe for an easement over their own land; in para 4.44 below we recommend that it should be possible for a registered proprietor to set up easements (etc) over a defined plot of his or her own land before selling it, in order to facilitate the conveyancing of large developments, and so the draft Bill makes this provision so as to ensure that there is no suggestion of any further abrogation of the "unity of seisin" rule.

[133]   See the Analysis of Responses, paras 4.137 to 4.155.

[134]   See para 2.61 above.

[135]   Note that unregistered legal easements for drainage will typically survive, even if unsuspected, due to frequent use. But such easements are rarely a trouble to the servient land.

the purchaser's title.[136]

### (3) The new scheme must be consistent with the law and practice of land registration

3.134 It will be clear from what we have said above that the new statutory scheme will apply in the same way to registered and unregistered land. Where the dominant land is registered the dominant owner should, in his or her own interests, apply for the easement to be registered once it comes into being; the occasion to do so may arise when land changes hands and, indeed, the prescriptive easement may be overridden by a registered disposition if it is not the subject of a notice on the register for the servient land and is neither obvious nor frequently used.

3.135 Our provisional proposal in the Consultation Paper was rather different: that qualifying use for the prescription period should give rise not to an easement but to a right to apply to have a notice entered on the register of title against the servient land.[137]

3.136 The Consultation Paper did not resolve what would happen if title to the servient land was not registered so that the process of prescription could not be completed. This was left as an open question for consultees, but we noted that the answer might well be that qualifying use for the prescription period would simply give rise to an easement over unregistered land, without any registration requirement.[138] We did not address the situation where title to part of the servient land is registered and part unregistered.

3.137 Consultees were unhappy with a scheme that depended upon registration. They pointed out that it left the claimant vulnerable to interference (or to overriding by a disposition of the servient land) after the completion of the prescription period but before the easement was registered; and they strongly objected to the replication of the "next before" requirement. Moreover, the idea that a proprietary right comes into existence at the point of registration imposes upon Land Registry an inappropriate role. Land Registry is not a tribunal and does not adjudicate disputes. To have registration itself be the decisive point at which the easement came into being would give Land Registry a judicial role.[139]

3.138 The scheme we recommend therefore does not pursue our provisional proposals to use the entry of a notice on the register as the linchpin for the acquisition of a prescriptive easement. It gains in simplicity as a result, and is consistent with

---

[136] Note also that our recommendation at para 3.230 below will make abandonment a more effective answer to the problem of obsolete easements.

[137] And, of course, the right to have the easement itself registered if title to the dominant land was registered. See the Consultation Paper, paras 4.221(2) and 4.222.

[138] Consultation Paper, paras 4.251 to 4.256.

[139] It is because Land Registry does not adjudicate disputes that the Adjudicator exists as an independent tribunal; but the Adjudicator has no involvement in applications to register.

registration principles.[140]

3.139 Nor have we developed the idea floated in the Consultation Paper, that a landowner, concerned about the possibility of prescription, might be able to register a notice of objection to prescription. The effect of such a notice would be to prevent use of the land by a neighbour from being qualifying use for the purposes of prescription.

3.140 The suggestion drew upon an analogy with notices under the Rights of Light Act 1959.[141] Its merit would be the introduction of a non-confrontational way to prevent prescription. Members of our Advisory Board liked it on that basis, but were concerned that the possibility of registering a notice of objection would lead to a practice of blanket registration as a defensive measure. The way to prevent this would be to permit the registration of objection only to specific easements, identified by description and with a plan. But that, too, would cause problems of its own: how accurate would the notice of objection have to be in order to prevent the easement that the neighbour might one day claim? How far could the line on the plan deviate from the precise route taken by the potential claimant? In addition, Land Registry was concerned about the idea of using a notice to register something that is not a right.[142]

3.141 Taken together, these points indicate that a system of notices of objection would be unprincipled as well as impracticable, and we have not pursued it.

### (4) The new scheme should not extend the scope for prescription

3.142 Although very few consultees wanted prescription to be abolished, we did hear a clear message to the effect that there is no enthusiasm for extending the reach of prescription. It should not become easier to establish; nor should it be open to a wider range of claimants.

3.143 Any scheme that is different from the current law is likely, perhaps certain, to make claims either easier or harder, and to allow a broader or narrower range of claimants than the current law. There is a risk that a less complex scheme may turn out to be an easier scheme; and we have taken steps to avoid that. In the light of consultees' concerns, with which we agree, we have shaped our policy so as to ensure that, where there is potentially a difference in scope between the current law and what we recommend, the outcome is a narrower law of prescription rather than a wider one. We discuss here some issues where we

---

[140] That means that there is no need to pursue our suggestions about the giving of notice to a registered servient owner (Consultation Paper, para 4.231), nor the possibility of giving the servient owner a veto similar to that he or she enjoys when faced with an application by an adverse possessor (Consultation Paper, para 4.232). If prescription has a practical role to play, it is not appropriate to make it subject to a veto. See the Analysis of Responses, paras 4.171 to 4.187. Land Registry will, of course, serve notice on the servient owner when there is an application to register a prescriptive easement and the servient owner has the opportunity to contest the validity of the claim.

[141] See para 3.109 above.

[142] See the Analysis of Responses, paras 4.183 to 4.187. A notice of objection could, in theory, be registered as a local land charge, as are notices under the Rights to Light Act 1959; but that would have an unacceptable impact upon the dozens of local authorities who would then have to be involved.

made that choice.

PRESCRIPTION BY AND AGAINST A FREEHOLDER

3.144    Currently prescription must be by, and against, a freeholder. A tenant cannot suffer prescription, although a prescriptive easement can arise against the freeholder while land is let. A tenant cannot prescribe against his or her landlord, although prescriptive use by a tenant against a third party may give rise to an easement in favour of the freeholder.[143]

3.145    In *China Field Ltd v Appeal Tribunal (Buildings)*,[144] a decision of Hong Kong's Court of Final Appeal, Lord Millett considered in great detail the law on prescriptive acquisition of easements in England and Wales and, in particular, the "fee simple" rule[145] and the "common landlord" rule.[146] He said:

> The [fee simple] rule is both counter-intuitive and contrary to the policy of the law. It is counter-intuitive because it is difficult to see why it should be impossible to presume a lost grant of an easement by or to a lessee for the term of his lease when such a grant may be made expressly ... . It is contrary to the policy of the law, for if the disturbance of long established *de facto* enjoyment of a right is contrary to legal policy, then this is equally the case whether the enjoyment is by or against a freeholder or a leaseholder.[147]

3.146    We asked in the Consultation Paper whether those rules should be relaxed in order to enable leaseholders to make claims to rights that were important to the use of their properties.[148] The law in this area might be viewed as unduly restrictive; on the other hand, to permit prescriptive acquisition by or against a leaseholder would expand the circumstances in which prescription may take place. It would also lead to the creation of prescriptive easements of a limited duration, since they could last no longer than the leases to which they were appurtenant and/or the leases against which they arose.

3.147    Our question (we did not make a proposal on the point) drew a wide range of responses and comment. A number of consultees saw little justification for any change and drew our attention to practical consequences that might result from a

---

[143] See *Gray and Gray*, paras 5.2.58 to 5.2.60; *Megarry and Wade*, paras 28-040 to 28-042; *Gale on Easements*, paras 4-59 to 4-76.

[144] [2009] HKCU 1650.

[145] "The ... rule ... that in order to acquire an easement by any form of prescription, including lost modern grant, the user must be by or on behalf of the owner in fee simple against an owner in fee simple". See *China Field Ltd v Appeal Tribunal (Buildings)* [2009] HKCU 1650 at [51].

[146] "The principle that the possession of a tenant is considered to be that of his landlord. If the fee simple rule stands, then it follows that a claim by prescription cannot succeed where both dominant and servient tenements are held under a common landlord". See *China Field Ltd v Appeal Tribunal (Buildings)* [2009] HKCU 1650 at [66].

[147] *China Field Ltd v Appeal Tribunal (Buildings)* [2009] HKCU 1650 at [54]. See G Healey, "Easements and tenancies" (2010) 1(Jan) *Woodfall on Landlord and Tenant Bulletin* 1 and M Merry, "A matter of authority but not of principle – acquisition by lessees of easements by long enjoyment" [2010] *Conveyancer and Property Lawyer* 176.

[148] Consultation Paper, para 4.238 and following.

relaxation of the restriction. We were asked[149] what would happen where a lease was originally granted for less than 20 years but was subsequently renewed under the Landlord and Tenant Act 1954, Part II. Would each renewal restart the clock or would the period be treated as cumulative? Consultees foresaw significant difficulties in practice, on the basis that if tenants could prescribe against their landlord's property the task of regenerating housing estates would be made very much more difficult.[150]

3.148    We explored the practicalities further with both Land Registry and our Advisory Board. We came to the conclusion that the problem, if it can be characterised as such, has the potential to affect only tenants of long leases,[151] and that any benefit reform might bring would only be achieved by disproportionately complex legislative provisions, and at the cost of widening the scope of prescription to an unknown extent.

3.149    Accordingly, we have not pursued the suggestion raised in the Consultation Paper and recommend that the new scheme reflect the current position. We have therefore not followed the views expressed by Lord Millett, quoted above at paragraph 3.145; we agree with consultees that the scope of prescription should not be extended.

**3.150    We recommend that qualifying use must be carried out by, and against, a freeholder.**

3.151    That recommendation is reflected in clause 16(2) of the draft Bill. In view of the fact that it is possible (albeit not particularly likely) for a prescriptive easement to arise against a freehold while land is let,[152] the draft Bill also provides, by way of clarification, that an easement so arising will bind the owners of all the interests subsisting in the servient land, not merely the freeholder.[153]

PRESCRIPTION BY THOSE IN ADVERSE POSSESSION OF LAND

3.152    We also asked whether there should be special rules about the acquisition of prescriptive easements by those in adverse possession of land.[154] Those who acquire title to land by adverse possession may face a problem; the prescription period is longer than the period for adverse possession, and they may therefore find that they have acquired title to land but have not acquired the easements they need to access it or for drainage.

3.153    However, there are obvious problems in granting special privilege – in the form of a shorter prescription period – to those in adverse possession of land. Consultees felt that this was unjustified, and we agree; and indeed, there is little

---

[149] By Gregory Hill (Barrister, Ten Old Square Chambers).

[150] See the Analysis of Responses, paras 4.188 to 4.201.

[151] The shorter the lease, the less worthwhile it will be to claim a prescriptive easement.

[152] See para 3.169 and following below.

[153] Draft Bill, cl 16(3).

[154] Consultation Paper, para 4.247.

or no evidence that the law causes real problems in practice in this respect.[155]

RIGHTS TO LIGHT

3.154 Rights to light are treated in the same way as all other easements in the recommendations that we make for the reform of prescription. But we have to make one special provision in the context of the Custom of London.

3.155 The Custom of London applies in relation to the buildings in a defined area within the boundary of the City of London.[156] It gives freehold owners[157] the right to build or rebuild on the ancient foundations of their buildings to any height regardless of whether this will result in any loss of light to neighbouring properties.[158]

3.156 The effect of the Custom is twofold. It can prevent the acquisition of a right to light where it is claimed on the basis of lost modern grant or on common law prescription,[159] and it can be a defence to a claim for the infringement of an existing right to light.[160] We are concerned with the first effect.

3.157 The Custom does not prevent all possible prescriptive claims to rights to light within the city boundary. It is ineffective – and so does not prevent prescription – when a right to light is claimed under section 3 of the Prescription Act 1832 because it is overridden by the wording of that section which applies "any local usage or custom to the contrary notwithstanding".

3.158 We have recommended that the three existing methods of prescription should be abolished and be replaced with a new statutory scheme of prescriptive acquisition. This then raises the question of how the Custom and the new scheme should operate in relation to one another. Should the new scheme for prescription be subject to the Custom of London, so as to prevent all claims to prescriptive rights to light within the city boundary? If the new scheme is not made subject to the Custom then the scope for prescriptive acquisition will be wider than in the current law; if the new scheme is overridden by the Custom then the reverse is true.

3.159 As we have explained above,[161] it is an underlying principle of the new scheme that it will not extend the scope for prescription. For that reason we have chosen

---

[155] See the Analysis of Responses, paras 4.202 to 4.210.

[156] The area that comprises the City of London is that land that falls within the City of London Corporation's boundary. The boundary has changed over time; the City Solicitor holds information on the current and previous extent of the boundary. See more generally: S Bickford-Smith and A Francis, *Rights of Light: The Modern Law* (2nd ed 2007) para 6.13(4).

[157] Originally the Custom applied only to residential properties but in the case of *Perry v Eames* [1891] 1 Ch 658 it was held to extend to non-residential properties as well.

[158] The terms of the Custom were set out by the Recorder of the City of London in *Plummer v Bentham* (1757) 1 Burr 248, 97 ER 297.

[159] See *Bowring Services v Scottish Widows Fund and Life Assurance Society* [1995] 1 EGLR 158.

[160] See S Bickford-Smith and A Francis, *Rights of Light: The Modern Law* (2nd ed 2007) para 6.13(4) and *Gale on Easements*, para 7-30.

[161] See paras 3.142 and 3.143 above.

to make the acquisition of a right to light by long use under the new scheme and within the boundary of the City of London Corporation subject to the Custom of London.

3.160 We have been able to identify one other custom – the Custom of York – which is in similar terms to the Custom of London.[162] We believe that Custom is now defunct but there may be other local customs or usages that have an equivalent effect to the Custom of London but of which we are not aware. Our policy in regard to these, if any exist, is the same as for the Custom of London.

**3.161 We recommend that rights to light created under the new scheme shall be subject to any local usage or custom to which they are currently subject.**

3.162 Clause 16(4) of the draft Bill enacts this policy.

THE PRESERVATION OF CURRENT IMMUNITIES

3.163 All that we have said so far ensures that our scheme does not widen the range of potential prescription claimants. The final step we took in order to limit the scope of the law relates to servient owners, because we were also concerned not to widen the range of those against whom a successful prescription claim can be made.

3.164 Our recommendations would set up an acquisitive scheme (one where the statute generates the easement) rather than an evidential scheme (whereby the statute sets up the conditions under which a grant is presumed, even though all concerned know that there was no grant).[163] But in order not to widen the scope of prescription, the scheme will have to incorporate some features derived from the current law in order to replicate, as closely as we can, some of its restrictions. There is therefore an element of pragmatism in the recommendation we make in relation to the capacity of the potential servient owner, and our recommendation about prescriptive use when land is let. Elements of the old system have to be retained, in both these cases, in order to avoid unintended consequences of a new scheme.

*Capacity*

3.165 First, then, capacity. The current law of prescription is based upon the fiction of grant, which means that a landowner who could not have granted the easement claimed cannot suffer prescription; the fiction of grant is impossible and therefore so is prescriptive acquisition.[164] Consultees offered a range of views about this.[165] However, since the close of the formal consultation we have heard deep concern

---

[162] S Bickford-Smith and A Francis, *Rights of Light: The Modern Law* (2nd ed 2007) para 6.13(4).

[163] In *R v Oxfordshire County Council, ex parte Sunningwell Parish Council* [2000] 1 AC 335, 349, Lord Hoffmann analysed the law of prescription and alluded to the theoretical bases for prescription, comparing the Roman law acquisitive model with the evidential model seen in English law. See also S Anderson "Easements and Prescription – changing perspectives in classification" (1975) 38 *Modern Law Review* 641.

[164] *Megarry and Wade*, para 28-050, *Gale on Easements*, paras 4-71 to 4-75, *Gray and Gray*, para 5.1.43 and 5.1.44.

[165] See the Analysis of Responses, paras 4.211 to 4.232.

from bodies who are currently, in effect, exempt from prescription due to a lack of capacity to grant easements and do not wish to see that exemption disappear.

3.166 It is difficult to judge who "ought" to be able to be subject to prescription.[166] What is clear to us is that it would not be appropriate for reform to subject to potential claims persons who are not currently subject to them, in the absence of a good reason for such a change. They would include freeholders with no capacity to grant easements as a result of a statutory restriction upon the terms on which they held the land;[167] freeholders who cannot grant an easement without the consent of another body;[168] and freeholders suffering from mental incapacity to an extent that prevents them from making a grant.

3.167 We want to ensure that freeholders, who currently cannot suffer prescription because they do not have capacity to grant an easement, have a defence to a claim.[169] This does not bring back a fiction of grant; but it replicates a feature of the old law in order not to extend the scope of prescription. It means that where land cannot be made subject to an easement by grant, it cannot be made so subject by prescription either. Accordingly, we make an additional recommendation, embodied in clause 17(3) of the draft Bill.

**3.168 We recommend that use of land cannot be qualifying use, for the purposes of prescription, at any time when the land is in the freehold ownership of a person or body who is not competent to grant an easement over it.**

*Prescriptive use when land is let*

3.169 The second step we have to take to ensure that reform does not make landowners any more vulnerable to prescription arises from consideration of what happens when there is potentially prescriptive use of land that is let.

3.170 The current law requires use "as of right" and, as we argued above, "as of right" means not by force, nor by stealth, nor by permission.[170] There is no separate requirement to prove that the freeholder knew or ought to know of the qualifying use. But there is one exception to that principle: one instance where the requirements for knowledge and acquiescence have an independent role to play. It arises from the requirement that prescriptive use be by and against a fee

---

[166] Mr William Pumphrey, one of the curators of the Monken Hadley Common, suggested that the protection should be extended to any land granted by Act of Parliament to a body for a particular purpose. We took the view that this was not practicable; it would be impossible to assess the impact of such a change, but it would appear to be an immunity considerably wider than the current law affords.

[167] These will be unusual bodies similar to the Conservators in the *Housden v Conservators of Wimbledon and Putney Commons* [2008] EWCA Civ 200, [2008] 1 WLR 1172 case. However, it would appear that any restriction in the articles of a limited company that might restrict its capacity to grant an easement will no longer prevent a prescriptive claim: Companies Act 2006, s 39(1) (the statutory successor to the European Communities Act 1972, s 9).

[168] This includes a rector, who needs the consent of the bishop – see *Gale on Easements*, para 3-07.

[169] The current law is seen in *Gale on Easements*, paras 4-71 and following, and 3-04 and following.

[170] See para 3.89 and following above.

simple owner.[171] When land is let, prescriptive acquisition of an easement can succeed only against the freeholder, and only if the freeholder acquiesces in the prescriptive use. Normally acquiescence follows from the fact of qualifying use.[172] But when land is let, the fact that a neighbour walks across it openly does *not* mean that the freeholder knows of it or has means of knowing of it; the land is let and so the tenant is in exclusive possession. And when land is let the fact that the use is without force may mean that the tenant acquiesces in it – but that is immaterial, and that quality of use does not mean that the landlord acquiesces. Accordingly, landlords are in effect protected from prescription while their land is let unless it can be proved that they did indeed know of the use, and did indeed acquiesce in it in the sense that (under the terms of the lease) he or she could have taken action but did not.[173]

3.171   We have sought to replicate that protection by a recommendation, reflected in clause 17(4) and (5) of the draft Bill.

3.172   **We recommend that use of land which is let shall not amount to qualifying use at any time when the servient freehold owner does not have power to prevent the use while the lease continues, or does not know about it and could not reasonably have discovered it, unless:**

   **(1)   the use began before the lease was granted; and**

   **(2)   at the time when the lease was granted the landlord knew about the use or could reasonably have discovered it.**

3.173   The purpose of that proviso is to ensure that a freeholder who knows about prescriptive use does not then become immune from prescription in the event that the land is let; but that if the use began so shortly before the lease was granted that the landlord had no opportunity to take action, he or she is protected from prescription.

3.174   If a claim to a prescriptive easement is litigated, it should be for the servient owner to raise the issue of capacity, or of lack of knowledge or power if the land was let, as defences. He or she will be in a position to prove that he or she did not have the requisite knowledge,[174] in a case where the land was let at the start of the period, and likewise to show that the 20-year period claimed included a time where there was no capacity to grant an easement. It should not be for the claimant to prove that the freeholder did have knowledge, or that the servient owner at all times did have capacity.[175]

---

[171]   See para 3.87 above.

[172]   See para 3.94 above.

[173]   *Williams v Sandy Lane (Chester) Ltd* [2006] EWCA Civ 1738, [2007] 1 P & CR 27, particularly at [24] and following and see *Llewellyn (Deceased) v Lorey* [2011] EWCA Civ 37, [2011] NPC 14.

[174]   Note the comments in *Gale on Easements*, para 4-114.

[175]   Draft Bill, cl 17(3).

**Prescription and the Crown**

3.175    Generally, the reforms that we recommend would bind the Crown; but reform of the law relating to prescription calls for further comment in relation to Crown land.

3.176    Generally Crown land is treated in the same way as any other for the purposes of the law of prescription. But while the Prescription Act 1832 makes special mention of the Crown in sections 1 and 2, it does not do so in section 3. Accordingly it is not possible to prescribe for a right to light, under the Prescription Act 1832, against Crown land. We take the view that that position should be replicated in the new statutory scheme.

**3.177    We recommend that it shall not be possible to prescribe for a right to light, under the new scheme, against Crown land.**

3.178    Clause 17(6) and (7) puts this recommendation into effect.

**Transitional provisions**

3.179    The reform of the law of prescription raises the issue of transitional provisions: prescription takes time. What is to be done about potential claims that have not been completed – to put it very loosely – at the point when reform takes place? Clearly the priority here is to ensure that vested rights remain secure and that reform does not operate to take away from anyone what has already been acquired.

3.180    The most obvious transitional issue is the potential claimant who has started, but not completed, a period of prescriptive use at the point when the new scheme comes into force. Let us suppose that A has been making qualifying use of B's land for 10 years at the point of reform. In this context it is important to bear in mind that whereas the law relating to possession of land dictates that a squatter has an interest in land from the outset, and before the expiry of the limitation period,[176] the law of prescription has a different theoretical foundation; prescriptive use gives rise to nothing until the prescriptive period has expired.

3.181    It would have been possible for us to provide that qualifying use under the old law should be added on to qualifying use under the new law, so that 10 years later A will acquire an easement but would have to establish his or her claim – if disputed – under two different sets of rules. That is unduly complex and would lead to the survival of the old law for up to 19 years and 364 days following reform.[177] Our preferred approach is to apply the new scheme to pre-commencement use.

3.182    The requirements of the new scheme are simpler, and in some respects more restrictive; use of light, for example, preceded by oral consent, will be disqualified under the new scheme. To that extent, the application of the new rules to pre-reform use may amount to a retrospective adjustment of the criteria, but no more. There is no question of interference with property rights, because until the prescriptive period is completed there is no question of the claimant having an easement; applying the new law to the pre-reform use seems to be a lesser evil

---

[176] *Asher v Whitlock* (1865-66) LR 1 QB 1.

[177] Because of the possibility of prescriptive use that started one day before the reform.

than requiring people to do battle with the old law for nearly 20 years after reform.

3.183    However, the Prescription Act 1832 generates a special transitional case because of the peculiarities of its drafting. We noted above that the special meaning of "continuous" use under the 1832 Act means that there comes a point when prescriptive use cannot be defeated by interruption.[178] So once a potential claimant has 19 years and one day's use then, provided that he or she does not abandon the use thereafter, success is guaranteed, provided that an "action" is taken at the requisite time.

3.184    Such claims should not be defeated by reform. Accordingly we make two recommendations about transitional cases.

3.185    **We recommend that the new statutory scheme for prescription that we recommend shall apply to use that commenced before the implementation of reform, subject to the recommendation that follows.**

3.186    **We recommend that the Prescription Act 1832 shall continue in force for one year after the implementation of reform, in order to enable potential claimants who, at the date of implementation, are in a position to take advantage of sections 1, 2 or 3 of that Act or are within one year of being able to do so to make their claim.**

3.187    Obviously if a landowner has already met the demands of common law prescription or, far more likely, lost modern grant, at the date of reform then an easement has already arisen by prescription and there is no transitional issue at all: reform changes nothing. Accordingly the draft Bill provides that the new scheme applies to use that took place before reform if it continues afterwards,[179] while ensuring that if an easement has actually been acquired under the old law at the point of reform then any dispute about it will be determined according to the old law.[180] Clause 18(2) of the draft Bill preserves the Prescription Act 1832 insofar as is necessary to ensure that potential claimants who are in a position to claim under that Act or are in the last year of use where interruption cannot defeat the claim will not be disadvantaged by reform.[181] Where a potential claimant does not take advantage of this continuation of the old law they will become subject to the new law and any claim to the benefit of an easement acquired by prescription will have to be proved under the new rules.

### (5) EASEMENTS THAT CONFER THE RIGHT TO EXTENSIVE USE

**The legal principles**

3.188    We now turn to an issue that relates to the characteristics of an easement, namely the problem of easements that confer a right to extensive or even exclusive use of the servient land. The problem that we discuss may occasionally

---

[178]  See para 3.104 above.

[179]  Draft Bill, cl 16(5).

[180]  Draft Bill, cl 18(1) and (2).

[181]  That preservation of the Prescription Act 1832 applies equally to profits.

be relevant to profits too,[182] but we discuss it here in relation only to easements since that is where it is known to give rise to practical difficulties.

3.189 Clearly, not every arrangement for one person to make use of another's land can be an easement. In Part 2 we explained that, in order to qualify as an easement or profit, a right must comply with the requirements set out in *Re Ellenborough Park*.[183] The fourth of those requirements is that the right must be "capable of forming the subject matter of a grant". To determine whether this is so, certain questions must be asked:

> Whether the right conferred is too wide and vague, *whether it is inconsistent with the proprietorship or possession of the alleged servient owners*, and whether it is a mere right of recreation without utility or benefit.[184]

If any of these is answered in the affirmative, then the "right" cannot be an easement.

3.190 In the Consultation Paper we discussed the implications of the words we have italicised, because they have caused particular problems during recent years in the context of easements, or purported easements, that confer a right to park or otherwise seem to give the grantee an extensive or intensive right to use the servient land.[185]

3.191 The difficulty is this: an easement or profit is an interest in land, not an estate. If what the dominant owner can do on the servient land actually amounts to an ownership right – regardless of the words used – then it cannot be an easement. That much is clear. What is more difficult is to delineate precisely the point at which the dominant owner's right can be said to be "too much" to be merely an interest in land.

3.192 The earlier cases, up to and including *Re Ellenborough Park*, answered this question in terms of what the dominant owner is allowed to do. Peter Luther has demonstrated that the nineteenth century cases were concerned about the scope of the right asserted, and regarded as valid easements that permitted a narrowly-defined activity.[186] Mixing muck on a neighbour's field,[187] occupying a church pew while attending services,[188] and placing stones on the foreshore to protect land from erosion[189] were all acceptable; a right to do pretty much anything that the dominant owner liked, or a right that was too uncertain in its extent, was not.[190]

[182] *Polo Woods Foundation v Shelton-Agar* [2009] EWHC 1361 (Ch), [2010] 1 P & CR 12.

[183] [1956] Ch 131.

[184] *Re Ellenborough Park* [1956] Ch 131, 175 to 176, by Lord Evershed MR (emphasis added).

[185] Consultation Paper, paras 3.34 to 3.55.

[186] P Luther, "Easements and exclusive possession" (1996) 16 *Legal Studies* 51.

[187] *Pye v Mumford* (1848) 11 QB 666, 116 ER 623.

[188] *Hinde v Chorlton* (1866-67) LR 2 CP 104.

[189] *Philpot v Bath* (1905) 21 TLR 634.

[190] *Reilly v Booth* (1890) LR 44 Ch D 12.

And that was the difficulty with the claimed right in *Copeland v Greenhalf*,[191] where the defendant claimed an easement that allowed him to park any number of vehicles on the plaintiff's land, for as long as he liked. That was too extensive to be an easement; a right to store coal in a shed, in *Wright v Macadam*,[192] was held not to be.[193]

3.193 However, in recent decades the emphasis has changed. In *Street v Mountford*[194] the House of Lords held that the grant of a right to exclusive possession, for a term, is a sufficient condition for the creation of a lease. Exclusive possession is the right to exclude others, involving both factual control and the legal ability to exclude others.[195] That principle gives rise to a problem when set beside the earlier cases. If exclusive possession is the *right* (rather than just a practical ability) to exclude all others,[196] then it becomes inadequate to define an easement merely by reference to the range of activities it permits, because a right to do only one thing may nevertheless confer exclusive possession – as does a lease for storage, for example.[197] That dilemma did not arise in the earlier cases, at a time when the defining characteristic of an ownership right had not been formulated in this way. Lopes LJ, in *Reilly v Booth*, was able to say "there is no easement known to law which gives exclusive and unrestricted use of a piece of land"[198] without specifying whether the important word was "exclusive" or "unrestricted". But exclusive possession is now the hallmark of an estate in land;[199] and therefore *Wright v Macadam* is now regarded as problematic, and as inconsistent with *Copeland v Greenhalf*. How can a right be an easement (and not an estate) if it confers exclusive possession of the servient land?[200]

3.194 So the turning point represented by *Street v Mountford* in the law of leases has had the effect of teasing out into two principles the requirement that an easement must not be "inconsistent with the proprietorship or possession of the alleged

---

[191] [1952] Ch 488.

[192] [1949] 2 KB 744.

[193] We note that there are difficulties in reconciling those two decisions; but the principle is clear.

[194] [1985] AC 809.

[195] *Gray and Gray*, para 2.1.6 and following.

[196] See para 2.3 above.

[197] We disagree with the view expressed by Peter Luther (see para 3.192, n 186 above) that exclusive possession necessarily involves an unlimited range of activities. A lease confers exclusive possession, even where its terms limit the uses to which the tenant may put the building. Exclusive possession is the right to take possession of land and to exclude others.

[198] (1890) LR 44 Ch D 12, 26.

[199] Subject to the exceptions set out in *Street v Mountford* [1985] AC 809, 821.

[200] By that is meant the portion of the servient land over which the easement is exercised. Difficulties cannot be resolved by looking at the whole of the land of the servient owner (because such a solution would enable the grant of an easement to build a house and live in it if the servient owner has a large estate but not if he or she has a small one): see *Moncrieff v Jamieson* [2007] UKHL 42, [2007] 1 WLR 2620 at [57].

servient owners".[201]

3.195   First there is the concern with exclusive possession. A grant that confers exclusive possession for a defined term must be a lease; a grant of exclusive possession without a term is almost certainly a fee simple. That much is clear, although it does call for care where land is sold and the parties wish to grant or reserve easements – both in consideration of the practical arrangement and in drafting.

3.196   On the other hand there is the "ouster principle", distilled from the older cases, that an easement must not leave the servient owner without any reasonable use of his or her land. This is a shift in focus from the dominant owner to the servient; it can be seen in the words of Mr Justice Upjohn in *Copeland v Greenhalf*,[202] and traced back to the Scottish House of Lords decision in *Dyce v Hay*,[203] where Lord St Leonards said:

> There can be no prescriptive right in the nature of a servitude or easement so large as to preclude the ordinary uses of property by the owner of the lands affected.[204]

3.197   Judge Paul Baker QC put it this way:

> The essential question is one of degree. If the right granted in relation to the area over which it is to be exercisable is such that it would leave the servient owner without any reasonable use of his land … it could not be an easement though it might be some larger or different grant.[205]

3.198   The extent of the ouster principle is unclear, and that gives rise to problems in the context of any purported easement that confers a right to make extensive use of the land, even if not actually to exclude the servient owner.

**Extensive or exclusive use**

3.199   Both these principles cause difficulty where there is a purported grant of a right to make particularly extensive use of land. The most controversial and frequently encountered example (as well as the most economically important) is the right to park, although similar difficulties arise with a right to make sole use of a bin area or balcony. A parking space may be transferred as part of a freehold, or demised as part of a lease; alternatively a right to park may be conferred alongside an estate (usually along with a lease), and that is where particular pitfalls may lie.

---

[201] *Re Ellenborough Park* [1956] Ch 131, 176, by Lord Evershed MR.

[202] [1952] Ch 488, 498 (quoted in the Consultation Paper, para 3.36).

[203] (1852) 1 Macq 305.

[204] *Dyce v Hay* (1852) 1 Macq 305; quoted by Lord Scott in *Moncrieff v Jamieson* [2007] UKHL 42, [2007] 1 WLR 2620 at [54].

[205] *London & Blenheim Estates Ltd v Ladbroke Retail Parks Ltd* [1992] 1 WLR 1278, 1288.

3.200    Clearly if such arrangements are in effect the grant of exclusive possession, they cannot be easements. A right to park in a lockable garage on terms that the dominant owner (that is, the person benefiting from the easement) will have sole access to the only key will not pass the test. A grant that gives the right wholly to exclude the owner of the land, all the time, is not an easement.

3.201    However, the ouster principle is a different matter. Alexander Hill-Smith has provided a useful survey of parking cases, in an endeavour to determine at what point of intensity the use of a parking space becomes impermissible.[206] Establishing where that point may be is problematic and the cases do not give consistent answers. A right to park a vehicle at any time anywhere in a car park has been held to be a valid easement[207] while the exclusive right to park in several car parking spaces for 9.5 hours on each weekday has been held to be invalid.[208]

3.202    The ouster principle in the context of car parking was explored by the House of Lords in *Moncrieff v Jamieson*, where Lord Scott explained:

> It has been argued that the rights of parking claimed by the pursuers in respect of the [putative servient land] deprive the defenders of any reasonable use of that land, are therefore inconsistent with their ownership of [the land] and should not be recognised as servitudal rights in rem … . This is the so-called "ouster" principle.[209]

3.203    Lord Scott suggested that a "test of degree" was unhelpful, and might be replaced by a test that asked whether the servient owner retained possession and control of the land. As we noted in the Consultation Paper, the factual background of the case,[210] as well as the fact that the decision concerned the law of Scotland, mean that it cannot be said to determine the issue conclusively for English law.

3.204    So the extent of the ouster principle, and the point at which it prevents an easement from being valid, is unclear, and that lack of clarity puts many valuable parking rights at risk. Future litigation could produce a decision that invalidated many of them, yet such rights are constantly being created.[211] The law also causes difficulties for Land Registry, whose staff have to determine whether what is being created is an easement or an estate in land. The difficulty is exacerbated by current drafting practices, which often employ terms such as "exclusive use" or

---

[206] See A Hill-Smith, "Rights of parking and the ouster principle after *Batchelor v Marlow*" [2007] *Conveyancer and Property Lawyer* 223.

[207] *Newman v Jones* (22 March 1982) Ch (unreported); cited in A Hill-Smith, "Rights of parking and the ouster principle after *Batchelor v Marlow*" [2007] *Conveyancer and Property Lawyer* 223, where it is noted that extracts from the judgment are cited in *Handel v St Stephens Close* [1994] 1 EGLR 70.

[208] *Batchelor v Marlow* [2001] EWCA Civ 1051, [2003] 1 WLR 764.

[209] *Moncrieff v Jamieson* [2007] UKHL 42, [2007] 1 WLR 2620 at [54].

[210] The case concerned an expressly granted right of way; the issue was whether that included an ancillary right to park.

[211] Recent Land Registry data supplied to us suggests that over 7,500 exclusive rights to park were created in 2009/2010.

"exclusive right". It may not be clear whether what is being conferred is a right to exclusive possession, in other words excluding all others including the dominant owner, or simply the sole use of the land for a particular purpose together with a promise not to grant a conflicting right to use the land to others (without excluding the owner).

**Reform**

3.205 As the law stands, then, an easement must not confer exclusive possession of the servient land; nor must it prevent the servient owner from making reasonable use of it. These two different principles were both discussed in the Consultation Paper. We endeavoured there to devise a test which would ensure that the grant of exclusive possession did not prevent that grant being an easement,[212] but further consideration, and the responses of consultees, have led us to revise our view.[213] As we said in the Consultation Paper, "easements and possessory interests in land must be mutually exclusive";[214] reform of the law that made it impossible to discern whether a particular right was a lease (or fee simple) or an easement would be unsustainable.

3.206 The law should remain that if the dominant owner is granted exclusive possession of land then, while it may be a grant of a lease or a freehold, it cannot be an easement.

3.207 The ouster principle is a different matter. We have explored the difficulties to which it gives rise; it is hard to see that the principle is particularly useful. Easements will not, of course, normally deprive the servient owner of any reasonable use of the servient land, but if the parties wish to make such an arrangement (without conferring exclusive possession) it is hard to see why they should not do so. In line with that thinking, the courts have been moving to a less conservative view of parking easements.

3.208 We conclude therefore that while an easement must not grant exclusive possession, the ouster principle should be abolished.[215] An easement that stops short of exclusive possession, even if it deprives the owner of much of the use of his land, or indeed of all reasonable use of it, is valid. The effect of this would be to reverse, for the future, the decision in *Batchelor v Marlow*,[216] for example, and therefore to validate a potentially wide range of parking easements. In particular, easements that confer an "exclusive right to park" would be clearly valid, provided

---

[212] Consultation Paper, para 3.55.

[213] See the Analysis of Responses, paras 3.29 to 3.41.

[214] Consultation Paper, para 3.34.

[215] The effect of this would be to effectively reverse the decision in *Copeland v Greenhalf* [1952] Ch 488 (see paras 3.192 and 3.196 above).

[216] [2001] EWCA Civ 1051, [2003] 1 WLR 764.

that the servient owner can access the land (to however limited an extent).[217]

**3.209** **We recommend that a right to use another's land in a way that prevents that other from making any reasonable use of it will not for that reason fail to be an easement.**

3.210 Clause 24 of the draft Bill puts our recommendation into effect.

3.211 The only further comment we make in relation to this is that some easements, particularly those allowing pipes to be exclusively used, would appear to give the user exclusive possession of the land through which the pipe runs. We do not wish to cast doubt upon easements that are, under the current law, "undoubtedly" valid.[218] History here seems to provide the explanation: long before *Street v Mountford*, it was well-established that certain easements such as those for pipes were valid. They remain an exception to principle and one upon which we do not wish to cast doubt.

### (6) THE EXTINGUISHMENT OF EASEMENTS AND PROFITS BY ABANDONMENT

**The current law**

3.212 In the following paragraphs we look at the law relating to the termination of an easement or profit by abandonment.[219] In the Consultation Paper we explained that an easement or profit can be extinguished by abandonment[220] where there is some act or omission on the part of the owner of land benefited by it, accompanied by an intention to abandon the right.[221]

3.213 Whether abandonment has occurred is a question of fact.[222] There are various factors that lead a court to infer that abandonment has occurred; for example, where a dominant owner has made alterations to the dominant tenement which make the enjoyment of an easement or profit impossible or unnecessary.[223]

3.214 Consideration of the possibility of extinguishment by abandonment requires us to take into account two competing concerns. One is the need to preserve property rights and avoid any unlawful deprivation of property, while the other is the need

---

[217] *Virdi v Chana* [2008] EWHC 2901 (Ch), [2008] NPC 130 concerned the right to park in a space that was somewhat larger than a car, but not much larger. HHJ Purle QC considered that the ability of the servient owner to plant and tend to a tree, to maintain and repair a fence, to replace the fence with a wall or to put signage up (all without substantially interfering with the enjoyment of the right to park) were all indicators of possible uses which could be made of servient land which would prevent ouster having occurred.

[218] *Gale on Easements*, para 1-56.

[219] In this section on abandonment we refer, for the most part, only to easements; but what we say applies equally to profits.

[220] This is also called "implied release".

[221] Consultation Paper, para 5.14.

[222] Examples of when abandonment has been held to have occurred and where it has not are set out in *Megarry and Wade*, para 29-010 and *Gray and Gray*, para 5.2.91.

[223] See *Megarry and Wade*, paras 29-010 to 29-011.

to ensure that land is not burdened by rights that are obsolete. It benefits no-one to have titles encumbered by easements and profits that are never going to be used; but those who hold such interests should not be obliged to defend their rights by constant use.

3.215 The law relating to extinguishment by abandonment should balance those two concerns by enabling the law to respond to the fact that an interest is positively unwanted. This is particularly important because, although obsolete restrictive covenants can be discharged by the Lands Chamber pursuant to section 84 of the Law of Property Act 1925, there is at present no such jurisdiction for easements and profits. We recommend its extension to easements and profits created after the enactment of our reforms, but we cannot make that recommendation for existing interests,[224] and so reform to the law relating to abandonment remains important for existing rights. Even for those created in the future, the availability of section 84 and the possibility of abandonment are not mutually exclusive and both should be available.

3.216 In the Consultation Paper we expressed concern about the difficulty of establishing that an easement has been abandoned.[225] We referred to *Benn v Hardinge*,[226] where the fact that an easement had not been used for 175 years was not sufficient to establish abandonment of a right of way, because, the court held, "it might be of significant importance in the future".[227]

3.217 If abandonment is too hard to prove, then legal entitlements may bear little or no relation to the actual use of the land. Contrast the law relating to prescription, which brings legal entitlements into line with use. Prescription may be established by 20 years' use, whereas abandonment may be impossible to establish, because of the difficulties in finding intent, even after many years of non-use.

3.218 There are two possible responses to this problem. One is to devise another way for easements and profits to be brought to an end, by extending the jurisdiction of the Lands Chamber so that it can discharge obsolete easements and profits. We make a recommendation to that effect in Part 7 below but, for reasons we explain there, we can make that recommendation only for easements and profits created after the date of reform.

3.219 The other response is to reform the law relating to abandonment. We approach that with caution. Abandonment involves a positive intention on the part of the dominant owner to deprive him or herself of a property right, and therefore the courts have said that:

---

[224] See para 7.32 below, and the Analysis of Responses, paras 14.14 to 14.25.

[225] Consultation Paper, paras 5.14 to 5.22.

[226] (1993) 66 P & CR 246.

[227] *Benn v Hardinge* (1993) 66 P & CR 246, 262, by Hirst LJ.

Abandonment is not, we think, to be lightly inferred. Owners of property do not normally wish to divest themselves of it unless it is to their advantage to do so, notwithstanding that they may have no present use for it.[228]

## The proposals in the Consultation Paper

3.220 In the Consultation Paper we made two proposals in relation to abandonment:

(1) that, where title to land is registered and an easement or profit has been entered on the register of the servient title, it should not be capable of extinguishment by reason of abandonment; and

(2) that, where title to land is not registered or title is registered but an easement or profit has not been entered on the register of the servient title, it should be capable of extinguishment by abandonment, and that where it has not been exercised for a specified continuous period a presumption of abandonment should arise.[229]

3.221 We made those proposals in the light of another concern: the integrity and security of the register of title. We took the view that once an easement or profit had been protected by an entry on the register of title to the servient land, there should be no possibility of abandonment at all. However, where an easement or profit was not so protected, we proposed to bolster the possibility of proving abandonment by introducing a presumption of abandonment once it had not been used for a particular period.

3.222 Responses to the first proposal were mixed. Some consultees expressed agreement, with the proviso that it should be possible to secure the extinguishment of easements through the Lands Chamber. A number of consultees disagreed on principle, arguing that where the circumstances indicate abandonment, the fact that the easement is registered does not change that.

3.223 Two responses in particular have caused us to decide not to proceed with the first proposal. Both Herbert Smith LLP and the response of Michael Croker, Miriam Brown and Kevin Marsh[230] demonstrated that it would cause insuperable problems where a number of properties were burdened by an easement, some with registered titles and some without.[231] The result would be that the easement would be extinguished as to some servient tenements and not others, in a haphazard fashion which depended entirely upon the registration status of the burdened land.

3.224 In the light of these points we have decided not to pursue the proposal that there can be no abandonment of an easement where the burdened land is registered

---

[228] *Gotobed v Pridmore* (1971) 217 EG 759, 760, by Buckley LJ, cited with approval in *Williams v Usherwood* (1983) 45 P & CR 235, 256, by Cumming-Bruce LJ and *Benn v Hardinge* (1993) 66 P & CR 246, 257 to 261, by Dillan LJ.

[229] Consultation Paper, paras 5.30 and 5.31.

[230] Michael Croker, Miriam Brown and Kevin Marsh co-authored a single response, see the explanation at para 3.19 of the Analysis of Responses.

[231] See the Analysis of Responses, paras 5.1 to 5.11.

and the easement is noted on the servient title.

3.225 Our second proposal must therefore be approached on the basis that it should remain possible for any easement to be abandoned regardless of whether title to land is registered or not. Should a continuous specified period of non-use give rise to a presumption of abandonment?

3.226 The effect of this proposal would not be novel, because until 1993, when *Benn v Hardinge*[232] was decided, that was regarded as being the law. The 1984 edition of *Megarry and Wade* stated:

> If the dominant owner shows an intention to release an easement or profit, it will be extinguished by implied release. Mere non-user is not enough by itself, even if accompanied by a mistaken belief that the right has been extinguished; an intention to abandon the right must be shown. *Nevertheless non-user for a long period may raise a presumption of abandonment. For this purpose twenty years' non-user will usually suffice but even then the presumption is rebuttable if there is some other explanation.*[233]

3.227 Consultation responses revealed two particular questions arising from the idea of a presumption of abandonment. Some consultees asked whether there should be a different rule for interests that are, by their nature, exercised infrequently (for example, a right to haul timber). We were also asked whether our proposal would prejudice owners who had not been able, perhaps through ill-health, to exercise their rights. We take the view that neither example gives rise to concern; a presumption of abandonment would, in both these cases, be relatively easy to rebut.

3.228 The other concern, by contrast, was about the difficulty of proving non-use. Certainly this may not be easy. Nor should it be. Proving abandonment is almost impossible at present; we see the introduction of a presumption as the re-opening of a narrow door, but not of floodgates. It will still be for the applicant to prove continuous non-use for a specified number of years; and even then the presumption can be rebutted.

3.229 Subject to those points, the proposal attracted substantial support from consultees. The question remains what period of non-use should give rise to a presumption of abandonment. Twenty years was the period supposed to give rise to that presumption before *Benn v Hardinge*,[234] and there is an obvious parallel with the prescription period.

---

[232] (1993) 66 P & CR 246.

[233] R Megarry and H W R Wade, *The Law of Real Property* (5th ed 1984) pp 897 to 898 (emphasis added). See *Moore v Rawson* (1824) 3 B & C 332, 339; 107 ER 756, 759 to 760 and *Lawrence v Obee* (1814) 3 Camp 514, 170 ER 1465, which concerned an easement of light to a window. A presumption of abandonment arose after it was found that the window had been bricked up for 20 years.

[234] (1993) 66 P & CR 246.

**3.230    We recommend that where an easement or profit has not been used for a continuous period of 20 years, there should be a rebuttable presumption that it has been abandoned.**

3.231    Clause 27 of the draft Bill gives effect to this recommendation.

## (7) THE TERMINATION OF THE ESTATE TO WHICH AN INTEREST IS APPURTENANT

### The decision in *Wall v Collins*

3.232    It is clear from the words of the Law of Property Act 1925 that, in order to take effect at law, an "easement, right or privilege" must be "for an interest equivalent to an estate in fee simple absolute in possession or a term of years absolute".[235]

3.233    An easement or a profit can be granted to, or by, a leaseholder; and such interests exist, obviously, for the duration of the lease and no longer.[236] They are therefore granted for a term "equivalent to ... a term of years absolute".[237] The question which then arises is: what happens to an easement that benefits a lease if the lease itself ceases to exist? This could happen in a number of ways. The estate could be terminated by notice to quit (whether given by the landlord or by the tenant), forfeited for breach of condition or covenant, disclaimed on the tenant's insolvency,[238] surrendered or merged. Surrender takes place where the leasehold terminates because the landlord acquires the lease. Merger may, but will not always, occur when a tenant acquires the superior estate (usually the freehold); there is merger if, in accordance with equitable principles, there is an intention that there be a merger.[239]

3.234    The question we are asking here is not about interests that *burden* a lease.[240] It is well-established that an easement that has been granted by a leaseholder, burdening his or her lease, in favour of a third party, will be extinguished by forfeiture of the lease.[241] When a lease is surrendered, an easement which burdened the lease will become a burden upon the superior estate (usually the freehold, but it may be a superior lease).[242] When the lessee acquires the superior estate, there is the possibility of merger; but merger is an equitable doctrine and there is a presumption that merger was not intended if it was "only

---

[235] LPA 1925, s 1(2)(a).

[236] *Wall v Collins* [2007] EWCA Civ 444, [2007] Ch 390 at [15] by Carnwath LJ: "the grantee has an interest at least co-extensive with the period of the easement".

[237] LPA 1925, s 1(2)(a).

[238] A lease may be disclaimed by the trustee in bankruptcy of an individual tenant, or by the Treasury Solicitor when the lease becomes *bona vacantia* on liquidation of a company. In these circumstances the lease comes to an end – whereas a freehold, in these circumstances, escheats (see Lewison and others, *Woodfall on Landlord and Tenant: Volume 1* (2010) para 16.118 and following and paras 17.271 to 17.275).

[239] Under LPA 1925, s 185.

[240] This is one of the issues raised by Andrew Lyall in his article "What are Easements Attached or Appurtenant to?" [2010] *Conveyancer and Property Lawyer* 300, 306; but this is not the problem addressed by our proposals in the Consultation Paper.

[241] *Megarry and Wade*, para 18-031.

[242] *Barrett v Morgan* [2000] 2 AC 264, 270, by Lord Millett.

consistent with the duty of the party that the merger should not take place".[243] This means that, if X (a lessee) grants an easement to Y and then acquires the superior estate to his lease, merger will not be permitted because merger would extinguish Y's easement and thus be inconsistent with the duty X owes to Y.

3.235 So the position as to burdens is clear. Rather, we are concerned here with rights that *benefit* a lease and burden the land of a third party.[244]

3.236 Until recently it was relatively clear that such interests did not survive the ending of the lease. We have to say "relatively"; the answer was perfectly clear so far as forfeiture was concerned:

> If a lease is forfeited, then any subordinate property rights fall with it.[245]

3.237 There was rather less authority about surrender, disclaimer and merger, but the view generally taken was, as the 17th edition of *Gale on Easements* put it, that:

> An easement granted expressly or impliedly to a tenant determines with the expiration or determination by any means of the tenancy.[246]

3.238 That was also the view taken by Land Registry; where a lease came to an end by merger, surrender, disclaimer or forfeiture then any easements over third party land were treated as coming to an end along with the estate to which they were regarded as being appurtenant.[247]

---

[243] Lewison and others, *Woodfall on Landlord and Tenant: Volume 1* (2010) para 17.054.

[244] Generally they will have been granted by a third party; rights granted to a lessee by the landlord over the latter's retained land will determine, as a result of unity of seisin, when the lease comes to an end. But in *MRA Engineering Ltd v Trimster Co Ltd* (1988) 56 P & CR 1 an easement had been granted by a landlord to his tenant over retained land, which he then sold, and the issue was whether the easement (over the third party's land) survived to benefit the landlord after surrender of the lease. See paras 3.248 and 3.249 below.

[245] R Smith, *Property Law* (6th ed 2009) p 408. See also *Bendall v McWhirter* [1952] 2 QB 466, 487, by Romer LJ: "every subordinate interest must perish with the superior interest on which it is dependent". Compare the clear position in relation to sub-leases: *Gray and Gray*, paras 4.4.83 and 4.4.84 and *Great Western Railway Co v Smith* (1875-76) LR 2 Ch D 235, 253.

[246] J R Gaunt and P Morgan, *Gale on Easements* (17th ed 2002) para 1-31 at n 12, citing *Beddington v Atlee* (1887) 35 LR Ch D 317 and *MRA Engineering Ltd v Trimster Co Ltd* (1988) 56 P & CR 1.

[247] On the other hand, Andrew Lyall takes a different view in his article "What are Easements Attached or Appurtenant to?" [2010] *Conveyancer and Property Lawyer* 300. He does not, however, refer to the authorities cited in para 3.237, n 246 above.

3.239    However, the Court of Appeal arrived at a different position in *Wall v Collins*.[248] The claimant sought to enforce a right of way which, the parties agreed, had been expressly granted in 1911 to the leaseholder of the property of which the claimant was now the freehold owner. The lease was for a 999-year term, granted in 1910. Some time after that grant, that leaseholder acquired the freehold estate in the dominant land. At first, the freehold estate was expressed to be subject to the 1910 lease and an entry was made in the charges register of the freehold title noting the lease. However, in 1999, when the claimant bought the freehold and leasehold titles from the individual who then owned both, the entry in the charges register noting the lease was removed on the express instruction of his solicitor. There seems little doubt that at that moment the freehold and leasehold estates merged, so that the leasehold estate ceased to exist.[249]

3.240    The question for the court was the effect on the 1911 easement of the merger of the leasehold with the freehold. The judge at first instance had held that as the right of way was attached to the lease, the right was lost when the lease was extinguished by merger. The Court of Appeal rejected this analysis. Whilst accepting that the easement could last no longer than the 1910 lease, the court asserted that whatever its legal source (whether a conveyance, a lease, or a separate grant) the easement was attached to the land it was intended to benefit. Accordingly, the merger of the leasehold with the freehold did not extinguish the right of way. It survived to benefit the freeholder, albeit only for its original term. Lord Justice Carnwath stated:

> As a matter of common sense, it is difficult to see why a lessee should be worse off, so far as concerns an easement annexed to the land, merely because he has acquired a larger interest in the [benefited land].[250]

3.241    In the next edition of *Gale on Easements* we find the text quoted at paragraph 3.237 above updated as follows:

---

[248] [2007] EWCA Civ 444, [2007] Ch 390.

[249] See *Wall v Collins* [2007] EWCA Civ 444, [2007] Ch 390 at [12].

[250] *Wall v Collins* [2007] EWCA Civ 444, [2007] Ch 390 at [18].

An easement granted expressly or impliedly to a tenant determines with the expiration or determination of the tenancy ... . A different conclusion was reached where the lessee of the dominant tenement, with the benefit of an easement for the term of his lease, acquired the freehold reversion on his lease and the lease merged in the freehold; it was held that the person who was the lessee and who was now the freehold owner of the dominant tenement retained the benefit of the original easement for a period equivalent to the original term of the lease: *Wall v Collins* [2007] Ch 390 ... . In any event, it was held in *Wall v Collins* that the lessee who acquired the freehold acquired the same easement (in fee) under s.62 of the Law of Property Act 1925 ... . This second conclusion seems sound whereas the first conclusion is more doubtful.[251]

### Reactions to *Wall v Collins*

3.242   Responses to *Wall v Collins* tend to be expressed by reference to the metaphor of attachment or appurtenance. For those who regarded the easement in these circumstances as appurtenant to the lease, the decision was wrong. But if the easement was attached to the land, it rings true; and of course the practical advantages of the decision are clear.

3.243   In the Consultation Paper we inclined to the former view. We added that the position was in acute need of clarification. We provisionally proposed that where an easement is attached to a leasehold estate it should be automatically extinguished on termination of that estate; but we invited the views of consultees not only on that proposal but also on whether there should be any qualifications or restrictions added to it.[252]

### Responses to our consultation

3.244   There was support for that proposal,[253] in particular from Land Registry. However, a significant number of consultees disagreed with us. In many cases, the disagreement was not with our analysis of the law, but rather with the effect of our proposal; consultees felt that the practical benefits of the decision outweighed the theoretical indignation that it aroused. They found persuasive the idea that just because a tenant acquires a greater interest in the land, he or she should not lose the benefits attached to the estate if he or she chooses to extinguish, by merger, the redundant lease. The Chancery Bar Association summed up the conflict between principle and pragmatism:

---

[251] *Gale on Easements*, para 1–32 at n 112.

[252] Consultation Paper, para 5.86.

[253] See the Analysis of Responses, paras 5.52 to 5.62.

We agree that where an easement is attached to a leasehold estate, the easement should be automatically extinguished on termination of the estate. As a matter of principle that must be correct. Nevertheless, we note the concerns of Hooper LJ in *Wall v Collins* [2007] Ch 390 at paragraph 58 of the judgment and the potentially disastrous consequences which might ensue from the proposed amendment and thought should therefore be given as to whether the dominant owner who stands to lose his right through merger in these circumstances should be able to apply under the revised section 84 for its preservation.

3.245 HHJ Ian Leeming QC put it like this:

I take the points made in the paper, but I have sympathy for the plight of a dominant owner who loses a valuable right through inadvertence to the consequences of merger, even if the merger has been expressly declared or sought. I would favour some saving provision for that situation, which the Court of Appeal appears to have afforded in an unsatisfactory analysis of the law.

3.246 We take these practical concerns seriously. The loss of rights appurtenant to a lease is unavoidable where the lease is terminated by forfeiture;[254] but *Wall v Collins* does remedy the problem of the loss of rights on merger. If the decision were reversed then there would again be a potential for the inadvertent loss of rights where merger is effected without appreciation of its effect. The only way to avoid that would be for a tenant acquiring a superior lease or freehold to ensure that the estates do not merge, in order to enable a right attached to the inferior estate to survive.[255] That would involve unnecessary costs on future dispositions of the land because of the need to deal with two estates rather than one.

3.247 Further consideration of the issue following consultation has left us concerned about consistency in the law in this area. The reasoning that an easement granted to a leaseholder is annexed to the land rather than to the lease would seem to imply that such an easement would therefore survive forfeiture, surrender and disclaimer. Yet we have found no suggestion in legal writing since *Wall v Collins* that the effect of the decision extends beyond merger. We can say with some confidence that it would not be applied to forfeiture; the axiom that forfeiture brings to an end every aspect of a lease is so well-embedded in the law that we think it implausible that any court would extend the ratio of *Wall v Collins* thus far. To do so would be to give landlords an incentive to forfeit in some cases, in order to obtain valuable rights attached to the lease, and that would be highly controversial.

3.248 Surrender, on the other hand, is a consensual transaction very similar to merger.

[254] Although in that instance it is the landlord who loses out by not picking up the appurtenant right, rather than the tenant who now has no estate and therefore no interest in the survival of any easement.

[255] The pre-*Wall v Collins* version of the Land Registry Practice Guide No 26 advised former tenants to do this. See http://www1.landregistry.gov.uk/assets/library/documents/lrpg026.pdf (last visited 13 May 2011).

Generally surrender involves the tenant leaving the picture; there is unlikely to be any unfairness in the landlord not taking the benefit of an easement granted to the tenant by a third party. Indeed if *Wall v* Collins extends to surrender then he or she will take that benefit. That may in some circumstances be a useful result. Moreover, it is clear law that when a landlord and tenant agree an extension (or indeed a reduction) of the term of the lease, that transaction operates as a surrender and re-grant. In those circumstances, if the easement comes to an end with the surrender, the tenant loses rights that he or she formerly enjoyed with the lease; *Wall v Collins* (if the decision extends to surrender) avoids that consequence.

3.249    It is not known whether the ratio of *Wall v Collins* extends to surrender. The Court of Appeal's decision in *MRA Engineering Ltd v Trimster Company Ltd,*[256] in which it was held that an easement did not survive in those circumstances, was not cited to the court in *Wall v Collins*. Land Registry has proceeded on the basis that the decision applies only to merger,[257] yet it is hard to see why it should not extend to surrender, and our consultees generally regarded the two forms of termination as being akin to each other because they are each consensual transactions.

3.250    As to disclaimer, this is closer to forfeiture than to merger or surrender in that it is not a consensual transaction; and again we think that the orthodox view is too well-established to be questioned.

**Our recommendation**

3.251    In reaching a conclusion on this issue we have found it helpful to conceptualise the problem simply as a practical question: what happens to an easement or other right granted to a tenant, by a third party rather than by the landlord, when the lease comes to an end? This is more useful than excessive reliance on the metaphors of attachment or appurtenance.

3.252    We continue to take the view that the pre-*Wall v Collins* understanding of the legal effect of merger should be restored. This would bring consistency with the position on forfeiture and disclaimer and it would clarify the position on surrender which currently is not known.[258] We note that that would make it possible to say that in all cases of termination of a lease, an easement that benefits the lease is brought to an end. It would enable Land Registry practice to remain consistent with the structure of estates upon which title registration is built.

---

[256] (1988) 56 P & CR 1.

[257] Land Registry Practice Guide No 26, revised following *Wall v Collins*. See http://www1.landregistry.gov.uk/assets/library/documents/lrpg026_addendum2.pdf (last visited 13 May 2011).

[258] The reform proposed below would make it clear that an interest benefiting a leasehold estate is terminated on the surrender of that estate, but that an election can be made to keep the benefit. The certainty that an interest attached to a leasehold estate is ordinarily terminated on the demise of the estate itself will be welcomed by Land Registry.

3.253 Yet we hear the practical concerns of consultees and we agree that a saving mechanism is needed. This should not be achieved through obliging the parties to take proceedings.[259] Instead, we are attracted to a solution along the lines suggested by HHJ Leeming.

3.254 Accordingly, we take the view that the decision in *Wall v Collins* should be statutorily reversed, but that the position of the parties involved in merger and surrender can be improved – compared with the situation pre-*Wall v Collins* – by providing a simple mechanism to enable interests appurtenant to leases to be preserved on merger or surrender.

**3.255 We recommend:**

(1) **that the decision in *Wall v Collins*, that an easement that benefits a lease survives the termination of the leasehold estate by merger with the freehold, be reversed by statute but**

(2) **that statute should provide a mechanism to enable the reversioner, on merger and surrender, (or the tenant, where there is a surrender and re-grant) to elect to keep the benefit of interests appurtenant to the lease surrendered or merged.**

3.256 Clause 26 of the draft Bill puts that policy into effect.[260] While subsection (1) sets out the general position, the subsections which follow it enable the holder of the superior estate on surrender or merger (or the leaseholder where there is a deemed surrender and re-grant by operation of law) to elect to keep any interests that were appurtenant to the lease. In the event of that election the interest(s) concerned become appurtenant to the superior estate (normally the freehold, except in the case of deemed surrender and re-grant, but sometimes a superior lease) but would nevertheless remain interests "equivalent to ... a term of years absolute".[261]

3.257 How is that election to be made? Both merger and surrender require some positive action; merger does not happen automatically when the tenant acquires the freehold, and surrender is often – but not always – effected by deed.[262] Even when surrender occurs by operation of law, on an agreement to vary the term of a lease, there will be a deed bringing the varied term into existence. The precise nature of what is done will depend upon whether the title to the relevant estate is registered or unregistered.

---

[259] We are not attracted to the suggestion made by the Chancery Bar Association that the problem be dealt with in the Lands Chamber. See the Analysis of Responses, para 5.56 and following.

[260] Note that it refers not only to easements and profits but also to land obligations, which we introduce in Part 5 below, and which must be subject to the same rules.

[261] LPA 1925, s 1(2)(a).

[262] Surrender by operation of law remains possible. It occurs when the parties do something inconsistent with the terms of the lease – for example where a tenant gives the keys to the landlord and the landlord accepts them. See LPA 1925, s 52 and *Megarry and Wade*, paras 18-069 and 18-070.

3.258 Where title to the relevant estate[263] is registered,[264] we think that all that is needed for the proprietor to make clear an intention to keep the relevant interest is to ask the registrar to transfer it to the title to which it is now to be appurtenant. That will be done when requesting amalgamation of freehold and leasehold titles upon merger, when requesting the removal of the lease from the register in the case of a "true" surrender, or when registering the extended lease in the case of a deemed surrender and re-grant. The request should be made in accordance with land registration rules[265] and paragraph 16 of schedule 3 to the draft Bill adds a power for Land Registry to make rules about this to schedule 10 to the Land Registration Act 2002.

**3.259 We recommend that Land Registry make rules to enable an election to be made in cases where title to the relevant estate is registered, or where application is made to register that estate because the transaction concerned is a registrable disposition.**

3.260 More difficult is the case where the relevant estate (that is, the estate to which the interest is now to be appurtenant) is not registered. There must be a record of the election, but that record does not have to have the function of giving notice to another party, because the continuation of the appurtenant interest does not disadvantage anyone (the burdened land is in the same position as it was before the transaction). So we think that the most convenient way for the freeholder (or on occasions, an unregistered lessee) to elect to preserve one or more appurtenant interests would be for him or her to endorse a note of the election on a document of title.[266] Sometimes this will be the lease, or a new lease; sometimes it will be the still-unregistered conveyance of the freehold.[267]

**3.261 We recommend that where title to the relevant estate is unregistered, the election should be made by endorsement on the document that evidences the title of the person who made the election.**

3.262 Where an unregistered lease is extended, and therefore is the subject of a deemed surrender and re-grant, then the new lease (if the term is in excess of seven years) will trigger first registration.[268] In cases where it does not, again endorsement of the lease would be the appropriate way for the election to be made. Occasionally, there is an agreement between landlord and tenant to make the term of the lease shorter; that, again, will operate as a deemed surrender and re-grant. Technically, it brings to an end an interest appurtenant to the lease,[269]

---

[263] That is, the estate to which the interest is now to be appurtenant.

[264] Including those cases where the transaction concerned triggers first registration.

[265] Draft Bill, cl 26(5).

[266] This is a normal technique of unregistered conveyancing; for example, when there is a sale of part of an unregistered title a note of the sale is endorsed on the seller's title deed.

[267] Draft Bill, cl 26(6) refers in broad terms to a "document evidencing the title", so as to cater for cases where the original lease is lost and a certified copy, for example, is being used.

[268] See LRA 2002, s 4(4)(b).

[269] This may not be widely appreciated: see *MRA Engineering Ltd v Trimster Company Ltd* (1988) 56 P & CR 1. Unless *Wall v Collins* applies to surrender, our recommendation makes no change to the current law in this respect.

and so our clause enables an election to be made to keep the interest. The interest will then be longer than the new lease, and will determine when the lease expires by effluxion of time.

3.263    The effect of clause 26(1) is that in all cases, if no election is made, the interest in question determines when the surrender or merger takes place. The clause provides that no election can be made in the case of an oral lease, because of course in that case there is no document of title to endorse.

# PART 4
# REFORMS FOR REGISTERED TITLES

## INTRODUCTION

4.1 This Part continues the theme of Part 3 by examining reform that would impact upon easements and profits by changing details within the current law without introducing any wholly new concepts. In Part 3 we looked at a number of issues that impact equally upon registered and unregistered land; in particular implication and prescription but also easements conferring a right to extensive use and some issues about the termination of interests.

4.2 In this Part we recommend four reforms that would have effect only when the title to the relevant land is registered. They are:

(1) a clarification of the scope of the guarantee of validity of registered easements;

(2) reform of the "unity of seisin" rule;

(3) a point about the express release of registered interests; and

(4) short-form interests.

4.3 As the law stands, these reforms would affect only easements and, in some cases, profits, because of the three interests we examine in this project only those two are currently legal interests. If our recommendations in Parts 5 and 6 are implemented then what we recommend here would apply also to land obligations. We discuss that again in Part 6 when we explain the structure we recommend for land obligations; and the relevant provisions of the draft Bill (clauses 23 and 28, and paragraph 16 of schedule 3) would apply to all three types of legal interest. But in this Part, for the sake of simplicity, we discuss only easements and profits.

4.4 In order to explain why there are reforms that we recommend only in the context of registered titles, we have to recall the purposes and functions of title registration.

4.5 The primary purpose of the register is to guarantee title. Section 58 of the Land Registration Act 2002 guarantees the accuracy of the register:

58 Conclusiveness

(1) If, on the entry of a person in the register as the proprietor of a legal estate, the legal estate would not otherwise be vested in him, it shall be deemed to be vested in him as a result of the registration.

(2) Subsection (1) does not apply where the entry is made in pursuance of a registrable disposition in relation to which some other registration requirement remains to be met.

4.6     Schedules 4 and 8 to the Land Registration Act 2002 complement section 58 by setting out when the register may be altered or rectified and providing for an indemnity where loss is suffered as a result of the rectification of the register.

4.7     That guarantee of title means that there are instances where title is valid, or invalid, in circumstances where the opposite result would obtain if title were unregistered. The most obvious case is where a forged transfer is registered; unless and until the register is rectified, the transferee pursuant to the forged transfer holds the legal estate, whereas at common law he or she would have nothing. Whether the register is rectified or not depends upon the circumstances of the forgery and the position of the transferee; the provisions of schedule 4 mean that an innocent transferee in possession of the land will almost always keep it, while the person who lost the land as a result of the forgery (again, assuming their innocence) will be indemnified. The guarantee of title gives some security to those who rely upon the register, with the indemnity fund shouldering a degree of risk.

4.8     Another function of the register of title, which we discussed in Part 2, is to control enforceability. Section 29 of the Land Registration Act 2002 sets out the circumstances in which a registered disposition will take effect subject to prior interests; as we noted, it is therefore the registration rules, rather than the status of an interest as legal or equitable, that determine whether it is enforceable "against all the world".

4.9     Finally, the register is a public record of information. This function is very much subordinate to its other roles – it is notable that full public access to the register came very late, in 1990,[1] although it has always been possible for those involved in a transaction to search the register.

4.10    The reforms that we recommend in this Part are all linked with the functions of title registration: the guarantee of title, the management of enforceability and the provision of public information. In some cases, those functions make reform desirable, while in others they facilitate reform.

**SECTION 58 OF THE LAND REGISTRATION ACT 2002: A CLARIFICATION**

4.11    We set out the terms of section 58 above. It is central to the purpose and operation of the title registration system. From it stem the provisions in schedules 4 and 8 to the Land Registration Act 2002, relating to the alteration of the register in cases of mistake and so on, and to the payment of indemnity.[2]

4.12    It is clear law that the "statutory magic" of section 58 has the effect of guaranteeing the validity of a legal estate in circumstances where there would have been no title at common law. In unregistered land, a forged conveyance cannot pass a legal estate. Where title is registered, and a forged transfer is then registered, section 58 vests the legal estate in the transferee despite the invalidity of the transfer. Whether the register is then rectified, when the mistake comes to

---

[1]    Land Registration Act 1988 (Commencement) Order 1990 SI 1990 No 1359.

[2]    See para 2.60 above.

light, depends upon the circumstances of the case and the terms of schedule 4.[3]

4.13 Equally, therefore, if an easement is created by a forged grant, and the grantee registered as proprietor to the easement,[4] then the validity of the easement is guaranteed. Rectification will have to be considered if and when the forgery comes to light.

4.14 That much is uncontroversial. However, we have discussed with our Land Registry working group the position where a different kind of mistake is made, namely the registration of an easement or profit appurtenant that does not meet with the common law requirements for validity, in particular because the interest does not in fact accommodate and serve the dominant land. In those circumstances, if the register is later altered, can there be any liability for the indemnity fund?[5] In other words, is the effect of section 58 that Land Registry was guaranteeing the validity, not (as in the forgery case) of a legal interest that was not in fact transferred, but of a legal interest that could not have been created at common law?

4.15 This is not an issue upon which the courts have had to pronounce. Our understanding is that section 58 does not create anything in those circumstances. The alteration of the register, following the registration in error of such an easement, gives rise to no indemnity because there is no loss. Nothing valid was created in the first place. The situation is the same as the purported creation of an easement for a view.

4.16 Land Registry has expressed the wish to have this placed beyond doubt.[6]

**4.17 We recommend that statute should state, for the avoidance of doubt, that section 58(1) has no effect in relation to an entry made in pursuance of an instrument that purports to create an easement that does not accommodate and serve the dominant land.**

4.18 That clarification is effected by paragraph 16(3)(b) of schedule 3 to the draft Bill.

### THE "UNITY OF SEISIN" RULE

4.19 The first group of recommendations that we make here relate to both the creation and the extinguishment of interests in registered land. They relate to the rule known, by way of shorthand, as the "unity of seisin" rule.

4.20 We noted in Part 2[7] that there is no definition of an easement or of a profit,

---

[3] Schedule 4 to the Land Registration Act 2002 enables the register to be altered in order to bring it up to date or to correct a mistake in it; special considerations apply to rectification, which is an alteration to correct a mistake which prejudicially affects the title of a registered proprietor. See *Megarry and Wade*, para 7-131 and following.

[4] That is, the easement is registered as an interest appurtenant to the grantee's registered estate.

[5] Indeed, the alteration may not even be rectification; a rectification is an alteration that "prejudicially affects the title of a registered proprietor". If it is not rectification, there is no right to indemnity regardless of loss.

[6] The point is equally relevant to land obligations, as we explain in Part 6 (paras 6.75 to 6.78).

because of the antiquity of those interests. However, what we do have is the statement of the requirements for a valid easement or profit appurtenant (meaning one that has a dominant tenement and is not held in gross) in *Re Ellenborough Park*.[8] As we outlined in Part 2, the Court of Appeal's judgment asserted the four characteristics of such interests:

(1)    there must be a dominant and a servient tenement;

(2)    an easement must accommodate the dominant tenement, that is, be connected with its enjoyment and for its benefit;

(3)    the dominant and servient tenements must not be owned and occupied by the same person; and

(4)    the right claimed must be capable of forming the subject-matter of a grant.

4.21    The unity of seisin[9] rule is expressed at point (3) above. Set out more fully, the rule is that an easement or profit cannot exist where the dominant and servient tenements are in common ownership and possession. That has two practical effects. One is that the owner of a plot of land who plans to sell part, cannot (prior to and in preparation for sale), create an easement that benefits one part and burdens the other.[10]

4.22    The other practical effect is that if land that has the benefit of an easement is bought by the owner of the servient land, in circumstances where he or she is then entitled to possession of both, the right ceases to exist.

4.23    We proposed in the Consultation Paper that this requirement be abolished,[11] provided that titles to the dominant and servient estates were both registered and under separate title numbers.

4.24    There is no logical reason why the dominant land, in relation to an easement, and the servient land, should not both be owned and in the possession of the same person in the same capacity;[12] but people do not need easements over their own land. However, the proposal in the Consultation Paper was made in order to

---

[7]    See paras 2.18 and 2.31 above.

[8]    [1956] Ch 131.

[9]    The term "unity of seisin" is a convenient abbreviation for unity of both possession and ownership.

[10]    If one plot of land is leased, then there is no unity of possession and an easement can be created in favour of the leasehold estate

[11]    Consultation Paper, paras 3.66 and 8.88.

[12]    Albeit that (absent the unity of seisin rule), where X held both Blackacre and Whiteacre in fee simple, and Blackacre had the benefit of an easement over Whiteacre, then in crossing Whiteacre to get to Blackacre X would be exercising his rights as owner and is not using the easement. The easement could be said to be suspended or in abeyance in the sense that no-one is using it while X owns both plots: see *Canham v Fisk* (1831) 2 Cr & J 126, 149 ER 53; *Megarry and Wade*, para 29-014 and *Gray and Gray*, para 5.2.88.

resolve some practical problems arising from the current law; it was described by one consultee[13] as "the single most important proposal in the CP".[14] We wish to make a recommendation that follows, in large part, that provisional proposal for a number of reasons. The first reason for doing so relates to the treatment of development plans by Land Registry.[15] A second relates to the need to resolve the difficulties that arise on mortgages of part.[16] Third, there are concerns about what happens in the context of registered title when the dominant and servient tenements with respect to an easement come into common ownership. We go on to explain those three points here, and then to set out and explain the recommendation that we make and the relevant clauses in the draft Bill.

### Land Registry practice and development plans

4.25 The traditional scenario for the creation of an easement involves a sale of half of Blackacre by X to Y, where X reserves an easement over Y's land. But that scenario is now unusual. The usual context for the creation of appurtenant rights, and a considerable proportion of Land Registry's workload, involves the creation by developers of large residential estates followed by multiple sales of part. Land Registry offers to developers with a registered title the facility to plan the legal design of those sales with Registry staff in advance with a view to ensuring that the correct easements and covenants benefit each property.

4.26 The problem that arises in the course of those multiple sales is easiest to describe if we take a very simple case.

4.27 X has built two houses on his land, with a shared driveway. The boundary goes down the middle of the two plots and each plot is to have an easement over the other plot's half of the drive.

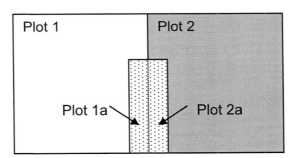

4.28 Accordingly, plot 1 is sold with the benefit of an easement over area 2a, with the vendor (still the owner of plot 2) reserving for plot 2 the benefit of an easement over area 1a. Later plot 2 is sold, with the benefit of that reserved easement, but subject to the easement already granted over 2a.

4.29 That arrangement works very well as stated. But "later" may be anything from minutes to months; and in practice it is as likely as not that the transfer of plot 2

[13]  Michael Croker, Miriam Brown and Kevin Marsh.

[14]  See the Analysis of Responses, paras 3.42 to 3.54

[15]  See para 4.25 and following below.

[16]  See para 4.34 and following below.

will reach Land Registry – and the transfer be registered – before the transfer of plot 1. And that means that plot 2 purports to benefit from, and be subject to, easements that do not yet exist at law.

4.30    If that scenario is multiplied over even a small housing estate involving, say, twenty houses, each sharing the estate road and perhaps driveways or drainage we can see that that situation is multiplied many times and becomes more complex. The problem was summarised by the response of one consultee:

> The legal process for easement creation now follows the path of five stages: no contract, contract, protecting search, transfer of part, registration ... developers cannot now control the order of creation of easements because any one of these stages can occur at any time. In an estate of ten properties with a single easement of vehicle access across nine of them, the possible number of combinations of stages (ie whether each unit is at one of the five stages) reaches a maximum of one million possible combinations. Where as is normal, units are to have the benefit of or be burdened by five or six different easements (not necessarily over the same adjacent units), the number of combinations is nearly infinite ... .[17]

4.31    It is therefore impossible for the developer or anyone else to ensure that the registration of transactions, and therefore the creation of legal interests, happens in the "correct" order.

4.32    The complexity of these situations creates additional work for Land Registry staff; the potential inaccuracies in such a system create risk both for Land Registry's indemnity fund and for its customers. The risk for the purchaser of property (whether an individual or a developer) is that there will be litigation – and we have heard, anecdotally, of instances where there have been attempts to trace back the transactions with a view to challenging the validity of rights created and registered. The risk for Land Registry is that it will guarantee interests that turn out to have been invalid, or improperly created – and therefore, again, there is an expense for customers because costs to the indemnity fund will be passed on in terms of levels of fees.

4.33    The solution must be to enable developers not only to plan the estate lay-out with Land Registry before the sales, delineating the plots to be sold on Land Registry plans, but also to create valid appurtenant rights between them. The objective is that when each plot is sold, each will have appurtenant rights that are not vulnerable to challenge later. To make that possible the unity of seisin rule would need to be set aside *only* in the situation where title to the land involved is registered.[18] We take the view that that is a proportionate response to a situation that is currently unavoidable, and that represents a considerable risk of later legal proceedings against home-owners, developers and to Land Registry.

---

[17]    Michael Croker, Miriam Brown and Kevin Marsh.

[18]    Developers seeking to sell unregistered land will therefore be able to benefit from the reform by registering their titles before sale.

**Mortgages of part**

4.34 The reform we recommend would also solve a serious problem for mortgagees,[19] brought to our attention before the publication of the Consultation Paper by the Council of Mortgage Lenders and emphasised by them in their consultation response. They said:

> Lenders have real issues with the current requirement that the dominant and servient [estates] be owned by separate persons ... should the lender need to take possession the lender will need appropriate rights over the part of the borrower's land that does not come within the charge. However, because of this rule this is very difficult to achieve.

4.35 The problem arises when a borrower mortgages only part of his or her land, and that land is not self-sufficient; if the mortgagor were to sell it, in order to realise the security, the buyer might require, say, an easement over the mortgagor's retained land in order to access the highway, or perhaps an easement of drainage or support.

4.36 The mortgagee is not troubled by this lack of independence during the currency of the mortgage; the mortgagee is not in possession and the land is not being used separately. But if the mortgagor defaults, and the mortgagee's power of sale is exercised, the land has to be sold without the easements that it needs. There is no power for the mortgagee to grant those easements. It has power only to sell the mortgaged land.[20]

4.37 The only solution to this problem would appear to be for the mortgage deed to contain personal covenants by the mortgagor to grant the required rights if necessary, on sale of the mortgaged part. But that is a contractual solution, and it may prove to be impossible to enforce the contract.

4.38 The reform we propose would mean that when granting the mortgage, the mortgagor could also set up any easements required between the mortgaged land and the free land, so that if the power of sale were exercised the detached portion would have all the appurtenant rights that it needed. The mortgagor too would be protected; he or she could ensure that the mortgaged land was burdened by any easement that he or she wanted to reserve.

**Land that falls into common ownership**

4.39 The other practical problem that we wish to solve is the anomaly that occurs when two titles come into the same ownership. When the dominant and servient land, in respect of an easement, fall into common ownership and possession the easement disappears (although the landowner or a purchaser may be unaware of the disappearance).[21] However, if both plots are registered, and are not merged

---

[19] See E Slessenger, "Precedent Editor's notes (March/April)" [2011] *Conveyancer and Property Lawyer* 92.

[20] LPA 1925, s 101.

[21] Note that the easement is not resurrected if the dominant and servient land are later separately owned. See Co Litt 313a, quoted in *Gale on Easements*, para 12-02.

into one title, the easement is likely to remain registered.[22] It therefore remains guaranteed. This could give rise to liability for Land Registry's indemnity fund, if someone wished to go behind the registered title and establish that land, currently subject to an easement, had once been in common ownership with the dominant land, so that the easement was in fact no longer in existence and the register liable to be rectified.

4.40 Our recommendation would remove the anomaly. Where two registered titles came into common ownership, an easement or profit benefiting one and burdening the other would survive unless the common owner makes an application to extinguish it.

### Consultees' responses

4.41 Most of the consultees who addressed the relevant questions in the Consultation Paper agreed with our provisional proposal.[23]

4.42 However, on one point of detail we changed our views following consultation. Our provisional proposal was that the unity of seisin rule should be set aside only in the event that the two plots of land were registered with separate title numbers. However, we came to the conclusion that registration with separate title numbers was neither necessary nor desirable. The members of our Land Registry working group were unhappy with this requirement, because of their experience that decisions about sale boundaries, on large developments, are often made and re-made several times over quite a long period, and that it would be disproportionately difficult to undo the division of the land into separate registered titles each time arrangements were changed prior to sale. The important point, in the interests of certainty, is that the registration of the title means that the benefited and burdened land would be delineated on Land Registry's title plan.

4.43 We note that the New Zealand legislation that enables the creation of appurtenant interests despite unity of seisin does not require separate title numbers for the benefited and burdened land.[24]

### Our recommendation

**4.44 We recommend that provided that title to the benefited and burdened land is registered, the fact that they are in common ownership and possession shall not prevent the creation or existence of easements or profits.**

---

[22] Land Registry cannot automatically remove it, because the registrar cannot know whether there is in fact unity of ownership and possession; for example there might be an unregistered lease affecting one or both plots.

[23] We expressed our proposal separately for easements and Land Obligations: Consultation Paper, paras 3.66 and 8.88 respectively; See the Analysis of Responses, paras 3.42 to 3.54 and 8.88.

[24] Land Transfer Act 1952, s 90E.

4.45    That recommendation would set aside the unity of seisin rule, but it would do so only where title to both the dominant and servient land was registered. The reason for that limitation upon the reform is that our recommendation is intended to solve problems specific to registered land. It would enable Land Registry to offer a more effective service in the context of developments involving multiple sales off a co-ordinated development plan, and it would eliminate potential problems arising when an easement is extinguished, at common law, by unity of seisin yet remains on the register. The issue is less relevant where title is unregistered.[25] Land Registry offers its services to facilitate development schemes only where title is registered, and a developer with unregistered land has to register its title in order to take advantage of that service.

4.46    The limitation of the reform to registered titles means that in all cases there will be a public record of the dominant and servient land, on Land Registry's plan and a record of the interests that affect each of them on the registered title. That will make it easy to ensure that the boundaries of land subsequently sold will match the boundaries of the land benefited or burdened, as the case may be, by the relevant rights. To extend the reform to unregistered titles would be unnecessary, and would create risks of uncertainty because that public record of the land involved would be absent.[26]

4.47    The recommendation is embodied in clause 23 of the draft Bill, which amends the Land Registration Act 2002 by inserting two new sections, 27A and 116A.

4.48    The new section 27A would extend an owner's powers so as to enable the creation of appurtenant rights despite the fact of common ownership and possession. The way in which such rights might be created is a matter for Land Registration Rules. Subsection (4) of the new section would enable those rules to prescribe a method that did not involve the use of a deed; we envisage that a straightforward application form would be prescribed. The creation of an appurtenant interest in these circumstances would be a registrable disposition (section 27A(3)): moreover, the disposition would be ineffective until the registration requirements were met (section 27A(5)). That means that there would be no question of the interest taking effect as an equitable interest prior to registration; the reform would permit the creation of registered interests only.[27]

4.49    The new section 116A addresses the other aspect of reform: the fact that an easement or profit would no longer be extinguished when the dominant and servient tenements fall into common ownership, provided that title to the dominant land – and therefore to the interest itself – is registered.

---

[25]    There is still the potential that, on first registration, easements are registered as benefiting or noted as burdening the land being registered despite having been extinguished at an earlier time. However, it is more likely that this would be picked up in examining title for the purposes of registration.

[26]    The limitation to registered title means that the reform will solve the problem of mortgages of part only where title to the land is registered prior to sale. The mortgage will in most cases trigger first registration of the mortgaged part in any event; LRA 2002, s 4(1)(g).

[27]    Any attempt by the registered proprietor to create an easement that extended also to unregistered land owned by him or her would be ineffective so far as the unregistered land was concerned.

4.50 That reform is to apply to interests whenever created or acquired, including therefore those in existence prior to the introduction of the reform.[28]

4.51 It remains open to the registered proprietor of the interest to release it. He or she might choose to do so because there was no longer any need for the interest since the land was to remain in common ownership; or because he or she planned to sell part of the land without the benefit or burden of the easement (as the case might be). Subsection (3) of the new 116A enables Land Registration Rules to prescribe the way in which the release can be effected, again without the necessity of using a deed.

## THE EXPRESS RELEASE OF REGISTERED INTERESTS

4.52 Once registered, as discussed above, the validity of an easement or profit is guaranteed by Land Registry.

4.53 Once granted, or indeed once it has arisen by implication or prescription, an interest may be varied or brought to an end by an agreement executed as a deed.[29] Currently the express variation or release of a registered easement or profit can generate strange results because neither is a registrable disposition under section 27(2) of the Land Registration Act 2002. An express variation or release therefore operates at law without registration. This means that Land Registry will continue to guarantee the existence of an easement that has in fact been released, or whose terms are now different, at law.[30]

4.54 Clearly this is unsatisfactory and leads to an unacceptable disjunction between registration and reality. It may cause confusion to Land Registry's clients; it may entitle a claimant to an indemnity payment because he or she has relied on the registration of an easement that no longer exists. Land Registry gave us the example of a case where there is an express release of an easement and the dominant tenement (the title to which is registered) is then mortgaged, or sold, with the benefit of the interest still on the register. The validity of the interest is therefore guaranteed, yet it has been released at law; the register is inaccurate and the registered proprietor may seek compensation from the indemnity fund when the mistake comes to light and is put right.

4.55 The creation of such an interest, if it is appurtenant to a registered title, must be completed by registration and will not take effect at law until this is done.[31] What is wanted is a reform that relates, we might say, to the other end of the lifespan of the easement or profit, ensuring that its express variation or release does not operate at law until the register is brought up to date. If the express variation or release of a registered interest were a registrable disposition, it could not operate at law until reflected on the register. Then in the example above, the interest

---

[28] Gregory Hill (Barrister, Ten Old Square Chambers) put it this way in his consultation response: "I do not believe it is either necessary or appropriate to limit the principle to easements created after the implementation of reform. There is, with respect, no reliance interest in the existing law still applying to an easement created before then".

[29] *Gray and Gray*, para 5.2.89.

[30] This is therefore a very similar problem to the one we noted in connection with the extinguishment of easements by unity of seisin; see para 4.39 above.

[31] LRA 2002, s 27.

would remain valid at law, and a transfer or mortgage would pass a wholly valid easement or covenant to the purchaser (since the latter would be unaffected by the equitable release). There would be no liability on the indemnity fund. In practice, of course, properly advised parties would therefore register an express release or variation immediately.

4.56 This is not a point on which we consulted, but it has been brought to our attention by our Land Registry working group. It seems to us that it is in the interests both of Land Registry and the public to change the position. The potential confusion is undesirable; and if Land Registry has to pay indemnity as a result, that is likely to be reflected, ultimately, in the level of fees that it must charge. Far better to have the register in tune with reality.

**4.57 We recommend that the express variation or release of a registered appurtenant interest shall be a registrable disposition pursuant to section 27 of the Land Registration Act 2002.**

4.58 The draft Bill makes provision to that effect in clause 28, by adding to section 27(2) of the Land Registration Act 2002 the express release of a registered interest as a registrable disposition.[32] It then adds a further section 114A to the 2002 Act, providing that the variation of an appurtenant right that benefits or burdens a registered estate has effect as the grant of a new right and the release of the old, so that registration requirements apply.[33]

## THE USE OF SHORT-FORMS FOR THE CREATION OF EASEMENTS

4.59 In the Consultation Paper we provisionally proposed that it should be possible for parties to create short-form easements by reference to a prescribed form of words.[34] Where that form of words was used, a fuller description of the substance of the easement would be implied into the instrument creating the right. We noted that such short-forms are extremely popular in those jurisdictions where they are available.

4.60 In Australia, a number of states have produced statutory definitions of certain relatively commonly used easements. One example is to be found in the New South Wales Conveyancing Act 1919. The statute enables the parties to use a "short-form" definition for the easement which they intend to create. If the parties elect to use that short-form, then the statutory definition (provided in the case of New South Wales in a schedule to the Act) is imported and will apply to the

---

[32] The clause in the draft Bill refers also to land obligations and we discuss this at para 6.87 below. Note that the recommendation, and the clause, refer to appurtenant interests only; there may be difficulties associated with failure to remove profits in gross from the register once they have been released, but this is a very different problem, akin to the problem of leases remaining registered once they have been released; it is therefore an instance of a general problem that falls outside the scope of this project. If the profit is held in gross, the problems associated with the transfer of land to a third party while an appurtenant interest remains registered by mistake will not arise.

[33] Without this provision, there might well be some difficulty in determining whether a given variation in fact amounted to the release of the old right and the grant of a new one.

[34] Consultation Paper, para 4.34; we made the same provisional proposal for Land Obligations at para 12.25. We mention short-forms for land obligations in Part 6 at paras 6.88 and 6.89 below.

easement being created. Short-form easements comprise over 90% of new easements created in South Australia and Tasmania, and 99% in the Northern Territory.[35]

4.61    A large majority of the consultees who answered this question about short-forms thought that they would be appropriate, provided that they were simply and clearly drafted.[36] We also asked if the parties should be free to vary the terms of short-form rights. Most consultees thought they should; and indeed, since the existence of short-forms would not preclude practitioners from drafting easements themselves, it would seem logically necessary for the short-forms to be variable.

4.62    However, if short-form easements are to be made available, who is to draft them? Other jurisdictions have statutory wording;[37] but we envisaged that Land Registry should draft the appropriate wording, and discussions were held with Land Registry before the Consultation Paper was published about the desirability of doing this.

4.63    We take the view that the appropriate vehicle for short-form easements and covenants would be Land Registration Rules. Due to its unique position within the conveyancing process, Land Registry is best placed to determine, in consultation with its day-to-day users, what easements might be made available as short-forms and whether and how this list is maintained and updated. This would also ensure that there was further consultation about the wording of the short-forms, which a number of consultees thought would be important. Accordingly, no provision is needed except for a rule-making power, which exists already within the Land Registration Act 2002.[38] Clearly this is an issue that Land Registry will be able to address only when resources permit.

**4.64    We recommend that Land Registry investigate the feasibility of making provision for short-form easements in Land Registration Rules and, if provision is thought feasible, that it draft and consult upon the necessary Rules.**

---

[35]   Figures obtained for the purposes of the Consultation Paper from correspondence with relevant land services divisions of state governments.

[36]   See the Analysis of Responses, paras 4.14 to 4.32.

[37]   New South Wales Conveyancing Act 1919, s 181A and sch 8.

[38]   LRA 2002, sch 10, para 8.

# PART 5
# COVENANTS: THE CASE FOR REFORM

## INTRODUCTION

5.1 In Parts 3 and 4 of this Report we have recommended reforms to the existing law of easements and profits. Here we turn to covenants. These are generically different from easements and profits, because they cannot exist as legal interests in land.[1] We look again at the problems in the law relating to covenants that we identified in the Consultation Paper, and examine first the difficulties associated with the current law of restrictive covenants. We then turn to positive covenants, which currently cannot "run with" or "bind" land; in other words, whilst it is possible to make a restrictive covenant enforceable against not only the current owner of land but also future owners, the same cannot be done with positive covenants. That means that only the original covenantor is bound by a positive covenant.[2]

5.2 Consideration of the issues relating to both restrictive and positive covenants together leads us to recommend that for the future they take effect as a new legal interest in land, known as a land obligation. Part 6 then examines the provisions of the draft Bill that would put into effect the recommendations we make in this Part, together with some further material on the registration and enforceability of land obligations, and in Part 7 we recommend consequential reform to the jurisdiction of the Lands Chamber.

5.3 As a preliminary, we reiterate that we are here concerned with what are commonly referred to as freehold covenants. The contrast is with leasehold covenants, by which we mean those made between landlord and tenant that relate only to the demised premises.[3] Leasehold covenants have developed along very different lines and are governed by different legal principles and statutory provisions.[4] We make no recommendations about them, and they are not affected by the recommendations that we do make. The covenants that fall within our project are called freehold covenants by way of shorthand, but we have to bear in mind that they may be entered into between leaseholders (that is, the lessee of Blackacre may covenant with the lessee of Redacre not to use his or her property for business purposes). For the rest of this Report references to "covenants" are to freehold covenants in the sense just defined, except where we refer specifically to leasehold covenants.

---

[1]   See para 2.14 above.

[2]   A positive covenant requires the covenantor to perform a positive act or to spend money in order to comply with the covenant.

[3]   In the Consultation Paper, para 8.100 and following, we looked at instances where covenants made between landlord and tenant nevertheless, under the current law, have to be registered as restrictive covenants. They fall outside the exclusion just defined – for example because although made between landlord and tenant they do not relate to the demised premises – and are therefore within the scope of our project. See the Analysis of Responses, paras 8.108 to 8.113.

[4]   For information on leasehold covenants generally, see *Megarry and Wade*, ch 20.

**PROBLEMS IN THE LAW RELATING TO COVENANTS**

5.4   In Part 2 we explained that while easements and profits are legal interests in land, covenants are not. They are contractual rights, although restrictive covenants have a hybrid status in that they can be made to bind a purchaser of land.[5] In the Consultation Paper we listed the problems associated with the law of covenants as follows:[6]

(1)   It is difficult to identify who has the benefit of a restrictive covenant for two reasons:

(a)   there is no requirement that the instrument creating the covenant should describe the benefited land with sufficient clarity to enable its identification without extrinsic evidence; and

(b)   the benefit of a restrictive covenant, being an equitable interest, cannot be registered as an appurtenant interest on the register of title to the dominant land.

(2)   There are differing and complicated rules for the running of the benefit and burden of restrictive covenants.

(3)   The contractual liability between the original parties to a covenant persists despite changes in the ownership of the land; when the land is sold, the original covenantor remains liable.

(4)   Whereas the benefit of a positive covenant can run at law, the burden of a positive covenant does not run so as to bind successors in title.

5.5   The first three items arise from the contractual status of covenants. They take effect primarily as contracts. They are not legal interests in land, and therefore cannot be registered.[7] That means that there is no public record of the benefited land, because while the burden can be protected on the register of title, there is no legal mechanism for the registration of the benefit.[8] That absence of information causes difficulties when there is a need to vary or extinguish the interest (whether by agreement or by application to the Lands Chamber under the provisions of section 84 of the Law of Property Act 1925).[9] The original benefited land may have been subdivided many times since the covenant was imposed.

5.6   A number of consultees expressed concern about the fact that the benefited land is not identified on the register, including the Chancery Bar Association and the Council of Mortgage Lenders.[10] The latter said:

---

[5]   We use "purchaser" here in its technical sense to mean anyone who purchases the land or an interest in it – for example, a mortgagee.

[6]   Consultation Paper, paras 7.36 to 7.45.

[7]   LRA 2002, s 2.

[8]   See para 2.62 above.

[9]   See Part 7 below.

[10]   See the Analysis of Responses, paras 7.1 to 7.11.

A large number of restrictive covenant indemnity policies are therefore purchased by borrowers. In a market where property prices are rising one policy may not be enough – new lenders may require top up policies to cover greater sums advanced. This can involve the borrower in expense where realistically there is very little likelihood that a covenant will be enforceable.

5.7 Turning to the second item in the list, one of the major defects in the current law relating to covenants is the sheer complexity of the multi-layered rules on the running of the burden and the benefit of restrictive and positive covenants. As the Consultation Paper explains,[11] the rules on the running of the burden of a covenant are distinct from the rules on the running of the benefit, although their practical effect for restrictive covenants is very similar.[12] Further, there are several different and overlapping methods by which the benefit of both positive and restrictive covenants might run, at law and in equity, and covenants created before and after 1925 are subject to different rules.[13]

5.8 Third on the list is the problem of contractual liability; the landowner who gives a restrictive covenant may be liable upon it for ever, which is clearly inappropriate since without possession of the land he or she can no longer comply with it.

5.9 That problem cannot be resolved for existing restrictive covenants. Nor can the difficulty of identifying the land benefited by existing restrictive covenants. Likewise, reform of the rules for the running of benefit and burden for existing covenants would be problematic, because any tidying of the rules is likely to lead to an adjustment of their effect. Retrospective changes that led to landowners losing the benefit of vested rights, or to the imposition of new burdens on their land, might be incompatible with Article 1 of the First Protocol to the European Convention on Human Rights.[14] We also received consultation responses from several individuals and groups strongly opposed to any change to the law that might affect the transmissibility of existing restrictive covenants.[15] Restrictive covenants have social functions (such as preserving parks or green spaces) that are of collective significance to a neighbourhood as a whole, and so even in cases where the loss of a covenant would not infringe the rights of an individual landowner, the local community might have valid objections to any such loss.

5.10 The future is a different matter. The problems listed 1 to 3 in the above list stem from the contractual status of covenants. If restrictive covenants were to take effect, for the future, not as contractual rights whose burden is transmitted through the rule in *Tulk v Moxhay*,[16] but as legal interests in land, then all three problems would be resolved. As a legal interest, the benefit of the covenant could

---

[11] Consultation Paper, paras 7.9 to 7.33.

[12] That is, the benefit will run if the covenant "touches and concerns" benefited land and in the absence of an express intention that it should not run: LPA 1925, s 78 as interpreted in *Federated Homes Ltd v Mill Lodge Properties Ltd* [1980] 1 WLR 594.

[13] See *J Sainsbury plc v Enfield London Borough Council* [1989] 1 WLR 590.

[14] See para 1.32 above.

[15] See the Analysis of Responses, paras 13.1 to 13.28.

[16] (1848) 2 Ph 774, 41 ER 1143. See the Consultation Paper, para 7.26.

be registered and there would then be a public record of it. The benefit and burden of the covenant could be transmitted as it is for easements and profits. And if a covenant took effect as an interest in land and no longer as a contract, the person who gave the covenant would no longer be liable on it forever.

5.11 The case for changing, for the future, the current contractual status of covenants becomes far stronger when we look at the most far-reaching of the problems we have listed, namely the final item in the list, and ask whether the burden of positive covenants (or indeed of positive obligations generally, whatever their form) should run with land.

5.12 The rule has deep roots, and is generally traced back to the 1834 decision in *Keppell v Bailey,*[17] which settled the conclusion that although positive leasehold covenants ran with land in accordance with *Spencer's Case,*[18] positive freehold covenants did not. *Austerberry v Corporation of Oldham*[19] is also regarded as authority for the rule.

5.13 Reform would mean that the burden of a positive obligation (for example to mend a fence) could be attached to an estate in land so as to bind a purchaser. Such a step should not be taken lightly. It was held by the Lord Chancellor in *Keppell v Bailey* that:

> Great detriment would arise and much confusion of rights if parties were allowed to invent new modes of holding and enjoying real property, and to impress upon their lands and tenements a peculiar character, which should follow them into all hands, however remote.[20]

5.14 In *Rhone v Stephens* the House of Lords expressed the view that only legislation could change the status of positive covenants:

> It is plain from the articles, reports and papers to which we were referred that judicial legislation to overrule the *Austerberry*[21] case would create a number of difficulties, anomalies and uncertainties and affect the rights and liabilities of people who have for over 100 years bought and sold land in the knowledge, imparted at an elementary stage to every student of the law of real property, that positive covenants, affecting freehold land are not directly enforceable except against the original covenantor. Parliamentary legislation to deal with the decision in the *Austerberry* case would require careful consideration of the consequences.[22]

5.15 The problem of positive covenants is part of the very roots of the Law

---

[17] (1834) 2 My & K 517, 39 ER 1042.

[18] (1583) 5 Co Rep 16a, 77 ER 72.

[19] (1885) LR 29 Ch D 750.

[20] (1834) 2 My & K 517, 536; 39 ER 1042, 1049, by Lord Brougham LC.

[21] *Austerberry v Corporation of Oldham* (1885) LR 29 Ch D 750.

[22] [1994] 2 AC 310, 321, by Lord Templeman.

Commission for England and Wales. In *Law Reform Now*,[23] making their case for the establishment of a Law Commission, Gerald Gardiner and Andrew Martin gathered together articles by leading scholars. Gerald Dworkin's chapter on land law identified as one of the major issues crying out for reform the fact that positive covenants do not run with land. The work of the Wilberforce Committee,[24] and the Commission's own work in the 1970s and 1980s, picked up this challenge.[25]

5.16    Our recommendations in 1984[26] would have enabled positive obligations to run with land. However, they were not implemented by the Government of the day; efforts were instead concentrated on the introduction of commonhold, as a new system for the freehold ownership of interdependent properties.[27] Those efforts came to fruition with the enactment of the Commonhold and Leasehold Reform Act 2002.

5.17    However, commonhold is designed for truly interdependent developments such as flats, or business units that share facilities and physical structure. It requires the creation of a commonhold association, and enables the association to set up a "local law" in the form of a commonhold community statement.[28] Commonhold was not designed for situations where very little is shared and there is no need for a management structure; and it is not generally appropriate to create a commonhold where there are no "common parts" (that is, land in shared ownership such as the stairways and roof of a block of flats).[29] So commonhold will not be used for a bilateral arrangement, for example, where two neighbours wish to allocate responsibility for a fence. And it is unlikely to be a welcome arrangement, because of its administrative structure, where just one facility is shared by a small group of properties, for example where all that is needed is an allocation of obligations to repair and share the cost of a driveway used by three or four houses.

5.18    So commonhold leaves gaps; there are many situations where positive obligations are wanted, but cannot be achieved in a straightforward manner under the current law. In view of that we examine afresh whether the law relating to positive covenants should be reformed, while bearing in mind that commonhold is available for more complex situations.

5.19    In doing so, however, we refer to the more general issue and so speak of positive

---

[23]   G Gardiner and A Martin, *Law Reform Now* (1963).

[24]   See the Report of the Committee on Positive Covenants Affecting Land (1965) Cmnd 2719.

[25]   See para 1.6 and following above.

[26]   The 1984 Report, Part 8.

[27]   Known in many other jurisdictions as strata title – see, for example, Landgate, *A Guide to Strata Titles* (March 2009) http://www.landgate.wa.gov.au/docvault.nsf/web/for_lg_Strata_Titles_3.03/$file/for_lg_Strata_Titles_3.03.pdf (last visited 13 May 2011).

[28]   See D Clarke, *Clarke on Commonhold: Law, Practice and Precedents* (2006) and T Aldridge, *Commonhold Law* (2010) for further detail on commonhold.

[29]   D Clarke, *Clarke on Commonhold: Law, Practice and Precedents* (2006) part 2, ch 7, para 20.

obligations rather than positive covenants. The question is the practical one, of whether positive obligations should run with land (or, to put it another way, whether they should be able to be property rights that bind successors in title), rather than the more technical issue of whether or not those obligations should take the form of covenants as they do at present, or whether they should do so as legal or equitable interests.

5.20 We address that technical issue later. The text that follows considers the practical case for reform, the academic analysis of the issue, the comparative picture, the responses from our consultees and the views of our Advisory Board. We conclude that there should be reform to enable positive obligations to run with land, in a form that resolves – for the future – the difficulties associated with the law relating to covenants that we listed above. We reach that conclusion with the proviso that certain concerns must be taken seriously and appropriate safeguards must be put in place. Part 6 deals with the practicalities of achieving this.

## POSITIVE OBLIGATIONS: THE CASE FOR REFORM

### The practical problems connected with positive obligations

5.21 If A sells part of his land to B, and B covenants to maintain the boundary fence and not to use the land for business, and then sells to C, C will have to observe the restrictive covenant (no business use) if the conditions in *Tulk v Moxhay*[30] are met, but the positive covenant (to maintain the fence) will not run with the land. C is not bound to observe it, and there remain only indirect means to enforce the covenant.[31]

5.22 This can be a considerable practical problem. As we noted above, commonhold will not solve it. More generally, a range of different obligations may be wanted, but unless a commonhold is desired those obligations cannot be created as property rights so as to run with freehold land. There are a number of ways in which lawyers circumvent the problem.

### *Use of leasehold title*

5.23 As the burden of a positive covenant may run with a leasehold estate, long leases are often used to ensure that covenants will remain enforceable.[32] This involves unnecessary expense in negotiating a lease and requires the "burdened owner" (and, perhaps, its funder) to accept a lease rather than a freehold.

---

[30] (1848) 2 Ph 774, 41 ER 1143; see Consultation Paper, paras 7.26 and 7.28. Note that the requirement of notice in *Tulk v Moxhay* has been replaced, by statute, with a requirement of registration of the burden of the covenant: see para 2.40 above.

[31] Michael Croker, Miriam Brown and Kevin Marsh's group response to the Consultation Paper stated: "Every time there is a major storm, Land Registry enquiry lines are very busy with enquiries about the ownership and maintenance of boundary structures. Owners are very disappointed to learn that Land Registry cannot say who owns them or who is responsible for repairing or replacing them and that no-one indeed can actually be certain of those details if the land is freehold".

[32] Curiously, LPA 1925, s 153 provides that a lease created for more than 300 years, of which 200 remain unexpired, may be enlarged into a freehold which will be subject to the same covenants, obligations and provisions which burdened the lease. Whether and how this would cause the burden of positive covenants to run has not been tested.

### Chains of indemnity

5.24 These are managed as follows: A covenants with B to maintain a fence. A will remain liable on the covenant after A has disposed of the land, simply as a matter of contract law. A enters into a contract with his successor in title, C, whereby C promises to A to mend the fence, and to indemnify A for any loss arising from a failure to do so. C may then sell to D and enter into a similar contract, creating a chain of indemnity contracts.[33] This method of circumvention suffers from a number of shortcomings. First, if the covenantee is enforcing against the covenantor who no longer occupies the land, the covenantee will only be able to obtain damages rather than an injunction or specific performance to enforce the covenant. Secondly, a chain is only as strong as its weakest link, and will therefore fail if one successor in title is insolvent or cannot be found, or if the chain is not continued.

### Estate rentcharges

5.25 A rentcharge is an annual or periodic sum of money payable to someone who does not own the land charged with its payment.[34] If a rentcharge is coupled with a right of entry,[35] the owner of the interest may enter the land to enforce the rentcharge and/or the performance of covenants. The right of entry may be exercised not only for failure to pay the rentcharge, but also for breach of the covenant, subject to the court's jurisdiction to provide relief against forfeiture. Thus positive covenants can be effectively made to run with the land. The rentcharge itself may be for only a nominal sum and the covenants do not have to relate to the rentcharge or the land.[36] This method of circumvention is cumbersome, and disliked by many developers. It is also a very indirect method of enforcement. It is not the positive covenant itself that is enforceable, it is the threat of entry.[37]

### Benefit and burden principle

5.26 This is the principle in *Halsall v Brizell*,[38] that one may not take a benefit without accepting the burden that goes with it. So it is possible to enforce an obligation to pay for the upkeep of a driveway, where the obligee has and chooses to exercise a right of way over it. The principle does not work where the person benefited has no choice about accepting the benefit, as would be the case with, say, a right of

---

[33] Another approach is for the covenantee to require the covenantor to promise to compel his successor to enter into a direct covenant with the covenantee, and to promise to impose the same obligation on his successor. Where land is registered, this approach may be coupled with a restriction preventing disposal of the land without confirmation of compliance.

[34] Transfer of Land – Report on Rentcharges (1975) Law Com No 68, para 9.

[35] The rule against perpetuities does not apply to a right of entry annexed to an estate rentcharge: LPA 1925, s 4(3) (as amended by the Perpetuities and Accumulations Act 2009); Perpetuities and Accumulations Act 1964, s 11.

[36] Rentcharges Act 1977, s 2(4).

[37] It has been suggested that a property subject to a rentcharge may be unacceptable, or less desirable as a security, to a lender, depending on the terms of the rentcharge and the extent of the powers that may be given to the rent owner: S Bright, "Estate rentcharges and the enforcement of positive covenants" [1988] *Conveyancer and Property Lawyer* 99.

[38] [1957] Ch 169.

support.[39]

5.27 None of these methods is therefore ideal; they can all be made to work but only indirectly, with unnecessary cost and risk and, in the case of indemnity chains, only for a limited, and uncertain, period.

5.28 So in looking at the arguments for and against reform, we have to bear in mind that positive obligations can already be made to be enforceable against successors in title to freehold land. The problem we have to address is not that proprietary positive obligations cannot be created; it is that positive obligations can be made to run with land already, but only by indirect and ultimately flawed methods.

**The arguments for and against reform**

5.29 In 1987 Bernard Rudden, in his renowned article "Economic Theory v Property Law: The *Numerus Clausus* Problem"[40] asked why positive obligations do not run with land. He explored the contrast between property rights and "fancies", by which is meant contractual rights that are excluded from recognition as property rights.[41] Only property rights can be enforced against future owners of burdened land,[42] while contractual rights endure only between the original parties.[43] He explained that most legal systems restrict the acceptable range of property rights, and noted that at that stage very few systems included positive covenants (under whatever label) in that category.

5.30 Rudden explored the practical, economic and philosophical arguments for the exclusion of positive obligations, such as the protection of purchasers (so that they have only a fixed list of property rights to check when buying), the need to facilitate development by resisting the overburdening of property, and the difficulty of ensuring that rights can be discharged or varied. He argued that these points can be overcome if obligations are carefully defined and are integrated within a registration system. He concluded that the reasons generally given for the fact that the burden of a positive covenant does not run are not particularly strong. He noted that the existence of the "workarounds" described above –

---

[39] This is why the principle was unavailable in *Rhone v Stephens* [1994] 2 AC 310. As Lord Templeman made clear in the case, "conditions can be attached to the exercise of a power in express terms or by implication … . It does not follow that any condition can be rendered enforceable by attaching to it a right nor does it follow that every burden imposed by a conveyance may be enforced by depriving the covenantor's successor in title of every benefit which he enjoyed thereunder. The condition must be relevant to the exercise of the right" [1994] 2 AC 310, 322. See also *Gale on Easements*, para 1-94.

[40] In J Eekelaar and J Bell (eds), *Oxford Essays in Jurisprudence* (3rd series 1987) p 239.

[41] The Law Commission had used the same term in the 1984 Report; the term originated in Lord Brougham LC's judgment in *Keppell v Bailey* (1834) 2 My & K 517, 535; 39 ER 1042, 1049.

[42] See paras 2.4 and 2.5 above.

[43] Covenants are therefore rather odd, in that the effect of LPA 1925, s 78 treats the benefit of a covenant, positive or negative, as being annexed to land, like a property right; but the burden of negative covenants only runs in equity, and only on the basis that a purchaser with notice is bound. Accordingly positive covenants are "fancies", in Rudden's terms.

which he described as "fictitious (not to say preposterous)"[44] – tends to highlight the weakness of those reasons, in any event.

5.31 Within the last two or three decades, the comparative picture that Bernard Rudden saw has changed, in that a number of common law jurisdictions have implemented reforms making positive covenants run with land. Those that have done so now include New South Wales,[45] the Northern Territory,[46] Northern Ireland,[47] Trinidad and Tobago,[48] New Zealand[49] and Hong Kong;[50] the most recent addition to the list is the Republic of Ireland.[51] In addition, there have been major studies in two jurisdictions where positive covenants have run for centuries: the American Restatement,[52] and the Scottish Law Commission's Report on Real Burdens.[53] In all these contexts we find the issues highlighted by Rudden and other writers being explored, and various solutions embraced.

5.32 Our nearest neighbour, Scotland, has a well-established system which allows positive obligations to exist as property rights. Scots land law is the only civilian system with which it is useful for us to make any detailed comparison;[54] while the Scottish legal system is different from ours, many of the practical issues are the same.[55]

5.33 In the USA, the problem that has vexed English land law for so long has never been an issue; positive freehold covenants have always been enforceable. American land law diverged from English law after *Spencer's Case*[56] but before *Keppell v Bailey*[57] and so never drove a wedge between freehold and leasehold

---

[44] B Rudden, "Economic Theory v Property Law: The *Numerus Clausus* Problem" in J Eekelaar and J Bell (eds), *Oxford Essays in Jurisprudence* (3rd series 1987) p 262.

[45] Conveyancing Act 1919, s 88BA.

[46] Law of Property Act 2000 (NT), s 167.

[47] Property (Northern Ireland) Order 1997, art 34.

[48] Land Law and Conveyancing Act 1981, s 118.

[49] Property Law Act 2007, s 303.

[50] Conveyancing and Property Ordinance 1984 (as amended), s 41.

[51] Land and Conveyancing Law Reform Act 2009, s 49.

[52] The American Law Institute, *Restatement of the Law Third: Property (Servitudes)* (2000). The American Law Institute is an independent not for profit organisation with a membership comprising 4,000 legal professionals, which produces recommendations to clarify, modernise, and improve the law. For more information, see: http://www.ali.org/index.cfm?fuseaction=about.overview (last viewed 13 May 2011). The Restatement is considered authoritative and designed to act as a guide to courts and legislators.

[53] Report on Real Burdens (2000) Scot Law Com No 181, which led to the Title Conditions (Scotland) Act 2003.

[54] For a note on the approach to positive covenants in some European jurisdictions, see S van Erp, "Land Burdens: A Fragmented or Uniform Approach: When Will the Civil Law Debate Start?" (2004) 8.3 *Electronic Journal of Comparative Law*.

[55] In particular, we have made reference to some of the Scottish solutions to potential problems arising from enforceability in Part 6.

[56] (1583) 5 Co Rep 16a, 77 ER 72.

[57] (1834) 2 My & K 517, 39 ER 1042 and see para 5.12 above.

in this context. The Restatement draws together easements, profits and covenants both positive and negative into a unified system, and we have drawn inspiration from that work.

5.34 More recent academic analysis has sought to find a principled reason why the law should allow, or prevent, the creation of new property rights. It has been argued that such rights are desired and permitted in cases where it is better (cheaper, or "fairer") to create a right that will last, so that future owners do not have the cost of re-creating it, than to create a transient right that future owners will want to re-make. That balance can be explained in terms of economic efficiency,[58] or of mutual benefit.[59]

5.35 The other side of the coin is that once land has been burdened with an obligation that does not need to be re-created when it changes hands, the land may lose value because there may be little or no scope to vary or remove the burden by negotiation. And so it has been argued that wherever the range of property rights has been widened, the effect has been not to eliminate problems but to re-create them in different forms.[60] Pamela O'Connor, the Commissioner charged with the reform of easements and covenants for the Victoria Law Reform Commission, has drawn attention to problems of choice; she notes the potential for oppression particularly in large-scale housing development, where properties are burdened with positive obligations which have not been truly chosen by their purchasers (since positive obligations will simply be part of a package).[61]

5.36 All these are valid concerns. If it were not already possible to impose positive obligations that run with freehold land, albeit by indirect means, we would agree that it would be important to establish an economic case for doing so.[62] But we regard it as very significant that there is no obstacle to creating such obligations, through estate rentcharges, chains of indemnity and so on, as discussed above; the problem is not the inability to achieve the objective – for which we can see that the market has made its own case – but that the objective has to be achieved by roundabout methods.

5.37 It has been argued that the availability of these "workarounds" means that the basic rule, that positive covenants do not run, is acceptable.[63] It has been said in response that "it is undesirable that people be encouraged to take circuitous routes to avoid the effect of a legal rule".[64] We agree; more importantly, it is

---

[58] B W F Depoorter and R Parisi, "Fragmentation of Property Rights: A Functional Interpretation of the Law of Servitudes" (2003) 3(1) *Global Jurist Frontiers* 2.

[59] J R Gordley, "Servitudes" (2003) 3(1) *Global Jurist Frontiers* 3; see also B Akkermans, *The Principle of* Numerus Clausus *in European Property Law* (2008) p 440 and following.

[60] C M Rose, "Servitudes" *Arizona Legal Studies Discussion Paper No 09-13* (March 2009).

[61] P O'Connor, "Careful What You Wish For: Positive Freehold Covenants" (2011) 3 (May/Jun) *Conveyancer and Property Lawyer* (forthcoming).

[62] B McFarlane, "The *Numerus Clausus* Principle and Covenants Relating to Land" in S Bright (ed), *Modern Studies in Property Law: Volume 6* (2011) p 311.

[63] J Snape, "The Benefit and Burden of Covenants – Now Where Are We?" (1994) 3 *Nottingham Law Journal* 68.

[64] L Turano, "Intention, interpretation and the "mystery" of section 79 of the Law of Property Act 1925" [2000] *Conveyancer and Property Lawyer* 377.

expensive and time-consuming, and some of the methods used can be risky and uncertain. The existence of these indirect methods of enforcing positive obligations shows the desire for and practical importance of positive obligations; and the fact that the law permits these methods shows that there is no consistent policy that positive obligations should not be attached to land.

5.38    The "workarounds" described above are products of the determination of practitioners in the face of a prohibition imposed by *Keppell v Bailey* that impedes the arrangements that their clients want to make. So the task for this project is not to justify positive obligations, starting from a clean slate, but to recommend reforms that would provide a simpler and more practicable method to achieve what can already be done, in a way that minimises the economic burden upon properties and their owners.

5.39    In answer to our questions about the problems associated with freehold covenants,[65] the majority of consultees felt that the burden of positive obligations should run.[66]

5.40    Herbert Smith LLP, for example, said:

> It is clearly wrong in concept that parties should be required to adopt some, often complicated, mechanism or, worse, a legal estate structure which would not otherwise be adopted, in order to achieve security on positive covenants.

5.41    The Chancery Bar Association added:

> We agree that it is a serious practical problem and injustice that positive covenants cannot be enforced directly between the successors in title to the original land owning contracting parties, in particular in the case of fencing and maintenance covenants.

5.42    Letitia Crabb[67] and the Charities' Property Association expressed the view that if the main concern is inter-dependent units, the solution is to be found in specific legislation, such as commonhold. However, the main concern is not interdependent units but rather the gap in the current law, which commonhold does not address and for which it is not suitable. It remains impossible to use a simple legal structure to manage responsibility for mending a fence between properties, or a single facility shared by a few properties. Other consultees agreed that there is still a need for reform despite the introduction of commonhold.[68]

---

[65]    Consultation Paper, paras 7.59, 7.66, 7.79(1) and 7.80.

[66]    See the Analysis of Responses, paras 7.1 to 7.32.

[67]    University of Reading.

[68]    We asked this specifically in the Consultation Paper, para 7.66. See the Analysis of Responses, paras 7.12 to 7.20. Pamela O'Connor, in the article cited above at para 5.35 n 61, notes that very few jurisdictions have introduced *both* binding positive covenants *and* a strata title system. We have taken the view that the combination of both is desirable here, because of the use of alternative and cumbersome workarounds, because of the views of consultees, and because commonhold is so little used.

5.43 A very few consultees explicitly opposed such a reform, raising concerns about how positive obligations would be enforced and the litigation that might follow. We take those concerns seriously. Although we conclude that we should recommend that positive obligations should be able to run with land, we look carefully at the safeguards necessary to ensure that land cannot be burdened with an open-ended range of obligations, and that burdens on title are readily discoverable. We also address carefully in Part 6 the difficulties associated with enforceability.

## Safeguards to accompany positive obligations

5.44 The main concerns raised by the introduction of positive obligations are the potential for an open-ended range of obligations which overburden land, and the need to ensure that burdens on title are readily discoverable. These difficulties have already been faced, and addressed, by the different jurisdictions which have reformed their land law to allow positive obligations to run with land. We explore four different strategies for addressing these issues below.

### *A list of permissible positive obligations*

5.45 One response to that concern is to limit the range of positive obligations available. So in New South Wales it is possible to create positive covenants only for maintenance or repair of a site subject to an easement;[69] in Northern Ireland, too, the range of positive covenants is restricted to those listed in the statute.[70]

5.46 We asked consultees whether there should be any limitations or restrictions on the types of obligations that should be capable of creation.[71] All but four of the consultees who answered this question agreed that a list of permissible positive obligations was undesirable. A typical comment was:

> We can see no reason why there should be any limitations or restrictions on the types of Land Obligations[72] that should be capable of creation once they can be recorded on the register. It seems to us that knowledge of the burden is of fundamental importance and this can be assured by entry on the Register.[73]

5.47 The National Trust agreed that a list would be undesirable, but stressed the need for the Lands Chamber to be able to adjudicate applications to vary or discharge positive obligations if they became unworkable over time due to changes in circumstances.

---

[69] Conveyancing Act 1919, s 88BA.

[70] Property (Northern Ireland) Order 1997.

[71] Consultation Paper, para 8.24.

[72] The Consultation Paper proposed the introduction of "Land Obligations", spelt with initial capitals. We have not adopted that usage here; the land obligations we recommend in this Report differ in some technical details from those proposed in the Consultation Paper and so we have found it useful to retain the initial capitals when referring to the interests that that paper described and proposed.

[73] Diocese of Southwark.

5.48　In other words, consultees were concerned about registration and discharge, but unimpressed with the idea of a list. We agree that a list of permitted positive obligations may achieve very little, and creates the risk that something important is omitted.[74] We note the Scottish experience of an unlimited range of real burdens (corresponding to positive and negative obligations) and a list of permitted servitudes (corresponding to easements), which has given rise to difficulties when new types of servitudes are claimed.[75] A list also has to be kept under review and changed over time to meet changing conditions. We therefore do not propose to limit the range of obligations in that way.[76]

### *Controlling the range of positive obligations*

5.49　A different strategy is to restrict the range of obligations that may be permitted not with a list, but by a requirement as to the nature of the obligation. This can be achieved in two different ways.

5.50　First, most common law countries have a requirement that restrictive covenants must "touch and concern" the land of the covenantee if they are to bind the covenantor's land; that is to say, they must benefit the covenantee's land, rather than the covenantee personally. Another way to express this is to say that the covenant must be of benefit to the covenantee while the covenantee is the owner of the benefited land, and irrelevant to that covenantee otherwise. A way to control the permissible range of positive obligations would be to impose a touch and concern requirement, thus permitting, for example, an obligation to mend a fence but not an obligation to walk the covenantee's dog.

---

[74]　Dr Nicholas Roberts (Oxford Brookes University) pointed out that the Northern Irish list omits the obligation to insure property.

[75]　See *Romano v Standard Commercial Property Securities Ltd* [2008] CSOH 105 (OH).

[76]　We have to add a note of caution here: many consultees would have liked to see the range of obligations so free of restrictions as to include any form of financial obligation. But we are clear that that would be unsafe, and indeed other consultees pointed this out (particularly in response to our description of different types of Land Obligations in the Consultation Paper, para 8.23). Accordingly our conclusions on the "touch and concern" requirement represent something of a compromise: the range of possible covenants is not limited by a list, but is reined in by that conceptual restriction.

5.51 The policy of the American Restatement is to abandon the touch and concern requirement, for both positive and negative covenants; this has given rise to considerable controversy.[77] Our view, reinforced by consultees' responses[78] and by discussion with stakeholders, is that a "touch and concern" requirement is a robust control mechanism that prevents land being overburdened, even if it is vulnerable to the uncertainties of judicial interpretation at times. It acts as a filter, in limiting the range of enforceable covenants; it can therefore counter assertions that the enforceability of positive obligations would open the door to a wide range of unsuitable burdens. It is particularly important as a way of preventing the imposition of overage covenants that bind land.[79]

5.52 Overage is a form of payment, by a buyer to a seller, of value realised after the purchase, often on the grant of planning consent or on completion of a development;[80] it is therefore a form of deferred consideration for a sale. It does not touch and concern land, being as valuable to someone who does not own neighbouring land as to one who does. The use of positive obligations as a way of enforcing overage would be to use such obligations as a form of charge, which is inappropriate. We agree with those consultees who took the view that overage should not be able to be secured by positive obligations.[81]

5.53 A second way to control the range of possible positive obligations is through statutory definition. The Consultation Paper adopted a formalistic definition of a Land Obligation,[82] proposing that one could only be created by precise use of the term "Land Obligation".[83] Consultees were generally unhappy with that requirement, taking the view that it created a trap for the unwary.[84] We are very cautious about excessively formal creation requirements, and are not recommending their imposition.[85] What we now think is far more useful is to develop a functional definition of permissible positive proprietary obligations, which will serve not only to identify them and to distinguish them from other interests in land, but also to control the type of obligation that can be imposed. A requirement that a positive obligation may only be to do something on one's own land, or on a boundary structure, or to pay money in return for the performance of another obligation, will eliminate a number of possibilities that we would regard as excessive burdens on land. Obligations to do work on a neighbour's land, for example, might well touch and concern that land; but they would be far more likely to render the burdened land unmarketable than would an obligation to do

---

[77] The American Law Institute, *Restatement of the Law Third: Property (Servitudes)* (2000) § 3.2 p 411; J R Gordley, "Servitudes" (2003) 3(1) *Global Jurist Frontiers* 3.

[78] See the Analysis of Responses, paras 8.78 to 8.87.

[79] By contrast, the objective of the American Restatement in abandoning the touch and concern requirement was to "permit innovative land-development practices" (see The American Law Institute, *Restatement of the Law Third: Property (Servitudes)* (2000) § 3.2 p 411); that is not one of the aims of our reform.

[80] See *Crest Nicholson (Londinium) Ltd v Akaria Investments Ltd* [2010] EWCA Civ 1331.

[81] See the Analysis of Responses, para 8.10.

[82] See para 5.46, n 72 above.

[83] Consultation Paper, paras 8.25 to 8.28.

[84] See the Analysis of Responses, paras 8.13 to 8.19.

[85] See para 6.46 and following below.

work on one's own land, or to mend a fence between the two plots. And the work required might be to work in the neighbour's shop or factory, which is clearly not what this reform seeks to achieve.

5.54 So we take the view that as well as a "touch and concern" requirement, a careful functional definition can also be employed to control the range of positive obligations available.

### A jurisdiction to vary and discharge

5.55 The reason why the American Restatement regards the touch and concern requirement as unimportant, in terms of safeguards, is the availability of a jurisdiction to vary covenants.[86] In other words, if a covenant is flexible in the sense that it can be discharged or varied at relatively low cost, there is little or no need to control the range that can be made to bind land.

5.56 That argument has to be handled with care, as it is heavily dependent upon access to efficient and economic means to vary or discharge. Unless such proceedings are quick, cheap and stress-free, a touch and concern requirement remains essential and, as we have explained above, we do not wish to dispense with that requirement.

5.57 Conversely, even a robust touch and concern requirement does not obviate the need for a way to discharge or modify obligations. Section 84 of the Law of Property Act 1925 gives to the Lands Chamber a jurisdiction to modify or discharge restrictive covenants that have become obsolete; if positive obligations are to be able to run with land, it is essential that that jurisdiction be extended to positive obligations. We discuss that in Part 7.

### Registration

5.58 Finally, a pervasive technique for controlling the impact of binding positive obligations is registration. Susan French, the editor of the American Restatement, in an article written during the progress of the project, explains that the current position in English law as to freehold covenants came about because of the lack of a recording or registration system that could achieve adequate publicity for positive rights.[87] The American states, by contrast, operated deeds registration systems from relatively early days,[88] and so could enforce the burden of positive covenants in the confidence that only a really careless purchaser could be caught

---

[86] As noted in the Restatement (The American Law Institute, *Restatement of the Law Third: Property (Servitudes)* (2000) § 3.2 p 411-2): "one problem addressed by [the touch and concern doctrine], the persistent problem of affirmative obligations to pay money or provide services without any time limit, is addressed in this Restatement by the rule in § 7.2, which permits judicial modification or termination of such obligations …".

[87] S F French, "Design Proposal for the New Restatement of the Law of Real Property – Servitudes" (1987-88) 21 *University of California Davis Law Review* 1213. See also S F French, "Toward a Modern Law of Servitudes: Reweaving the Ancient Strands" (1981-82) 55 *Southern California Law Review* 1261, 1283 at n 114. For an analysis of other aspects of the different evolutions in the US and in England, see S Goulding, "Privity of estate and real covenants" (2007) 36 *Common Law World Review* 193.

[88] And still do; after an early experiment with title registration, the American states have continued with deeds registration backed up by title indemnity.

out by an unexpected burden. The countries that have introduced reform relatively recently all have sophisticated registration systems.

5.59 Clearly one of the issues that goes hand-in-hand with the question whether or not the burden of positive covenants should run with land is the need to ensure that that burden is registered against the title in some way, so that successors to the covenantor are not caught out by unexpected burdens. This is potentially far more of a priority for positive obligations than it is for restrictive covenants; it is conceivably much worse to find out unexpectedly that you have to pay to maintain a road every five years, than it is to find out that your land is subject to a covenant not to build in front of a building line, or not to use for business purposes, and so on. In any event, the system for registering burdens is well-developed, both within the title registration system and via the land charges system where title is unregistered.

5.60 The ability to register the burden of an obligation does not, we think, by itself justify the creation of positive obligations that run with land.[89] Registration enables a purchaser to choose not to buy; it does not prevent the imposition of an obligation that will render the land unmarketable. Hence the importance of careful definition, and of the touch and concern requirement, to control the initial imposition, and the jurisdiction of a tribunal to discharge or vary obligations that have become unworkable. But equally, a requirement for registration of the burden is essential.

5.61 However, there is another information problem, which we have already highlighted in relation to restrictive covenants, and which carries even more weight in the context of positive obligations. At present, it is not possible to record the benefit of a restrictive covenant on either the Land Charges Register (for unregistered land) or on the register of title (for registered land). The Land Charges Act 1972 provides for the registration of interests against the name of the owner only of the burdened land.[90] The Land Registration Act 2002 only provides for the registration of the benefit of legal interests in land.[91] In the absence of information about where the benefit lies it may be impossible to negotiate a release. Owners of land burdened by a restrictive covenant may therefore have to rely on indemnity insurance, or bring a claim to the Lands Chamber (and indeed may be compelled to do so if they wish to mortgage the land, in order to make the title acceptable to the lender). We noted these problems above.[92] They would be far more acute if positive obligations were introduced without the benefit being registrable, because positive obligations are arguably more vulnerable than negative ones to changes in circumstances and may be more likely to require discharge or modification.

5.62 So we think that if land is to be burdened with positive obligations, it is important that the land that benefits from the obligation be able to be identified with

---

[89] B Edgeworth, "The *numerus clausus* principle in contemporary Australian property law" (2006) 32 *Monash University Law Review* 387.

[90] Land Charges Act 1972, s 3(1).

[91] LRA 2002, s 2.

[92] See para 5.4 above.

certainty through a publicly accessible register. In practice that means title registration,[93] and that brings us back to the conclusion we suggested above[94] in response to the difficulties that arise from the contractual status of covenants: that such covenants should take effect for the future as legal interests in land and not as contractual rights.

## RECOMMENDATIONS FOR THE REFORM OF FREEHOLD COVENANTS

5.63 We have concluded that we should recommend the reform of positive obligations. But along with that must go recommendations about safeguards, in order to minimise practical and economic risk. We have not favoured the approach adopted in some jurisdictions of having a list of permissible positive obligations;[95] but we have taken the view that careful definition, a touch and concern requirement, the ability to register the benefit of the obligation (rather than just the burden) and the facility to have burdens discharged or modified are all important elements of reform.

5.64 Our conclusion about positive obligations has implications for the way in which the current law of positive and restrictive covenants should be reformed. One approach to such reform is simply to assimilate positive covenants to the current law of restrictive covenants. Some jurisdictions have introduced enforceable positive covenants on that basis. The New Zealand Property Law and Equity Reform Committee proposed that both positive and negative covenants should run with the land in equity, and rejected the creation of an entirely new range of obligations:

> The proposed new s 64A of the Property Law Act 1952 will assimilate positive covenants as closely as possible to the existing law of restrictive covenants and general contractual obligations. We agree with the Law Commission [for England and Wales] that it is not possible juristically to equate positive covenants totally with restrictive covenants, but we believe the simpler course is the one we propose.[96]

5.65 However, that simple course would perpetuate the other disadvantages we noted in connection with restrictive covenants: the inability to keep a public record of benefited land, the complexity of the rules relating to the running of benefit and burden, and the fact that even where the burden of a restrictive covenant runs with land, the original covenantor remains liable on it.[97]

---

[93] We comment on the implications of positive obligations in unregistered land at paras 6.54 to 6.58 below.

[94] See para 5.10 above.

[95] See paras 5.45 to 5.48 above.

[96] New Zealand Property Law and Equity Reform Committee Report, *Positive Covenants Affecting Land* (June 1985) para 30. The Law Commission's 1984 Report was published shortly before the Property Law and Equity Reform Committee published its report. The Committee took note of the Law Commission recommendations, but did not consider that it was necessary to create an entirely new range of obligations. See New Zealand's Property Law Act 2007, s 303.

[97] Consultation Paper, para 7.38.

5.66    That latter point in particular should not be replicated for positive covenants. If positive obligations are to be able to run with land, they should do so in the form of a property interest rather than as a covenant that involves continuing contractual liability.

5.67    Moreover, the requirement that the benefit of the obligation be able to be registered is as relevant to negative obligations as it is to positive. Consideration of that requirement takes us to the provisions of the Land Registration Act 2002, of which section 2 lists the legal estates and interests, title to which can be registered. This points to the desirability of reforming the law of freehold covenants – negative and positive – by enabling proprietors of land to create obligations in the form of legal interests, rather than simply extending the category of equitable interests to include positive covenants.[98] Reform that enables covenants to take effect as legal interests will allow consistency with easements and a natural fit with the grammar of our land law. It enables a regime where third-party rights in land can all be created and registered in the same, or very nearly the same, way. We explain this in greater detail in Part 6.

5.68    The introduction of a new legal interest was at the heart of our recommendations in 1984,[99] and was also advocated in the Consultation Paper. We argued that the problems inherent in the law of freehold covenants were so great that they could be resolved only by the introduction of a new legal interest rather than by extending or modifying the current system of equitable interests. Consultees expressed broad agreement with that argument, although they were concerned (as we noted above) about undue complexity.[100] Our recommendation is therefore for a simpler scheme, involving a new legal interest in land but without some of the more complex features (formal requirements for creation, for example) of the Land Obligation of the Consultation Paper.

5.69    **We recommend that the owner of an estate in land shall be able to create positive and negative obligations that will be able to take effect (subject to the formal requirements for the creation of legal interests) as legal interests appurtenant to another estate in land, and therefore as registrable interests pursuant to the Land Registration Act 2002, provided that:**

    **(1)    the benefit of the obligation touches and concerns the benefited land;**

    **(2)    the obligation is either:**

        **(a)    an obligation not to do something on the burdened land;**

---

[98]    It would not be impossible to extend the list of registrable interests, under the LRA 2002, to include an equitable interest, but we take the view that that would do considerable violence to the structure of title registration, and for no obvious benefit.

[99]    See para 1.6 and following above.

[100]    See the Analysis of Responses, paras 7.21 to 7.32,

(b)     an obligation to do something on the burdened land or on the boundary (or any structure or feature that is treated as marking or lying on the boundary) of the burdened and benefited land; or

(c)     an obligation to make a payment in return for the performance of an obligation of the kind mentioned in paragraph (b); and

(3)     the obligation is not made between lessor and lessee and relating to the demised premises.

5.70   **We recommend that for the future, covenants made by the owner of an estate in land and that satisfy the conditions set out above shall take effect, not as promises and not in accordance with the current law relating to restrictive covenants, but as legal interests in the burdened land, appurtenant to the benefited estate in land.**

5.71   These two recommendations work together, both enabling the creation of obligations as interests and ensuring that future covenants take effect as such interests, and indeed as legal interests when the formal requirements for their creation are met. That means that in terms of drafting, there is freedom – but no compulsion – for conveyancers to draft restrictive covenants as they currently do. There is no requirement to use any particular form of words, provided that the obligation imposed meets the requirements for a valid land obligation in the draft Bill.

5.72   Technically, these new obligations are akin to the land obligations of the 1984 recommendations and to the new legal interest that we proposed in the Consultation Paper, and "land obligations" is the most natural of the available labels for them. This is neither the scheme recommended in 1984 nor, in much of its detail, the scheme provisionally proposed in the Consultation Paper. What we recommend here is a much simpler arrangement and one that involves far more continuity with the current law. Yet it is clearly a scheme that provides for obligations to take effect as legal interests, and the word "obligation" is important. As will be seen, the word plays an important role in the draft Bill.

5.73   Equally important will be the ability to draft the new obligations in the familiar form of covenants, if practitioners so choose, even though the effect will be to create land obligations. We think that that will be welcome to practitioners and we imagine that negative obligations (that is, obligations not to do something) will generally be worded in that form.

5.74   We have therefore considered the possibility of calling the new obligations "new covenants" in order to emphasise the continuity with the current law; and we think that in some circumstances practitioners may find that a useful label. But the reality is that the debate that informs our policy decision is about obligations, and that a legal interest in land is not a covenant. If it is truly a legal interest it is no longer a contract and shares none of the important and often unwelcome features of a covenant – in particular, there is no privity of contract and no question of the benefited and burdened estate owners having to have made an agreement with each other. The right will be enforceable, as a legal interest and therefore one of those listed in section 1(2)(a) of the Law of Property Act 1925, by virtue of its

113

status as an interest in land, and not as a contract. The rules in *Tulk v Moxhay*[101] and in *Elliston v Reacher*[102] will have no relevance to the new interests because they will not be covenants.

5.75 The label "covenant", therefore, would technically be a misrepresentation of what we are recommending and may be misleading, and for the purposes of this Report we have retained the label "land obligations", although the draft Bill refers to the new interests, as will be seen in Part 6 below, simply as "obligations".

5.76 In Part 6 we turn to the provisions of the draft Bill, which we discuss in detail in order to explore the nature of land obligations, and their creation, registration and enforceability. We postpone to Part 7 our recommendations about the Lands Chamber.

## ADDITIONAL DETAILS

5.77 It remains to comment on a number of further matters:

(1) the availability of land obligations in unregistered land;

(2) the future status of the rule in *Tulk v Moxhay* and of the other current rules for the running of the benefit and burden of restrictive covenants;

(3) the relationship between the reform that we recommend and the availability of commonhold; and

(4) the relationship between the reform that we recommend and some current forms of easements.

### Land obligations in unregistered land

5.78 We proposed in the Consultation Paper that it should only be possible to create a Land Obligation if title to both the servient and dominant land was registered.[103] A proprietor of unregistered land who wished to grant or take the benefit of a Land Obligation would therefore have to register his title. We have decided not to recommend such a requirement for the creation of land obligations. Accordingly the provisional proposal at paragraph 8.110 of the Consultation Paper is no longer relevant.[104] To do so would generate an inconsistency within the system of appurtenant rights. It would be very strange if easements could be created in unregistered land, but not land obligations. A number of consultees (10 of the 35 who responded to the question, including Farrer & Co LLP, Andrew Francis,[105] Gregory Hill,[106] Network Rail and the Agricultural Law Association) were extremely unhappy with the idea of marginalising unregistered land in this way.

---

[101] (1848) 2 Ph 774, 41 ER 1143. See paras 5.82 to 5.89 below.

[102] [1908] 2 Ch 665. See para 6.84, n 62 below.

[103] Consultation Paper, para 8.38. See the Analysis of Responses, paras 8.20 to 8.29.

[104] See the Analysis of Responses, paras 8.100 to 8.107.

[105] Barrister, Serle Court Chambers.

[106] Barrister, Ten Old Square Chambers.

5.79    Since the enactment of the Land Registration Act 2002, the "triggers" for first registration (that is, events that make first registration necessary) have been extended by statutory instrument. They now include an appointment of new trustees; and that will bring in many large-scale landowners within a generation. Moreover, many proprietors of unregistered land are registering their titles voluntarily.[107] So to recommend that the creation of a land obligation be a trigger for registration, for benefited or burdened land, is scarcely worthwhile. On the other hand, there are landowners for whom it would be a disproportionate measure in view of the difficulties they experience in registering their title.[108]

5.80    We are mindful also of the fact, raised by Land Registry with reference to this point, that because of the general boundaries rule it may be impossible to tell whether land at or near the edge of a plot is registered or not.[109] That uncertainty could be crucial in determining, for example, whether a fencing obligation was enforceable.

5.81    It follows from what we have said already that it is unacceptable for there to be positive obligations attached to land that are hard to discover. Traditionally, a legal interest bound all the world. If the benefit of an obligation to mend the fence were a legal interest in land, and the traditional rule applied without modification (as it does for legal easements in unregistered land) then any successor in title to the owner first subject to the obligation to mend the fence would equally be bound by the obligation to mend it whether he or she knew about that or not. That would be unacceptable. Accordingly, in order to control enforceability and to protect purchasers we have to bring land obligations into the Land Charges registration system. We explain this further in Part 6.

**The future for the rule in *Tulk v Moxhay* and the current law of restrictive covenants**

5.82    Clearly there will remain many old restrictive covenants with proprietary effect, pursuant to the rule in *Tulk v Moxhay*,[110] for many years – perhaps forever. Our proposals do not jeopardise rights already created.[111] But should it be possible to create new covenants under the rule post-reform?

5.83    This would not happen without express provision. Land obligations are to be defined functionally, as obligations to do or not do something on one's own land, subject to a "touch and concern" requirement. The framing of a covenant in the

[107] Recent Land Registry figures suggest that by July 2009 69% of land in England and Wales was registered and that by July 2010 this figure had risen to 73%.

[108] Network Rail, for example, is heavily reliant on a web of easements and restrictive covenants. Its title is unregistered and its interests would be severely disadvantaged by a requirement to register in order to benefit from a covenant. There may well be other large organisations in this position.

[109] LRA 2002, s 60 provides that the boundary of a registered estate, as shown for the purposes of the register, is a general boundary and therefore does not determine the exact line of the boundary, unless shown as determined. Where the general boundaries rule applies, it is not certain which land is registered and which is not.

[110] (1848) 2 Ph 774, 41 ER 1143.

[111] We discuss in Part 7 the need for a mechanism to discharge old restrictive covenants, and post-reform land obligations in prescribed circumstances, when they are truly obsolete.

terms used at present to create a covenant under the rule in *Tulk v Moxhay* would create the new legal interest, in accordance with our recommendation and provided that the covenant was expressed in a deed and duly registered as discussed in Part 6. But should the parties be able to state expressly that the covenant is to take the old form, enforceable pursuant to the rule in *Tulk v Moxhay*?

5.84 Two commonsense points indicate that this should not be allowed. The first is that it would be undesirable to have the two systems operating and growing simultaneously, so that a purchaser has to check "is this a *Tulk v Moxhay* covenant or a land obligation?" The objective must be for a purchaser simply to be able to see that the vendor wants him or her to be subject to an obligation not to use the land for business purposes, and to be aware that that will now (post-reform) generate a legal interest. The second is that it is hard to see why such a covenant would be wanted.

5.85 A possible answer to that is that the covenantee might wish to retain the liability of the original covenantor. But we have identified as one of the major problems with the current law the fact that it is possible for a covenantor to retain liability – say, for ensuring that land is not used for business purposes – long after parting with the land.[112] There has been little or no litigation on that issue so far as the current regime of restrictive covenants is concerned, but we would anticipate considerable problems of injustice and complexity were original covenantor liability permitted to outlast land ownership in respect of positive obligations. It is not desirable for anyone to be pursued for a service charge or the cost of maintaining a boundary, long after they have sold their land.[113]

5.86 We asked consultees whether *Tulk v Moxhay* covenants should continue, either in general or in certain circumstances where it would not have been possible to create a Land Obligation in the way that the Consultation Paper proposed.[114]

5.87 In general, consultees agreed that it would be undesirable for the two systems to run in parallel with the option to create either restrictive covenants or Land Obligations. Some expressed caution on the basis that they were not convinced of the virtue of Land Obligations, and we think that the proposals we now make – being more firmly rooted in existing concepts – will reassure those consultees. Consultees were far less happy with proposals that old-style covenants should be possible where Land Obligations were impossible because the land was unregistered,[115] some referring back to their unhappiness with the idea that Land Obligations should be available only in registered land. Under our recommendations that difficulty does not arise.

5.88 It must of course remain possible to provide expressly that a covenant will be merely personal – in which case it will not have proprietary effect and will not bind

---

[112] See paras 5.4, 5.8 and 5.9 above.

[113] The same concern can be seen in the context of leasehold covenants; concern about original tenant liability was the principal reason for the enactment of the Landlord and Tenant (Covenants) Act 1995.

[114] Consultation Paper, paras 8.109 to 8.113. See the Analysis of Responses, 8.100 to 8.124.

[115] Consultation Paper, para 8.110.

the land. But it should not be possible to impose a restrictive covenant pursuant to *Tulk v Moxhay* once the new regime is enacted.[116]

**5.89** **We recommend that following the implementation of reform it should no longer be possible to create freehold covenants enforceable under *Tulk v Moxhay*.**

### Land obligations and commonhold

5.90 As we discussed above, reform to the general law of positive obligations has to be seen as catering for those circumstances where commonhold is unsuitable. What is needed is a straightforward method (without "workarounds") to impose simple bilateral arrangements, or to share obligations for a single shared facility among a very few properties. To that end, what we recommend is a relatively simple structure. We recommend provision for the situation where benefited or burdened land is subdivided,[117] and for the variation of arrangements where costs are shared;[118] but we have made no provision for management structures, nor for any financial structures such as interest payments or sinking funds. The latter can be managed within the terms of an obligation.[119] And a simple management structure could be achieved by the use of a management company, such as is currently used to support estate rentcharges and also in the leasehold context. Thus a management company in which all the relevant landowners were shareholders could take on responsibility for the maintenance of a driveway, for example, with the shareholders each obliged to pay a proportion of the cost.

5.91 However, where complex financial and management arrangements are needed for major, expensive work the simple imposition of positive obligations will not be appropriate and commonhold or leasehold will continue to be the correct approach.[120]

### Land obligations, negative easements and easements of fencing

5.92 Finally, we have to look at some of the current available forms of easements, which will be affected by an overlap with the new obligations.

5.93 First, fencing easements. The existence of an easement of fencing is an anomaly; it has been described as a "spurious easement".[121] It appears to be an exception to the principle that an easement cannot involve the servient owner in the expenditure of money.[122] It seems that it can arise by prescription, when the

---

[116] That said, our recommendations would not prevent anyone from imposing or giving two covenants in respect of an obligation: the one proprietary under the new regime (which would take effect as a land obligation), and the one personal. To prevent this explicitly would be a disproportionate micro-management; there may well be commercial deals where such an arrangement is entered into by fully informed and advised parties.

[117] See para 6.98 and 6.118 and following below.

[118] See para 7.73 and following below.

[119] See paras 6.33 to 6.36 below.

[120] See the Analysis of Responses, paras 7.12 to 7.20.

[121] *Coaker v Willcocks* [1911] 2 KB 124, 131, by Farwell LJ.

[122] *Megarry and Wade*, para 27-014.

servient owner has responded to requests to mend a fence, over many years.[123] This is clearly anomalous; for a fencing easement to arise by implication or by prescription would be as implausible and contrary to principle as the prescription or implication of any covenant.[124] Once positive obligations can be created as interests in land any argument for the recognition of easements of fencing falls away.

**5.94 We recommend that, for the future, an obligation to fence must take effect as a land obligation and not as an easement.**

5.95 Clause 25 of the draft Bill gives effect to this recommendation.

5.96 More difficult is the interaction of land obligations with negative easements. Our recommendation would define a land obligation as an obligation to do or not do something on one's own land. Easements, being in general rights to do something on, or receive something from or through, someone else's land would accordingly not be land obligations.

5.97 However, negative easements would overlap with the new interest. These are the rights to receive support, or air, water or light in a defined channel; they have been the subject of some controversy,[125] but it is now well-established that they can be easements.[126] There is therefore an overlap with land obligations: an easement of support, for example, might more naturally be regarded as an obligation not to undermine, and a right to light as an obligation not to obstruct.[127] And of course because our definition is functional, the way that the interest is worded does not matter; what makes it a land obligation is its substance.

5.98 Should we therefore recommend that it should no longer be possible to create any new negative easements (without disturbing the existing ones)?[128] We asked in the Consultation Paper whether some or all of the negative easements should be abolished. Four consultees gave cautious support to the abolition of negative easements other than rights to light. But most of those who answered the question did not support abolition. Comments focused on the important social function of negative easements, and in particular on the importance of their being able to be created by prescription or implication.[129]

---

[123] *Gale on Easements*, para 1-78.

[124] See paras 6.59 to 6.62 below.

[125] See Consultation Paper, para 15.32 and the discussion of *Moore v Rawson* (1824) 3 B & C 332, 107 ER 756.

[126] In the Consultation Paper, para 15.33, we quoted from *Hunter v Canary Wharf Ltd* [1997] AC 655, 726, by Lord Hope.

[127] In *Moore v Rawson* (1824) 3 B & C 332, 340; 107 ER 756, 761, Littledale J said "the right to insist upon the non-obstruction and non-interruption of [light and air] more properly arises by a covenant".

[128] We note that that step was taken in the Title Conditions (Scotland) Act 2003; s 80 converts negative servitudes (equivalent to easements) into real burdens. Scotland had fewer negative servitudes; and they could not be created by prescription.

[129] See the Analysis of Responses, paras 15.1 to 15.8.

5.99    We note these views and make no recommendations about negative easements. For the future, attempts to create negative easements expressly will give rise to land obligations if the requirements of clause 1 of the draft Bill are met; but all four negative easements will continue to be able to arise by implication or prescription, which meets consultees' concerns.

# PART 6
# A NEW LEGAL INTEREST IN LAND

## INTRODUCTION

6.1 In Part 5 of this Report we rehearsed the arguments for the reform of freehold covenants, and recommended that both positive and negative obligations should take effect as legal interests in land, which we called land obligations. We also recommended certain safeguards to prevent land becoming burdened by unworkable positive obligations. We rejected the idea of a list of permissible positive obligations, but concluded that the range of available obligations should be limited by a touch and concern requirement, that the benefit as well as the burden of positive obligations must be registrable so as to be readily discoverable, and that there should be a tribunal jurisdiction to discharge or modify them.

6.2 We also recommended that, for the future, covenants both positive and negative should take effect as land obligations, and not as covenants. For restrictive covenants, this is a change in form, which will have the useful practical consequence that in future the extent of the benefited land will be readily discoverable from the register of title, if title to that land is registered. For positive covenants the change is more far-reaching; it will be possible to enforce positive obligations against successors in title, within the constraints set out in the draft Bill.

6.3 The benefit and burden of land obligations, both negative and positive, will be transmitted on the basis of the same principles that apply to easements and other appurtenant legal interests, so that the current complex rules for the running of the benefit and burden of restrictive covenants will not apply to land obligations.[1]

6.4 We go on now to explore the nature of land obligations, and their creation and registration, making a number of further recommendations that follow from what we have recommended in Part 5. We also recommend the extension to land obligations of the recommendations that we made in Part 4. Finally we look at the enforceability of land obligations, and at remedies for breach.

6.5 The scheme we recommend here is relatively simple. Practitioners will need to bear in mind that where complex shared responsibilities, management structures, or communal financial arrangements are required, they should continue to make use of leasehold or commonhold structures rather than endeavouring to adapt the new land obligations to a purpose for which they were not designed. In particular, land obligations will not enable the creation of freehold flats.

6.6 It should also be borne in mind that the scheme we recommend here is intimately linked with our recommendations in Part 7 concerning the jurisdiction of the Lands Chamber. Unless there is a jurisdiction to discharge and modify positive obligations (building on the existing jurisdiction to modify or discharge restrictive

---

[1] They will continue to apply to covenants entered into before the implementation of our recommendations.

covenants), the reforms that we recommend in this Part cannot safely be implemented, because of the danger that land will become over-burdened as circumstances change over time.

## LAND OBLIGATIONS IN THE DRAFT BILL

### A new power for estate owners

6.7     We turn now to the provisions of Part 1 of the draft Bill[2] which put into effect the recommendations that we made at paragraphs 5.69, 5.70 and 5.89 above. Clause 1 makes available, and defines, a new legal interest in land; we refer to that interest as a land obligation. It will rank alongside the other legal interests listed in section 1 of the Law of Property Act 1925.[3] Clause 2 produces the result that future covenants, positive and negative, will take effect as land obligations.

6.8     In order to explain how clause 1 of the draft Bill makes the new legal interest available, we have to look back at section 1 of the Law of Property Act 1925, which sets out the legal estates and interests in land. Any estate or interest not listed in section 1(1) or 1(2) of the 1925 Act is an equitable interest. However, that section is not an absolutely fundamental proposition of land law. Rather, it assumes the existence of a range of interests in land and makes provision about which of them are capable of existing at law and which in equity only.

6.9     The draft Bill has the effect of extending the range of legal interests in land by extending the powers of disposition of an estate owner. It gives an estate owner power to make his or her land subject to obligations, just as he or she can make it subject to easements.[4] The power to create land obligations may be exercised in the ways set out in clause 1(2) of the draft Bill, and the obligation created must have certain characteristics, set out in clauses 1(3) and 1(4), which we examine in more detail below; if the obligation created in that way has those characteristics, then it will burden the owner's estate through the operation of clause 1(1).

6.10    Obligations give rise to corresponding rights; rights created in exercise of the new statutory power will necessarily fall within section 1(2)(a) of the Law of Property Act 1925.[5] Clause 1 therefore changes the background against which section 1 of the 1925 Act operates, bringing in a new kind of right to which section 1(2)(a) already applies:

---

[2]   See Appendix A below.

[3]   See paras 2.10 and 2.11 above.

[4]   LPA 1925, s 51 states that "land and all interests therein lie in grant", but that the word "grant" does not have to be used in order to create an interest in land. So we speak of creating a land obligation; the interest is granted by the owner's creation of an obligation.

[5]   This is because the characteristics of the right resulting from the creation of a land obligation are such that it can be characterised as a right in or over land; and clause 14 of the draft Bill ensures that section 1 of the 1925 Act is indeed construed in this way. See para 6.13 below.

(2) The only interests or charges in or over land which are capable of subsisting or of being conveyed or created at law are —

(a) An easement, right, or privilege in or over land for an interest equivalent to an estate in fee simple absolute in possession or a term of years absolute.

6.11    If a land obligation is created without being limited in time, it will be created for an interest in fee simple absolute in possession; if created for a definite period the interest will be created for an interest equivalent to a term of years absolute.

6.12    The approach taken in the draft Bill is therefore to enable a new kind of interest in land to be created, and to bring it within section 1(2) of the Law of Property Act 1925 without amending that section. Similarly, land obligations will fall within section 2(a)(v) of the Land Registration Act 2002, which states that the Act makes provision for the registration of title to:

any other interest or charge which subsists for the benefit of ... an interest the title to which is registered.

There is no need for express statutory provision for the registration of title to land obligations that benefit registered estates, because the new interest keys into the existing statutory language.

6.13    Clause 14 of the draft Bill reinforces the idea that rights created in exercise of the new power are rights in or over land, by providing that references in any existing statute to rights or interests in land, or to incumbrances affecting land, are to be read as including land obligations. The provision ensures that it cannot be suggested that such references apply only to interests, rights and so on that were recognised by the general law at the time the Act in question was passed.[6]

**The exercise of the power: creating an appurtenant right**

6.14    Clause 1(1) of the draft Bill gives the owner of an estate in land the power to create obligations that burden his or her land. Clause 1(2) sets two limitations upon the way in which that power may be exercised.

6.15    First, it must be exercised for the benefit of an estate in land. We discussed in Part 2 whether the law relating to easements should be reformed so as to enable the creation of easements in gross, that is, easements held independently of a freehold or leasehold estate. We concluded that it should not.[7] The same question has to be answered in relation to land obligations; should they be able to exist in gross, or should they be only appurtenant rights, like easements? We

---

[6]    An example that we discussed in the Consultation Paper, para 5.4 and following was the Town and Country Planning Act 1990, s 237 which gives to local planning authorities the power to override certain interests when land is acquired or appropriated for planning purposes. No express provision is needed to bring the new rights within the scope of such provisions. Some statutory provisions, by contrast, are expressed to apply only to rights of way, for example, and not to restrictive covenants: see Housing Act 1988, sch 10, para 4 and the Channel Tunnel Rail Link Act 1996, s 7. We make no recommendation to extend such provisions to land obligations.

[7]    See para 2.24 above.

have reached the conclusion that land obligations should not be able to be created in gross, for the same reasons as applied to easements.

6.16 In particular, one of the concerns about the introduction of positive obligations that run with land is the need to ensure that land does not become overburdened. To make possible a wide range of obligations that did not depend upon the holder of the interest having an estate in land to benefit from the obligation would potentially multiply many times the number of land obligations that could be created. Moreover, the objective in making it possible for land to be burdened by positive obligations is to facilitate arrangements between neighbours. The creation of obligations in gross would not assist with that objective.[8]

6.17 We therefore recommended, in Part 5,[9] that land obligations must be appurtenant to a benefited estate; it must benefit an estate in land, be it freehold or leasehold.[10]

6.18 The second limitation upon the exercise of the power also relates to the benefited estate; clause 1(2)(b) provides that the obligation must touch and concern the land in which the benefited estate subsists.

6.19 The law relating to covenants that "touch and concern" land is well-known. We discussed some of its features in the Consultation Paper, and in particular the analysis by Lord Oliver in *P & A Swift Investments v Combined English Stores Group Plc.*[11] We made a provisional proposal that the new obligations should be subject to the touch and concern test,[12] and consultees generally agreed that a test of this kind was desirable.[13] We have argued, in Part 5 above, that such a test is essential as a way of defining and controlling the potential range of new positive obligations.

6.20 In the Consultation Paper our proposal teased out the meaning of "touch and concern". The essential feature of the test is that the obligation should benefit the estate in land to which it is appurtenant, specifically, rather than being of benefit potentially to anyone. We came to the conclusion that the meaning of the test is so well-established that statutory description or definition would not add to the law, and so the draft Bill makes reference to the existing test rather than setting it out afresh.

---

[8] See the Analysis of Responses, paras 8.69 to 8.77.

[9] See para 5.69 above.

[10] Subject, of course, to the provisions of clause 1(4) of the draft Bill. See para 5.69 above.

[11] [1989] AC 632, 642; Consultation Paper, para 8.78.

[12] Consultation Paper, para 8.80.

[13] See the Analysis of Responses, paras 8.78 to 8.87.

6.21 Obligations that do not touch and concern the benefited land will remain personal, to be enforced in the law of contract if at all; they will not run with the land. An obvious example is overage; we wish to make it very clear that overage agreements will not be able to take effect as land obligations.[14]

## The nature of a land obligation

6.22 Clause 1(3) of the draft Bill sets out four alternative conditions that an obligation must fulfil if it is to qualify as a land obligation – provided, also, that clause 1(2) is satisfied as explained above.

### Negative obligations

6.23 The first alternative is that it is an obligation not to do something on the burdened land.

6.24 Such obligations are familiar already as restrictive covenants; any covenant drafted so as to be valid, under the current law, as a restrictive covenant relating to land will be a valid land obligation. That has no effect upon existing restrictive covenants, which will retain their current status; but it means that for the future, an obligation (whether or not it is expressed as a covenant, because of clause 2 of the draft Bill) not to do something on one's own land, which touches and concerns the land of another, will take effect as a land obligation.

6.25 Equally, an express obligation not to obstruct light, water or air, or not to withdraw support from neighbouring land, will take effect as a land obligation if the requirements of clause 1 of the draft Bill are met.[15]

### Positive obligations

6.26 The second alternative is for a land obligation to be a positive obligation to do something on one's own land or in relation to a boundary structure or feature.

6.27 What we have in mind here are obligations to repair a fence, to maintain a shared driveway, to keep trees trimmed below a certain height, and suchlike. The limitation to obligations to do something on one's own land is important; land obligations should not involve, for example, an obligation to work on someone else's land, because such an obligation would be likely to be unduly onerous for a future owner.

6.28 The reference to boundary structures is included because an obligation to repair a fence, for example, might well encompass work on one's own land and another's, or even perhaps wholly on neighbouring land, because the exact position of a boundary in relation to a fence or wall may be uncertain.[16] A "boundary structure or feature" would include a hedge or stream; a shared garage, straddling both the benefited and burdened land, might well be described

---

[14] We are aware that it is Land Registry practice to facilitate the enforcement of overage covenants by the use of restrictions, in effect providing that land subject to such a covenant cannot be sold unless liability is passed to the covenantor's successor in title.

[15] See para 2.19 above. It will remain possible to prescribe for a negative easement, or to have one created by implication.

[16] See C Sara, *Boundaries and Easements* (4th ed 2008) para 1.01.

as a boundary structure. On the other hand, a covenant burdening Blackacre to maintain the entire structure of a garage whose western wall formed the boundary of two properties, but which otherwise lay wholly on Whiteacre, would not be within what we intend to be a valid land obligation; the garage as a whole would not be a boundary structure but that its western wall would be. The example is all the more pertinent if the structure that lies along the boundary is not the garage but, as is so often the case, the whole house.

6.29 Clause 1(3) of the draft Bill also refers to a structure or feature that is treated as marking or lying on the boundary of the benefited and burdened land; fences are often erected on the basis of imprecise measurement and may not exactly lie on a boundary, and yet an obligation to repair a fence that functioned as the boundary between the properties should fall within the definition.

### Reciprocal payment obligations

6.30 Some land obligations will need to be imposed in pairs. Where one of two neighbours has an obligation to keep the shared driveway in repair, the other may be obliged to pay half the cost. An obligation to make a payment is not naturally described as an obligation to do something on one's own land, and so special provision is included to ensure that reciprocal payment obligations are valid land obligations.

6.31 The term "reciprocal payment obligation" is defined in clause 1(5) of the draft Bill as an obligation to make a payment in return for the performance of a positive land obligation. A simple obligation to pay, without the element of reciprocity,[17] is not sufficient and will generate, at best, a personal contractual liability.

### An obligation under an apportionment arrangement

6.32 Finally, clause 1 of the draft Bill has to make provision for a fourth type of land obligation, namely an obligation to make a payment under an apportionment arrangement. This arises where two or more estates in land are burdened by the same positive obligation and want to make a permanent arrangement about how they share liability between themselves; we explain such arrangements below at paragraphs 6.127 to 6.130.

---

[17] An overage covenant is an obvious example.

**Ancillary rights**

6.33 Clause 1(6) of the draft Bill makes a provision for ancillary obligations. We raised in the Consultation Paper the possibility of "supplementary provisions", by which we meant obligations which could be attached to "primary" Land Obligations if the parties chose to do so, and which would therefore be valid and run with the land even if they would otherwise fall outside the definition of the primary obligations. The options we raised were provision for a sinking fund, provision for interest payments, and provisions allowing the dominant owner to enter and inspect the land to see if an obligation had been complied with.[18] Consultees were generally in favour of such provisions, but not of prescribing a list of permissible ancillary obligations.[19]

6.34 Accordingly both our recommendation and the provisions of clause 1(6) of the draft Bill are open-textured. The range of additional obligations is determined by the fact that they must be "ancillary" to the primary obligation; they must assist in or supplement its performance. It will be possible – and it may be important – for the parties to a land obligation to make provision for the timing of payments or for interest on late payment. We anticipate also that a provision for self-help will be useful in some instances; where the servient owner is to maintain a boundary, provision may be made for the dominant owner to enter and carry out the work if the obligation is not met.

6.35 We do not suggest or recommend, however, that ancillary obligations are used in order to create sinking funds. We doubt that they would be useful or workable in the absence of complex provisions to deal with eventualities such as bankruptcy; obligations that are sufficiently complex or expensive to require a sinking fund are best dealt with through the existing methods of leasehold or commonhold, where the administrative machinery is already available.

6.36 **We recommend that it shall be possible to create obligations ancillary to the legal interests recommended above, and that such obligations shall also be able to take effect as legal interests in land.**

**FUTURE FREEHOLD COVENANTS**

6.37 We turn now to clause 2 of the draft Bill. It provides that for the future, positive and restrictive covenants given by the owner of an estate in land, that meet the definitional requirements of clause 1(3) and that touch and concern the land of the covenantee, will take effect as land obligations, unless they are expressed to be personal to the parties.

---

[18] Consultation Paper, para 12.16.

[19] See the Analysis of Responses, paras 12.1 to 12.27.

6.38    Accordingly, any of the following will take effect as land obligations:[20]

(1)    a promise not to do something on the covenantor's land;

(2)    a promise to do something on one's own land or on a boundary structure (as described in clause 1(3)(b)(ii)); and

(3)    a promise to make a reciprocal payment

provided that the benefit of the promise touches and concerns the land of the covenantee, and that the promise is not expressed to be personal to the promisor or the promisee.

6.39    Clause 2(2) specifically provides that such promises are "to be treated as not being the making by the covenantor of a promise". In other words, once made, those promises take effect as land obligations; they are not covenants. They run with the benefited land, and bind successors in title to the burdened land, not because they are covenants, and without reference to any of the existing law relating to the running of restrictive covenants; they do so because they are interests in land. They will be legal interests if the requirements for the creation of legal interests are met.[21]

6.40    Our draft Bill therefore differs in its approach from the New Zealand legislation for positive covenants, which makes them enforceable by equating them with negative ones,[22] while controlling their enforceability by statute rather than by the common law. It is closer to the approach taken in Ireland, in the Land and Conveyancing Law Reform Act 2009. Section 11 of that Act provides that freehold covenants are among the available legal interests in land, and again statutory rules for enforceability are provided at section 49. But our draft Bill goes beyond the Irish approach by making more explicit the transition from contract to property right,[23] while also giving flexibility: our land obligations can be drafted as covenants but need not be.

6.41    Clause 2 is therefore important for two reasons. One is that it reinforces the fact that there is no need for land obligations to be drafted in any particular way. The important issue is whether the obligation satisfies the statutory definition, which is functional in that it describes what it is that the owner of the burdened land is obliged to do or not to do. One of the complications of the scheme proposed in the Consultation Paper is thereby avoided; there is no need to use any particular form of words. We think that practitioners will wish to draft negative obligations in the same form as restrictive covenants, and so there will be some continuity in drafting practice. Positive obligations can be drafted as positive covenants; equally, conveyancers may prefer a more direct form of words: "the vendor and

---

[20]    Provided that they comply with the general requirements for the creation of interests in land. See para 6.46 below.

[21]    See para 6.46 below.

[22]    Property Law Act 2007, s 303.

[23]    Section 49(6) of the Irish statute (Land and Conveyancing Law Reform Act 2009) implies a continuing contractual status for covenants, as does the express abolition of the rule in *Tulk v Moxhay*.

his successors in title will [mend the fence every two years]", or perhaps "the vendor grants to the purchaser the benefit of a land obligation on the part of the vendor and his successors in title to [contribute 20% of the cost of the maintenance of the shared driveway]".

6.42 There are therefore numerous ways in which land obligations may be drafted. It will be important, however, for conveyancers to recognise that land obligations are interests in land. They therefore fall within all the usual rules relating to such interests, and in particular they must be clear and certain. That is already part of the general law relating to interests in land,[24] and we need make no recommendation to that effect. Vague obligations to maintain a fence "to a reasonable standard", or to maintain a driveway "when required" or "when necessary" will not be sufficient; the servient owner (who may not be the original grantor/covenantor) will have to know exactly what has to be done and when. So an obligation to maintain a shared drive will have to specify when it is to be done and what is to be done, for example by reference to the materials to be used.

6.43 The other reason for the provisions of clause 2, as well as giving drafting freedom, is a form of anti-avoidance. At paragraphs 5.82 to 5.89 above we recommended that for the future no further covenants should be created so as to take effect under the rule in *Tulk v Moxhay*. Clause 2 ensures that it is no longer possible to create freehold covenants that will be enforceable under the rule in *Tulk v Moxhay*; any future covenants take effect as land obligations and *not* as covenants.

6.44 That therefore leaves nothing left for the rule in *Tulk v Moxhay*, and the old rules as to the running of benefits and burdens, to bite on – save, of course, for the old restrictive covenants in existence at the date of reform. No separate statutory provision is needed to ensure that the old rules have no application to future obligations even if drafted as covenants;[25] but the status of existing restrictive covenants, and the old rules that apply to them, are unchanged.

6.45 We noted in the Consultation Paper that the old rules as to the running of benefit and burden of restrictive covenants are a significant defect in the law, because of their complexity.[26] Not all consultees agreed,[27] and we accept that practitioners have learnt to live with the rules and to operate them efficiently. We also note that the approach taken to teaching practitioners is to equate registration with enforceability. We would have liked to be able to recommend reform to simplify the old rules so far as existing restrictive covenants were concerned, but we concluded that that would not be possible. Any change to the rules must have the

---

[24] *Re Ellenborough Park* [1956] Ch 131, 140 to 141; for a recent discussion see *Magrath v Parkside Hotels Ltd* [2011] EWHC 143 (Ch) at [20] to [25].

[25] Contrast the approach taken in the Irish statute, Land and Conveyancing Law Reform Act 2009, s 49, which provides "the rules of common law and equity (including the rule known as the rule in *Tulk v. Moxhay*) are abolished to the extent that they relate to the enforceability of a freehold covenant". That provision is needed because the Irish statute creates positive covenants that take effect at law and run with land, but remain covenants. Such provision is unnecessary in our draft Bill because there will be no new freehold *covenants* post reform.

[26] Consultation Paper, para 7.37.

[27] See the Analysis of Responses, paras 7.1 to 7.11.

effect of changing, albeit perhaps at the margins, which covenants are enforceable and which are not. The value of restrictive covenants, in money terms but also in aesthetic terms, is considerable, and we would not wish to make recommendations that jeopardised the value of any covenant by changing its status of enforceability. Accordingly our recommendations relate to future obligations only.

## THE CREATION AND REGISTRATION OF LAND OBLIGATIONS

### The requirements for the creation of legal and equitable interests in land

6.46 The current formal requirements for the express creation of a legal interest in land are:

(1) it must be granted by deed (section 52 of the Law of Property Act 1925); and

(2) if the estate out of which the right is granted is registered, the grant of the right must be completed by registration (section 27 of the Land Registration Act 2002).

6.47 We made no proposals in the Consultation Paper to change those current requirements. They will apply to the creation of land obligations, unless statute provides otherwise; and, for the sake of simplicity and consistency within the law, statute should not provide otherwise unless there is a very good reason to do so.

6.48 In the Consultation Paper we proposed a number of special provisions for the creation of a Land Obligation:

(1) express labelling as such;[28]

(2) both the dominant and servient estate to be registered;[29]

(3) a plan identifying the dominant and servient land (which the Consultation Paper proposed would be necessary for a Land Obligation to exist as either a legal *or* an equitable interest); and[30]

(4) completion by registration.[31]

6.49 Of these, we have concluded that item (1) is unnecessary.[32] The validity of a land obligation is governed by the requirements of clause 1 of the draft Bill; an additional requirement that particular wording be used would merely create a category of purported land obligations that would be perfectly valid but for an oversight in labelling. Item (2) is no longer appropriate, if our recommendations in Part 5 are accepted. Item (3) is clearly important, but we would see this as a requirement to be imposed through Land Registry procedure. Statutory provision

---

[28] Consultation Paper, para 8.28.

[29] Consultation Paper, para 8.38.

[30] Consultation Paper, paras 8.40 and 8.41.

[31] Consultation Paper, para 8.47.

[32] Nor is there any need to require the use of the term "land obligation".

for a plan to be used in creating a land obligation expressly would not be appropriate, since such a provision would leave open the issue of the adequacy of the plan, and validity would therefore be a matter of considerable uncertainty.

6.50    Land Registry will not, as things stand, register a right of way without a plan, or a description sufficiently precise to enable the delineation of the route on a title plan or an accurate verbal description for inclusion on the register. Similarly, an application for registration of a land obligation would require an indication of the extent of the benefited and burdened land except where these are, respectively, co-extensive with a registered title.

6.51    Accordingly, we see no need to recommend a statutory requirement for a plan.[33] The statutory requirements for the creation of a legal land obligation should be the same, in fact, as those for the creation of a legal easement. The formal creation requirements follow without further provision from the background law, in particular section 52 of the Law of Property Act 1925 and sections 2 and 27 of the Land Registration Act 2002, and item (4) in the list above is a necessary consequence of the recommendations we have already made.[34]

6.52    We make no recommendation here about equitable land obligations, because none is needed. Once it is possible to create legal land obligations, the effect of the principle expressed in *Lysaght v Edwards*[35] will be to ensure that obligations that fall short of the requirements for legal validity – for example, for want of formalities or of registration,[36] will take effect in equity so long as the requirements for contractual validity are met.[37] Generally, of course, land obligations will be contained in transfers of land and will become legal upon registration, as do easements; there should be very few that remain equitable.[38]

---

[33]    Whether a plan is used or not, the description of the interest created would need to be sufficiently certain. See para 6.42 above.

[34]    See para 6.12 above.

[35]    (1875-76) LR 2 Ch D 449. The case is authority for the principle that, where the parties contract to create a legal estate or interest but fail to comply with the relevant formalities to do so (for example, use of a deed or registration), that contract will nevertheless take effect in equity so as to create an equitable estate or interest. See *Gray and Gray*, para 8.1.56.

[36]    See para 6.64 below.

[37]    The instrument creating the land obligation will have to meet the requirements for a valid contract to create or convey an interest in land; see Law of Property (Miscellaneous Provisions) Act 1989, s 2. See *Megarry and Wade*, para 15-015.

[38]    We asked consultees, Consultation Paper, para 8.54, whether it should be possible to create equitable Land Obligations, and most agreed that it should. We see no convincing reason not to leave the background law unchanged, so that obligations that meet the requirements of clause 1 but do not meet the requirements for the creation of legal interests will take effect in equity.

6.53    If the title to land burdened by an equitable land obligation is registered, the obligation will not be enforceable against a purchaser unless it is protected by a notice on the register of title.[39] The position as to enforceability, in registered land, is therefore exactly the same as it is for equitable easements. Again, no separate recommendation, and no statutory provision, is needed to achieve this.[40]

### Land obligations in unregistered land

6.54    The Land Charges Act 1972 requires the burden of certain interests in unregistered land to be registered, on pain of being void against certain classes of purchaser. Restrictive covenants that burden land the title to which is unregistered must, under the current law, be registered against the name of the owner of the burdened land by a Class D(ii) land charge; if unregistered, they are void against a purchaser for money or money's worth of a legal estate in the land charged with it.[41]

6.55    We explained in Part 5 that the position at common law is that a legal interest in unregistered land will bind all the world – that is, it will affect purchasers of any interest, legal or equitable, in the burdened land. But that position would be unacceptable for land obligations; a purchaser should not be taken by surprise by an obligation attached to his or her property. We can ensure that there is a public and searchable record of the burden of land obligations affecting unregistered land by extending the provisions of the Land Charges Act 1972 to land obligations, positive and negative, legal or equitable, and to provide that unless registered as land charges they are void against the purchaser of the burdened land.[42]

6.56    Finding a way to record the benefit of a land obligation where the dominant land is unregistered is more difficult. There is no provision within the Land Charges Register for the registration of the benefited land. It might be possible for the Land Charges Register to incorporate a scanned plan of the benefited land when a burden is registered. Essentially, however, it is not possible for the Land Charges Register to duplicate the advantages of registered title; it records burdens on land without registering titles. Nevertheless, we think that the advantages of allowing the creation of land obligations in both registered and unregistered land far outweigh the disadvantages.

---

[39]    See para 2.7 above.

[40]    We asked consultees about the enforceability of equitable Land Obligations in the Consultation Paper, paras 8.61 and 8.62. In the light of their responses, we have taken the view that no special provision is needed.

[41]    Land Charges Act 1972, s 4(6).

[42]    Note that the registration systems of England and Wales do not protect from the incidence of unregistered interests those who are not purchasers. Donees of land take it subject to all prior interests.

**6.57**   **We recommend that where title to the burdened land is unregistered, the burden of a land obligation be registrable as a land charge under the Land Charges Act 1972, and if not registered should be void against a purchaser of the burdened land or of any interest in that land.**[43]

6.58   Paragraph 10 of schedule 3 to the draft Bill would amend the Land Charges Act 1972 so as to create a new Class G land charge to put this recommendation into effect.

### Land obligations to be created only expressly

6.59   Under the current law, restrictive covenants are not capable of being created by either implication or prescription; and we are not aware of any jurisdiction where covenants or obligations, negative or positive, can so arise.[44] We proposed in the Consultation Paper that the new obligations should only be capable of express creation;[45] consultees agreed with that proposal.[46]

6.60   We continue to take the view that it would be inappropriate for land obligations to arise by prescription or by implication. This scarcely needs unpacking. The fact that X has done something helpful or useful for a neighbour for many years cannot found a claim that she is legally obliged to carry on doing so. Nor can the fact that Y has never used her land for business purposes found a claim that her neighbour has a prescriptive right to prevent her doing so.[47] Nor would it be practicable to imply a land obligation, in the light of the requirement that the terms of a proprietary right be clear and certain. Implication would be likely to lead to insoluble disputes about the terms of the covenant. Issues of necessity do not arise in the way that they do for easements; an obligation (rather than an easement) is not going to be essential to ensure access, and an important positive obligation (say, to provide services) must be a matter to be negotiated, and potentially paid for, rather than something to be supplied by implication.

6.61   For similar reasons section 62 of the Law of Property Act 1925 should not operate so as to create land obligations, or to "upgrade" them in the manner discussed in Part 3;[48] clause 21 of the draft Bill refers accordingly to land obligations as well as to easements and profits.

---

[43]   We are using here the words of section 4(5), (7) and (8) of the Land Charges Act 1972, so as to relieve any purchaser of any estate in the burdened land if the covenant is not registered as a land charge, rather than precisely mirroring the provisions for restrictive covenants in section 4(6).

[44]   We refer of course to the property law rules for implication. In limited circumstances contractual terms may arise by implication (see para 3.36 above), and our recommendations do not change that. But we think that it would be extremely unlikely that the contractual rules of implication could ever be used to infer a positive covenant, and that the implication of a restrictive covenant must be very rare.

[45]   Consultation Paper, para 8.38.

[46]   See the Analysis of Responses, paras 8.20 to 8.29.

[47]   Subject to the need to respect other rights of the neighbour, such as rights of way or a right to light.

[48]   See para 3.52 and following above.

**6.62    We recommend that land obligations, whether restrictive or positive, should be incapable of creation by implication or prescription, and that section 62 of the Law of Property Act 1925 should not operate so as to create a land obligation or to convert one from a leasehold to a freehold interest.**

## FURTHER PROVISIONS FOR REGISTERED TITLE

6.63    We now look at a number of further provisions that we have to recommend in connection with the title registration system. Some of these are consequential provisions that follow from what has been said above about the creation and registration of easements. The rest derive from Part 4 of this Report, where we made a number of recommendations about the creation and extinguishment of easements and profits, the title to which is registered. Each of these is equally relevant and desirable for land obligations; we look at them in turn.

### Consequential provisions about registration

6.64    As we have explained, no statutory provision is needed to bring land obligations within the ambit of the Land Registration Act 2002. That Act operates by reference to the general law. As previously mentioned, land obligations will involve the creation of rights in or over land and, as such, will fall within section 1(2)(a) of the Law of Property Act 1925 (read in the light of clause 14 of the draft Bill). From this it follows that the creation of a land obligation in relation to a registered estate will be a registrable disposition for the purposes of the 2002 Act (by virtue of section 27(2)(d) of that Act). They will not be able to take effect at law until the burden is registered on the title to the burdened land (and, if the benefited land is registered, the benefit is registered on the title to the benefited land) because of the provisions of section 27 of the 2002 Act. The burden of land obligations will appear in the charges register of the title to the burdened land, and it will be possible to note there the burden of equitable land obligations.[49]

6.65    So far, then, land obligations behave exactly like easements within the title registration system.

6.66    However, we have to highlight two differences between land obligations and easements.[50]

### *Land obligations will not be overriding interests*

6.67    The first is that we do not recommend that land obligations should be overriding interests. That means that they will not bind a purchaser of land pursuant to a registered disposition, under section 29 of the Land Registration Act 2002, unless their priority is protected on the register.

---

[49]    Although, as we have said, equitable land obligations will be unusual. See para 6.52 above.

[50]    And appurtenant profits, although for brevity we do not mention profits in the discussion that follows.

6.68    Legal easements, by contrast, have the status of overriding interests, pursuant to schedules 1 and 3 to the Land Registration Act 2002. That means that an easement that has arisen by prescription or implication and has not been registered thereafter, will nevertheless bind a purchaser. That is irrelevant for land obligations, which can be created only expressly. It also means that where a legal easement has been granted out of unregistered land, and the documentation has been lost so that on first registration of the burdened land the interest is not carried forward on to the charges register of that land,[51] it may nevertheless override first registration and subsequent dispositions and continue to bind purchasers. That should again be irrelevant for land obligations, which are to be registrable as land charges and so will not easily be lost on first registration.[52]

### Land obligations that are omitted on voluntary first registration

6.69    This second point arises from what we have just said about first registration.

6.70    Where first registration of land burdened by a land obligation arises from one of the "triggers" for first registration[53] then, where the burden of the obligation has not previously been registered as a land charge, it will, as a result of the disposition, be void against the disponee.[54] There is therefore no occasion for it to be noted on the register.

6.71    But if first registration is voluntary[55] then the land obligation, despite not having previously been registered as a land charge, will not be rendered void by that failure. The burden survives. If it is not recorded in the charges register of the newly-registered servient land there will be a mistake on the register. It can be put right by the rectification of the register pursuant to schedule 4 to the Land Registration Act 2002; and, without provision to the contrary, it may also give rise to the payment of an indemnity pursuant to schedule 8.

6.72    Such an error will not be one that Land Registry staff have the means of avoiding; and the payment of an indemnity as a result of that omission could be a considerable burden upon the indemnity fund – a burden that would inevitably be passed on in the form of higher fee levels to Land Registry's customers.[56] At Land Registry's suggestion, with which we agree, we make a recommendation that will prevent that possibility.

---

[51]    There is no facility for the registration of a legal easement under the Land Charges Act 1972 and it is therefore possible for the burden of such an easement not to be picked up.

[52]    Subject to what we say in para 6.71 below.

[53]    Set out in LRA 2002, s 4.

[54]    See the recommendation in para 6.57 above.

[55]    Pursuant to LRA 2002, s 3.

[56]    See Land Registry, *Framework Document* (2008) http://www1.landregistry.gov.uk/assets/library/documents/frameworkdoc2008.pdf (last visited 13 May 2011).

**6.73** **We recommend that where land burdened by a land obligation is registered voluntarily, and the obligation is not noted in the charges register because it was not registered as a land charge, this shall not amount to a mistake on the register for the purposes of schedule 8 to the Land Registration Act 2002.**

6.74 That recommendation is given effect by paragraph 16 of schedule 3 to the draft Bill. The paragraph refers to land obligations that were, at the time of first registration, registrable but not registered; it therefore excludes those cases where the obligation was not registrable – either because it had already been rendered void by a conveyance or transfer made at a point when the obligation was not registered as a land charge, or because the obligation was created by the disposition that triggered registration, in which case section 14(3) of the Land Charges Act 1972 provides that it is not registrable as a land charge.[57]

**Recommendations derived from Part 4 above**

*Clarification of the effect of section 58 of the Land Registration Act 2002*

6.75 In Part 4, we discussed the "state guarantee of title" that is at the heart of the registration system. Section 58 of the Land Registration Act 2002 guarantees the validity of a registered estate or interest during the currency of that registration. We explained that Land Registry has asked us to recommend statutory clarification of the fact that an easement that does not accommodate and serve the dominant tenement is not guaranteed by virtue of section 58.

6.76 The same issue arises in connection with land obligations; they are to be legal interests and therefore within the scope of the registration guarantee. But section 58 cannot confer a legal estate upon the holder of a purported land obligation that does not meet with the requirements for valid creation, in particular if it does not touch and concern the benefited land.[58]

6.77 Accordingly, the clarification effected by paragraph 16 of schedule 3 to the draft Bill extends equally to the case where a purported land obligation does not touch and concern the benefited land. This is not a derogation from Land Registry's functions; it is one thing to regard Land Registry as guaranteeing title to validly created estates and interests, and quite another to require it to guarantee the results of defective conveyancing.

**6.78** **We recommend that statute should state, for the avoidance of doubt, that section 58(1) of the Land Registration Act 2002 has no effect in relation to an entry made in pursuance of an instrument that purports to create a land obligation that does not touch and concern the dominant land.**

---

[57] Because such a registration would be, in effect, a waste of effort since the land was about to come onto the register of title. The omission of the section 14(3) case from the ambit of this clause means that if the interest was not registrable because of the operation of that section, and Land Registry failed to note it on the charges register of the newly registered servient land, an indemnity *would* potentially be payable as a result of that mistake.

[58] Draft Bill, cl 1(2)(b).

*Unity of seisin*

6.79   We take the view that the "unity of seisin" rule would be applied by the courts, were the matter to come before them, to land obligations as it is to easements and profits. The rule states that an interest cannot be created, and cannot continue to exist, where the benefited and burdened land are in common ownership and possession. It is not a logically necessary feature of interests in land;[59] but it is set out as one of the defining features of an interest in land in *Re Ellenborough Park*[60] and we do not suppose that the courts would depart from that. But clause 22 of the draft Bill puts that point beyond doubt.

6.80   However, the reasons we gave in Part 4 for the disapplication of that rule as regards easements over registered land only are equally applicable to land obligations. Part of the objective of enabling the creation of proprietary positive obligations is to facilitate arrangements between neighbours, and we anticipate that it will be useful for properties developed together to be subject to, and to benefit from, obligations that deal with the maintenance of boundaries or of a shared facility such as a driveway. The concerns about the validity of easements imposed one by one as plots are sold off, and the possibility of dispositions taking place in the "wrong" order so that land may be sold with the benefit of an interest that does not yet exist, apply with equal force to land obligations.

6.81   Similarly, there may be a need to attach land obligations, positive or negative, to land that is subject to a mortgage of part in order to ensure the marketability of the security in the event that the mortgagee has to exercise its power of sale.

6.82   Finally, the unity of seisin rule would cause the same problems as it does in the context of easements and profits if it were to extinguish land obligations the title to which is registered. In that event, and if the land is subsequently divided, Land Registry would have to guarantee (as a result of section 58 of the Land Registration Act 2002) the existence of land obligations that had been extinguished.[61]

**6.83   We recommend that provided that title to the benefited and burdened land is registered, the fact that they are in common ownership and possession shall not prevent the creation or existence of land obligations.**

---

[59]   See para 4.24 above.

[60]   [1956] Ch 131, 140. See para 4.20 above.

[61]   See para 4.39 above.

6.84 Land obligations created in this way, with the benefited and burdened land delineated across the whole of a developed estate, will be mutually enforceable by different landowners where required. For example, the developer might impose on each plot an obligation not to use the land for business use; the benefited land, as regards each such obligation, could be the whole of the rest of the developer's land prior to sale, although in practice great care should be taken to ensure that the benefited land extends only to land that can truly benefit from the obligation – in many cases this will just be the adjacent plots. Once the developer's land is sold off, each of the properties that takes the benefit will be able to enforce the obligation.[62]

6.85 Land obligations that survive the unity of ownership and possession of the benefited and burdened estates will nevertheless be able to be released expressly, as we discuss in Part 4 in the context of easements and profits.[63]

6.86 Clause 23 of the draft Bill, which amends the Land Registration Act 2002 by inserting two new sections, 27A and 116A, is drafted so as to apply to land obligations as well as to easements and profits.

### The release of registered interests

6.87 We explained in Part 4 why the express release or variation of a registered interest should be a registrable disposition; our recommendation and clause 28 of the draft Bill make reference to registered appurtenant interests and are therefore applicable to land obligations as they are to easements and to profits appurtenant.

### Short-form interests

6.88 Our discussion of short-form interests in Part 4 focused on easements, but we think that it would be equally helpful to have Land Registry consult upon and draft short-form land obligations that could be incorporated by reference into a transfer. Indeed, the arguments for such interests are rather stronger because these are new interests; we do not anticipate that practitioners will have any difficulty in continuing to use existing precedents for restrictive covenants in order to create restrictive land obligations, but we have no doubt that guidance with positive obligations would be useful.

6.89 **We recommend that Land Registry investigate the feasibility of making provision for short-form land obligations in Land Registration Rules and, if provision is thought feasible, that it draft and consult upon the necessary rules.**

---

[62] Currently, the mutual enforceability of restrictive covenants is managed by compliance with the rules concerning "building schemes" in *Elliston v Reacher* [1908] 2 Ch 665, which we discuss in the Consultation Paper, paras 7.32 and 7.33. Those rules relate to restrictive covenants and will therefore have no application to land obligations and, indeed, will not be needed. Express abolition of the rule in *Elliston* is unnecessary; contrast the different approach in the Republic of Ireland: Land and Conveyancing Law Reform Act 2009, s 49(3).

[63] See paras 4.52 to 4.58 above.

## THE ENFORCEABILITY OF LAND OBLIGATIONS

6.90   The objective of creating obligations as interests in land, rather than as personal covenants, is to ensure that the benefit and burden of the obligation is carried forward to future owners of the land.[64] Absent any express provision, the benefit and burden of a land obligation will be transmitted to future owners of the relevant estates in land just as is the case for easements and appurtenant profits.

6.91   When we look in more detail at enforceability, it is useful to distinguish vertical and horizontal transmission. Where an estate in land is passed on by conveyance or transfer, in whole or in part, we call that a horizontal transmission, as where A sells Blackacre to B, and then B sells half of Blackacre to C. But where A creates new estates (legal or equitable) out of his own, for example by granting a 99-year lease to T (who might then sub-let to S1 and S2), or making a declaration of trust in favour of D – or indeed all of these things – we call that vertical transmission.

### Transmission of the benefit of a land obligation

6.92   Clearly, where an estate in land that benefits from a land obligation is transferred as a whole to a new owner – whether by sale or gift – that benefit will pass with the estate.[65] Similarly, on transmission of part of an estate which benefits from a land obligation, the benefit will carry over onto the new title as well as continuing to benefit the original estate.[66]

6.93   More complex is the issue of the "vertical" transmission of that benefit to estates and interests derived out of the benefited estate. The structure of English land law lends itself to complex vertical transmission and to the creation of structured relationships that can be – at least in theory, and sometimes in practice – almost feudal in their complexity.

---

[64]   We looked in Part 5 at the economic argument behind this; one explanation for the desire to have a particular arrangement take the form of an interest in land is that it may be cheaper to set up such an interest than to have the arrangement re-negotiated every time the relevant land changes hands.

[65]   We suggested in the Consultation Paper that there might be occasions on which the transferor of the whole estate might expressly provide that an appurtenant benefit should not be passed on with it; we asked consultees if they thought that that was desirable (Consultation Paper, para 9.10). Consultees expressed doubts about the purpose or workability of such a provision (see the Analysis of Responses, paras 9.6 to 9.14). We think that on a transfer of whole, the benefit of an appurtenant interest should not be able to be extinguished simply by a decision not to pass it on, although of course it might be expressly released. For the same reason we have made no recommendation about the possibility of withholding an appurtenant benefit on a transfer of part, but the land obligation could be expressly released vis-à-vis the part transferred.

[66]   See the Analysis of Responses, paras 10.49 to 10.58.

6.94    Generally, the benefit of a land obligation would be transmitted – whether or not the parties expressly so provide (and unless they provide otherwise) – in the same way as is an easement. If the benefited land is leased to B, B takes that benefit and can enforce the obligation. There will then be more than one person entitled to enforce the obligation (as there will be when there is horizontal transmission of part of the dominant land), but the extent of the obligation is defined by its terms and is not changed by the presence of more than one person entitled to enforce it.[67]

6.95    We need to make two specific provisions, however, to control enforceability through the transmission of benefit.

6.96    One is that the benefit of a land obligation should be transmitted only to estates (that is, leases and fees simple, legal and equitable), and not to interests derived from the benefited estates. We have in mind the decisions *Re Salvin's Indenture*[68] (which decided that an easement can be appurtenant to another easement)[69] and *Hanbury v Jenkins*[70] (which concerned an easement appurtenant to a profit). We think that the benefit of a land obligation should not attach to interests derived from the benefited estate, and so we do not wish to replicate the effect of those cases for land obligations.[71]

6.97    The other specific provision relates to obligations to pay money. Because of the terms of clause 1 of the draft Bill, these can be land obligations only if they are reciprocal payment obligations; and we note that problems might arise where more than one person is entitled to demand payment. The solution here lies in the reciprocal nature of the obligation; however many parties hold estates that benefit from a covenant to pay, say, towards maintenance of a driveway, the only ones who should be entitled to recover payment are those who have incurred expenditure in carrying out the obligation to maintain it.[72]

**6.98    We recommend that the benefit of a land obligation shall be appurtenant to the estate in land for the benefit of which it is imposed and shall therefore be transmitted with that estate and to any estates (but not to interests) derived out of it.**

---

[67]   Where there is an obligation to mend a fence, for example, it does not particularly matter whether one or ten people are able to remind the servient owner to do it, or even to sue for a failure to do so. A similar situation arises in other jurisdictions, and we understand that it has not given rise to problems.

[68]   [1938] 2 All ER 498.

[69]   The case concerned an easement to run a pipe for the benefit of a waterworks company, which did not own neighbouring land. The court held that the easement was appurtenant to the whole of the company's rights in the land, including its easements over the neighbouring land.

[70]   [1901] 2 Ch 401.

[71]   Imagine A has the benefit of a land obligation burdening C. B is then granted an easement over A's land. B should not thereby acquire the benefit of C's obligation.

[72]   Whilst they may all be bound by the linked obligation to maintain the drive, there are likely to be arrangements in place as to who performs that obligation; see paras 6.114 to 6.116 below.

**6.99** **We recommend that where more than one estate has the benefit of a reciprocal payment obligation, only the proprietor of an estate who has incurred the relevant expenditure in carrying out the linked obligation shall be entitled to recover the payment (and if more than one, in proportion to their expenditure).**

6.100 Clauses 3 and 10 of the draft Bill put those recommendations into effect.

### Transmission of the burden of a land obligation

6.101 The horizontal transmission of the burden of a land obligation is governed simply by the registration provisions that we have already made. The burden passes straightforwardly, subject to those provisions, where the burdened estate is transmitted horizontally as a whole.

6.102 More difficult is the transmission of the burden of a land obligation to estates derived out of the burdened estate, and the transmission whether horizontal or vertical of part of the burdened estate. In discussing these, we have to distinguish between positive and restrictive, or negative, obligations; these terms are used in the draft Bill and they carry the same meanings as they do under the current law in the context of freehold covenants.

### *The vertical transmission of the burden of a land obligation*

6.103 Under the current law, a restrictive covenant is transmitted to all estates and interests derived out of the burdened estate, subject to any limitations in the grant itself and the general priority rules and the specific requirements of the land charges and land registration systems.[73] Restrictive covenants also bind mortgagees in possession, and occupiers of the burdened land.[74] We take the view that those provisions of the current law should be replicated for restrictive land obligations.

**6.104** **We recommend that the burden of a restrictive land obligation should be transmitted to all estates and interests derived out of the burdened estate, and to all occupiers of the burdened land, save for:**

   **(1)** **the owner of an estate or interest that has priority to the land obligation (and an occupier authorised by such an owner); and**

   **(2)** **a mortgagee of the burdened land who is not in possession of it.**

---

[73] Clearly there is no question of the burden being passed on to derived estates with priority to the land obligation. We asked consultees whether this should be the case (Consultation Paper, para 9.29(1)) and they agreed. See the Analysis of Responses, paras 9.61 to 9.73. We do not consider that any recommendation is necessary on this point, as it will necessarily follow from the general law.

[74] *Kelsey v Dodd* (1881) 52 LJ Ch 34; *Marten v Flight Refuelling Ltd* [1962] Ch 115. Exactly who is bound by a restrictive covenant under the current law is not entirely clear. The cases cited by C H S Preston and G H Newsom, *Restrictive Covenants Affecting Freehold Land* (9th ed 1988) para 8-02 all relate to parties in possession or occupation (licensees, squatters etc). However, LPA 1925, s 79 provides that any person "deriving title" out of the estate of the original covenantor or his successors (expressly including occupiers) is bound.

6.105    Clause 4 of the draft Bill puts the first part of that recommendation into effect; and a mortgagee who is not in possession of the burdened land is saved from liability for breach of a negative obligation by clause 6(3).

6.106    The position for the vertical transmission of positive land obligations is different and a little more complicated. We explained in the Consultation Paper that it is not desirable to extend liability for positive covenants to all derived estates:

> As the 1984 Report put it, "positive obligations ... [require] the expenditure of money. It is therefore inappropriate that all those with an interest, however small, in the servient land should be liable to perform a positive obligation".[75]

6.107    For example, it is clearly inappropriate for a weekly tenant to have to spend several thousand pounds re-surfacing a driveway. Equally, it would be inappropriate for a lodger to have to do so.

6.108    Accordingly we made a number of alternative proposals about the vertical transmission of the burden of positive obligations only.[76] Clearly we cannot recommend that there be no vertical transmission,[77] since that would make it possible to escape an obligation by transferring a burdened estate to a company, controlled by oneself, which one could abandon after granting oneself a 3,000 year lease.[78] So, generally, the burden has to be transmitted vertically except where the dominant owner has agreed in the grant, or in a subsequent release or variation, to the contrary.[79]

6.109    We take the view that the solution to the problem of vertical transmission of the burden of a positive obligation lies along lines similar to provisions in comparable common law jurisdictions, which generally provide that the burden should pass "downwards", but not to leases of particularly short duration – some jurisdictions say five years.[80] We take the view that the burden of a positive covenant should pass "vertically" to all estates derived from a burdened estate except to leases granted for a term of seven years or less.

---

[75]    Consultation Paper, para 9.12.

[76]    Consultation Paper, para 9.20.

[77]    This is "Option 2" in the Consultation Paper, para 9.20. The proposal attracted little support: see the Analysis of Responses, para 9.29 and following.

[78]    Nor do we wish to pursue the suggestion that if the burden of a land obligation passes to a lessee, it should cease when the lease has only a certain period left to run ("Option 3" in the Consultation Paper, para 9.20). This would require Land Registry to remove burdens from leases, inevitably without prompting from the parties in most cases, which would be impracticable. See the Analysis of Responses, para 9.32 and following.

[79]    Consultation Paper, para 9.28; the consultation question at para 9.29 asked if a burden should *not* pass if there was contrary provision in the instrument creating the Land Obligation, and the majority of consultees agreed (see the Analysis of Responses, paras 9.61 to 9.73), but equally, agreement by the dominant owner at the time of creation of the derivative estate would be effective.

[80]    For example, the Irish Land and Conveyancing Law Reform Act 2009, s 48 deals with the issue by defining a servient owner to exclude a lessee of less than 5 years.

6.110 This is close to one of the options suggested in the Consultation Paper.[81] However, it differs from that provisional proposal in two ways.

6.111 First, we suggested in the Consultation Paper that liability should pass down to leases of more than 21 years. The reasoning for our recommendation of a seven year term is that it matches the length of lease that is registrable.[82] Land Registry has pointed out to us that there must be a clear rule to enable its staff to know whether or not to note a burden on the title of any new estate; this would indeed be a clear rule, enabling transmission "downwards" to any registered lease.[83]

6.112 Second, we did not suggest in the Consultation Paper that equitable estates derived out of the burdened estate would be subject to land obligations. Yet if X enters into a positive obligation for the benefit of Y, and then declares a trust of the land, the beneficiary takes subject to all prior interests, subject to whichever registration requirements apply.[84] Under the current law, the beneficiary of land clearly takes subject to a prior restrictive covenant, or an easement. We think that the same must be true for restrictive land obligations post-reform. As to positive obligations, we have to except from liability the beneficiary of a trust who is not entitled to immediate possession of the land; where land is held on trust for A for life, remainder to B,[85] B has no access to the land during A's lifetime and so cannot be responsible to the benefited owner for performance of positive obligations.

6.113 There would of course be circumstances in which it would not be appropriate for a beneficiary of a trust, in possession of the land, to bear an expense, or the entire expense – for example, it might be incongruous for a life tenant to have to mend the roof. But the fact that a beneficiary takes subject to an interest in the land does not mean that he or she has to bear the entire burden; the trustees also remain liable as legal owners and as trustees must allocate expenses to the capital or income of a fund in accordance with the relevant legal principles;[86] and where a beneficiary is in possession of the property the trustees will either have express powers within the trust, or in any event will have power under the Trusts of Land and Appointment of Trustees Act 1996, to make arrangements for the incidence of expenses.[87] So the cost of complying with a positive covenant would

---

[81] "Option 1" in the Consultation Paper, para 9.20. It would be fair to say that none of the options we put forward attracted overall support; and we would not now wish to pursue precisely the terms of any of those options.

[82] Other than the special classes created by the LRA 2002, s 4, which are registrable, despite being granted for seven years or less.

[83] With a very small and easily identifiable class of exceptions, namely the special cases in the LRA 2002, s 4. Only within that exception would Land Registry have to distinguish between positive and negative land obligations.

[84] Whether under the Land Charges Act 1972 or the LRA 2002.

[85] B is said to be a remainderman: a person who has an estate in land when he or she is entitled to the possession of that land only in the future, after the termination of someone else's immediate entitlement to the land.

[86] Capital and Income in Trusts: Classification and Apportionment (2009) Law Com No 315; *Carver v Duncan* [1985] AC 1082; *Revenue and Customs Commissioners v Trustees of the Peter Clay Discretionary Trust* [2008] EWCA Civ 1441, [2009] Ch 296.

[87] Trusts of Land and Appointment of Trustees Act 1996, s 13.

be managed within the trust by the trustees.

6.114 We would expect that landlords and tenants would agree the incidence of positive obligations between themselves. Thus a ten year lease could be negotiated on terms that, as between landlord and tenant, the landlord would meet most positive obligations burdening the land in favour of the neighbour, whereas in a 99-year lease the landlord might well provide that the tenant would do so. In either case the parties might agree that one of them would indemnify the other against any pursuit by the dominant owner. These contractual arrangements require no statutory provision. However, there is a need for a default rule to deal with cases where the parties have not made any provision. All may be liable to the benefited owner for a breach of the obligation;[88] but as between themselves, the freeholder should be liable to the tenant in the absence of any contrary provision in the relevant leases.

**6.115 We recommend that the burden of a positive land obligation be transmitted:**

**(1) to estates derived out of a burdened estate which confer a right to immediate possession of the burdened land, in accordance with the normal priority rules, save that the burden of a positive obligation shall not pass to a lease for seven years or less; and**

**(2) to mortgagees when they come into possession of a burdened estate.**

**6.116 We recommend that where a landlord and a tenant are both burdened by a positive land obligation, the landlord shall be liable to the tenant if the tenant suffers loss as a result of the landlord's breach of the obligation unless the parties expressly provide otherwise in the relevant lease.**

6.117 Those recommendations are embodied in clauses 5 and 6(3) of the draft Bill and by paragraph 3 of schedule 1.

### Transmission of part of the burdened land

6.118 Our starting point here is that there is no difference in principle between dealings with whole and with part; a right appurtenant to the whole of an area of land will adhere, on a dealing with part, both to the retained land and to the land disposed of.[89] And the priority rules determine the transmission of the burden of interests in land on a dealing with part as they do on a dealing with whole.

6.119 But practical problems may arise on sub-division of burdened land, particularly where the obligation is positive. As we explained in the Consultation Paper, a restrictive obligation (or an easement) is less likely to give rise to disputes when land is split up because all that is needed to comply with it is inaction.[90] Where land burdened by a positive obligation is disposed of in part, problems may arise:

---

[88] We propose at para 6.126 below that burdened estate owners should be jointly and severally liable for breaches of positive land obligations.

[89] See para 6.92, n 65 above.

[90] Consultation Paper, para 10.28.

(1)     where the proprietor of one part of the land (whether retained or transferred) will not be able to comply with the obligation following a transfer of part. This could arise where the obligation was to maintain a fence, for example, and the transferred part did not have access to the fence; and

(2)     where the obligation was to make a monetary payment. Either the payment would have to be attributed to one or other part as a whole, or there would have to be an apportionment. In any event there has to be a default rule for liability of the servient owners amongst themselves.

6.120   It is worth stressing that good drafting practice will ensure that these problems do not arise. It will be important when creating land obligations to consider carefully the extent of the burdened land; thought should be given to the possibility of subdivision in the future.

6.121   So where X sells part of his land to Y, and Y takes on a positive land obligation to maintain the boundary fence, if Y's land is a single building plot then it may well be appropriate for the whole of Y's land to be burdened by the obligation. But if Y's land is rather more extensive, and it is possible that it will be sold off in the future – whether as two houses or twenty – then the problem described at paragraph 6.119(1) above will arise, unless careful consideration is given, at the time when the obligation is created, to the need to ensure that only properties adjacent to the fence are bound by the obligation.[91]

6.122   It is important to note that while two owners benefited by the same obligation might reasonably agree that one should no longer benefit from an obligation without that troubling the servient owner, it cannot be possible for two servient owners to agree that one should be released from an obligation, without reference to the dominant owner. The priority rules determine that, where the whole of land burdened by an obligation is divided, both or indeed all the parts must remain liable for the obligation as a whole; and we proposed in the Consultation Paper[92] and recommend below[93] that in the case of positive land obligations that liability should be joint and several.[94] To allow for division of the obligation by agreement between the servient owners would be potentially to prejudice the dominant owner, and indeed to allow landowners to escape from burdens.[95]

---

[91]  Similar considerations will arise in relation to X's land if it is to be burdened with a reciprocal payment obligation.

[92]  Consultation Paper, para 10.26.

[93]  See para 6.126 below.

[94]  The majority of consultees agreed that liability should be joint and several unless the dominant owner agreed to a variation or an alternative basis had been expressly set out in the deed creating the Land Obligation. See the Analysis of Responses, paras 10.21 to 10.28.

[95]  The majority of consultees agreed. The London Property Support Lawyers Group said (in response to Consultation Paper, para 10.26), "otherwise it would be very easy for the original owner to apportion to a part of the land which was then transferred to a company with no assets".

6.123   So any compromise of the burden of an obligation must be made by agreement with all concerned including the dominant owner, by way of deed of variation. Failing that, there must be a dispute resolution procedure. The Consultation Paper made a provisional proposal about this;[96] since the objective would be a variation of the obligation it must form part of the jurisdiction of the Lands Chamber to modify or discharge an obligation and is discussed in Part 7, below.[97]

6.124   As we discussed in the context of vertical transmission of burdens, there is a separate issue about the incidence of a positive obligation as between the burdened owners, even if there is no question of re-negotiating with the dominant owner. The burdened owners are jointly and severally liable to the dominant owner(s), but between themselves there has to be an apportionment of liability, whether for money payments or for practical obligations such as maintaining a drive (inevitably involving expense). Arrangements for that apportionment may be made expressly, but we first provide a default rule.

6.125   In the case of vertical transmission, we follow the Scottish solution and place liability with the lessor rather than the lessee in default of any express agreement to the contrary; but a different solution is needed in the case of a horizontal transmission of part. Accordingly, again adapting the Scottish precedent, we recommend a division of responsibility by area.[98]

6.126   **We recommend that where property burdened by a positive obligation is divided, the resulting estates should be jointly and severally liable on the obligation, but that liability between those estates should be apportioned in the proportions which, in the absence of express apportionment, will be based upon the areas which their respective parts bear to the area of the burdened property.**

6.127   The provisions of clause 6(4) and of schedule 1 to the draft Bill put that recommendation into effect. The schedule sets out some details about the area to be taken into account when the apportionment by area is calculated; the area concerned is that of the burdened land at the time the obligation was imposed, but subtracting land that has escaped from the burden because a subsequent disposition takes priority to it,[99] land in relation to which the obligation is no longer enforceable either because it has been discharged by the Lands Chamber or as a result of compulsory purchase, and land that has escheated. The schedule deals separately, but in analogous terms, with cases where a burdened lease is sub-divided, and it ensures that any express apportionment arrangement – which we go on to discuss below – takes priority to the default rules. The examples given in Appendix D illustrate the way that the apportionment rules will operate.

6.128   The schedule provides for a default apportionment system by area. Where the default apportionment is inappropriate – for example where the land is burdened with an obligation to maintain a boundary which is not shared by the area sold off

---

[96]   Consultation Paper, para 10.27.

[97]   See para 7.52 and following below.

[98]   Title Conditions (Scotland) Act 2003, s 11(1)(b).

[99]   The circumstances in which this might happen are rare, and most will arise as a result of conveyancer error. Nevertheless, the draft Bill must take account of the possibility.

– it would be in the parties' interests to negotiate a different division before (or sometimes after) completing the sale. The diagram below illustrates this point: the whole of the area bounded by the rectangle is subject to a positive obligation to maintain the fence, shown with a bold broken line, made by X in favour of Y; but now the shaded area is being sold by X to Z. It is highly unlikely that Z (the buyer of the shaded area) will agree to take on any liability for the fence, and if it is not possible to negotiate a release with Y (the owner of the benefited land), then Z will need to negotiate an apportionment with X, so that X will undertake the entire responsibility and give an indemnity to Z.

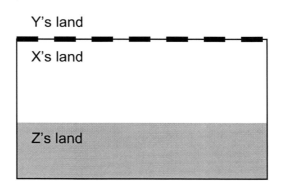

6.129    Such divisions of responsibility might be made by contract between the parties; but each will wish to ensure that the bargain holds when the other parts with the land and will therefore want to make such arrangements by using land obligations; in the diagram above the seller of the shaded area (X) will agree with the buyer (Z) that he (X) will bear the burden of repairing the fence, as between themselves only, and so to indemnify Z from any action taken by the dominant owner (Y). This is straightforward – although we hope that forward planning will make it unnecessary.

6.130    This takes us back to paragraph 6.32 above. We explained that an obligation to make a payment can be a land obligation if it is a reciprocal payment obligation, in effect paying for or contributing to the cost of the payee's doing something pursuant to a land obligation. An obligation to pay for the maintenance of a driveway, for example, is only valid if it is made in return for an obligation to maintain the driveway. However, an exception to that rule has to be made for obligations to make a payment arising from an apportionment of the burden of a covenant between parties who are jointly liable upon it.

**6.131    We recommend that where land burdened by a positive obligation is divided, and the parties (that is, the various servient owners) agree between themselves the extent to which both (or all) are liable to perform the obligation, the obligations arising under that agreement shall be land obligations.**

6.132    That recommendation encompasses the apportionment of responsibility for positive obligations both to do something on the burdened land (or a boundary structure) and to make a reciprocal payment. Insofar as it relates to payment obligations, it is the reason for clause 1(3)(d) in the draft Bill.

6.133    We would add that even in cases where the default apportionment rule by area would appear to present no difficulties, an express apportionment arrangement would be advisable in order to prevent disputes, perhaps about area, in the future.

## ADVERSE POSSESSION

6.134    We have to make special provision for the position of anyone in adverse possession of land that is subject to land obligations, whether positive or negative.

6.135    The legal position of an adverse possessor differs, as a result of the Land Registration Act 2002, according to whether the title of the dispossessed owner was registered or unregistered. From the outset, a squatter has a legal fee simple in the land of which he or she is in adverse possession.[100] The fee simple is generated by that possession, and enables the squatter to eject anyone attempting to take away possession of the land – except, of course, the proprietor whom the squatter has dispossessed and whose title is therefore better than the squatter's throughout the limitation period.

6.136    Where the dispossessed proprietor's title is unregistered, it is barred by the operation of sections 15 and 17 of the Limitation Act 1980 after the squatter has been in adverse possession for twelve years. At that point the squatter's fee simple becomes unchallengeable. The squatter still has the fee simple generated by adverse possession; he or she does not take over the dispossessed owner's title.[101]

6.137    But if the dispossessed owner's title is registered, then after ten years' adverse possession the squatter can apply to be substituted as the registered proprietor of the dispossessed owner's registered estate. The squatter will succeed only in tightly defined circumstances; it is now extremely difficult for a registered proprietor to lose title to an adverse possessor.[102]

6.138    If the squatter *does* succeed in being registered as proprietor of the dispossessed proprietor's estate, then the squatter will take that estate with its appurtenant rights and subject to all the burdens attached to it. The squatter will become able to enforce all the land obligations that benefit the estate, and will be subject to any land obligations, and old restrictive covenants, that burden it. No statutory provision is required to generate that result.

---

[100] *Asher v Whitlock* (1865-66) LR 1 QB 1.

[101] *Tichborne v Weir* (1892) 8 TLR 713, 714; [1891-94] All ER 449, 451.

[102] LRA 2002, sch 6.

6.139    But what of the squatter before registration; or in unregistered land both before and after the dispossessed proprietor's title is barred? In these situations we have one element of the current law to help us: *Re Nisbet and Potts' Contract*[103] established that an adverse possessor is bound in these circumstances by any restrictive covenants that bound the dispossessed proprietor. We do not think it fair that the squatter should be able to take the land free of restrictions that bound the legitimate owner.

6.140    So what should be the position of the squatter, whose title is not registered, so far as land obligations are concerned? First, the squatter would not be able to enforce obligations appurtenant to the estate of the dispossessed proprietor, unless we recommend special provision to that effect, since those obligations would not be appurtenant to the squatter's estate. We asked consultees[104] whether a squatter whose title is not registered should be able to enforce land obligations; the majority of consultees agreed with us that such a squatter should not be entitled to do so. We therefore make no recommendation to attach to the squatter's unregistered fee simple estate the benefit of land obligations appurtenant to the estate of the dispossessed proprietor.[105]

6.141    Should a squatter be bound by land obligations that burdened the dispossessed proprietor's estate? The overwhelming response of consultees was that the squatter should be bound.[106] We agree. This accords with the approach to restrictive covenants under the current law; and it meets a demand for fairness. There is no reason why the squatter should escape the liabilities to which the holder of the paper title is subject. We have already recommended that occupiers of land be bound by restrictive obligations, as they are under the current law;[107] additional provision is needed to make squatters liable for positive obligations since these do not generally bind occupiers. A squatter would also be subject to any other appurtenant rights that bound the dispossessed proprietor.[108]

6.142    A recommendation that a squatter whose title is not registered should be subject to all the land obligations that bound the dispossessed proprietor will be relevant in three situations:

   (1)    the squatter in unregistered land who has not yet barred the title of the dispossessed proprietor;

   (2)    the same squatter once the dispossessed proprietor's title has been barred; and

   (3)    the squatter in registered land who has not yet applied for registration.

[103] [1905] 1 Ch 391.

[104] Consultation Paper, para 9.34.

[105] Under the current law an occupier is entitled to enforce a restrictive covenant: LPA 1925, s 78(1). We have made no proposal to replicate that position for land obligations, and what we say here about adverse possessors is consistent with that.

[106] Consultation Paper, paras 9.36 and 9.37; see the Analysis of Responses, para 9.79 to 9.93.

[107] See para 6.104 above.

[108] This is the current law: LPA 1925, s 79(1) and see *Megarry and Wade*, para 35-063.

6.143 Finally, what of the squatter in unregistered land, who has barred the title of the dispossessed proprietor, and who has successfully applied to have his or her own title registered? The squatter then has an independent title and not the title of the dispossessed proprietor. And it follows from what we have said above that this squatter too should be bound by the land obligations that bound the dispossessed proprietor, and indeed by any easements or profits that bound that proprietor.

**6.144 We recommend that both an adverse possessor of land, who has not made a successful application to be registered as proprietor to that land, and an adverse possessor of unregistered land who has had his or her own title registered, should be subject to the land obligations that bound the estate of the dispossessed proprietor.**

6.145 This is reflected in clauses 4 and 5(1) of the draft Bill; in particular, a squatter in adverse possession of the burdened land is bound by positive obligations because his or her estate confers a right to immediate possession of the burdened land.

## LIABILITY AND REMEDIES FOR BREACH OF LAND OBLIGATIONS

6.146 We have explained above how the benefit and burden of a land obligation will pass to successive owners of the burdened and benefited land, and we explored the extent to which there should be exceptions to what would happen under the general law and the extent to which special additional provision should be made, in particular for where land is sub-divided. Next we ask what happens when an obligation is not complied with. What is the cause of action that will enable the dominant owner to take action, whom can the dominant owner sue, and what might be the remedies?

### The cause of action

6.147 Under the current law, interference with rights appurtenant to land, for example an easement, gives rise to an action in nuisance.[109] This is not appropriate for breach of an obligation, particularly a positive one that requires the servient owner to do something in order to comply. We therefore proposed in the Consultation Paper that there should be a new statutory cause of action available to those entitled to enforce an obligation.[110]

**6.148 We recommend that breach of a land obligation shall be enforceable by action.**

6.149 Clause 7 of the draft Bill provides for this.

### Liability for breach

6.150 We observed in the Consultation Paper that breach of a positive obligation was more closely analogous to a breach of contract than to a tort, and we remain of

---

[109] As an easement is not a possessory right, interference will not amount to a trespass, see *Paine & Co v St Neots Gas & Coke Co* [1939] 3 All ER 812.

[110] Consultation Paper, para 8.90 and following.

this view. In keeping with the contract analogy, it would only be necessary for a dominant owner to show that there has been a breach of the terms of the obligation.[111]

6.151 We also looked in the Consultation Paper at liability for breach. This has to be carefully distinguished from the issue of transmission of the burden of a land obligation. Take a land obligation not to use land for a business. There may be a number of parties holding burdened estates (for example the freeholder, a tenant of part, a beneficiary of a trust in possession, and the remainderman under the trust). All these hold burdened estates and so each will be liable if he or she breaches the obligation. If, say, the weekly tenant starts to run a business on the land, the weekly tenant can be sued; but can any of the other burdened parties be sued as well?

6.152 We proposed in the Consultation Paper[112] that a restrictive obligation should be enforceable against anyone bound by it if they have broken it, or "permitted or suffered" it to be broken by another. Consultees agreed with that proposal, although some queried the language used.[113] The phrase is derived from case law; the intention is that when a restrictive obligation is broken, those liable should be those who have actually broken it, or who have allowed someone over whom they have control to break it. Thus a landlord cannot escape liability where the breach was his or her tenant's; nor can a trustee avoid liability if the breach was committed by the beneficiary of the trust.[114] But none of these are liable if the breach is by a trespasser.

6.153 For positive obligations, the position is different. We can state more simply that those who are bound by the land obligation are jointly and severally liable for breaches, since all are responsible for ensuring that the work or payment required by the covenant is performed. We raised this point in the Consultation Paper, and consultees agreed with our provisional view.[115]

**6.154 We recommend that a person who is bound by a negative land obligation breaches it by doing something which it prohibits, or by permitting or suffering someone else to do so; and that a person who is bound by a positive obligation breaches it if the obligation is not performed.**

6.155 Clause 6(1) and (2) of the draft Bill puts this recommendation into effect.

6.156 However, we add a further recommendation to control liability for breach of a reciprocal payment obligation, in response to a point raised in discussions with practitioners: it was pointed out to us that it would be helpful to replicate, for

---

[111] By contrast where a claim is made alleging a disturbance of an easement it is necessary to show there has been a substantial interference with the right; *Gale on Easements*, para 13-03.

[112] Consultation Paper, para 9.41.

[113] See the Analysis of Responses, paras 9.94 to 9.98.

[114] Assuming in both those cases that the landlord and the trustee both held burdened estates.

[115] Consultation Paper, paras 9.42 and 9.43. See the Analysis of Responses, paras 9.99 to 9.107.

positive land obligations, the protection embodied in the statutory controls on service charges within landlord and tenant legislation.[116] These provisions ensure that payment only has to be made for reasonable costs, and only for work done to a reasonable standard. Without such provisions the possibilities for abuse are obvious.[117]

**6.157** **We recommend no amount should be payable under a reciprocal payment obligation in respect of work not carried out to a reasonable standard; and that in determining the amount payable under such an obligation, only costs which are reasonably incurred in performing the obligation for which payment is made are to be taken into account.**

6.158 Clause 9 of the draft Bill embodies that recommendation.

### Remedies for breach of a land obligation

6.159 Finally, we turn to remedies.

#### *Remedies imposed by court order*

6.160 A land obligation will be an interest in land. The primary remedy for breach should be an injunction or an order to perform the obligation.[118] An injunction would be the most appropriate remedy where the substance of the obligation is restrictive, while a positive obligation should be enforced primarily by an order to perform the covenant or, where it is a financial obligation, the payment of a sum of money. Where appropriate the court may order damages to be paid in substitution for an injunction.[119]

6.161 Our proposals[120] as to cause of action, liability for breach, and remedies were well supported by consultees. One consultee[121] thought we should go further and give the courts the widest possible discretion to make any order thought appropriate, such as an order for sale of the defendant's land. We are not minded to go so far; such a wide discretion, with a potentially draconian range of remedies, would not be generally supported.

6.162 Nor are we minded to pursue the suggestion made to us that damages for breach of positive obligations should be limited to the value of the land. To do this would subject the value of these obligations arbitrarily to fluctuations in the value of the underlying estate. There are no similar limitations in enforcing restrictive covenants or easements, both of which can result in damages which are in no

[116] Landlord and Tenant Act 1985, ss 19(1) and 19(2).

[117] And without a control on the amount payable, it would be easy to disguise an overage payment as a reciprocal payment obligation.

[118] Recently confirmed by the Court of Appeal in *Watson v Croft Promo-Sport Ltd* [2009] EWCA Civ 15, [2009] 3 All ER 249 where Sir Andrew Morritt VC reiterated that an injunction should be refused only in exceptional cases.

[119] We note here that, where damages are awarded, they should not be reduced solely because the claimant had a right to undertake the works themselves and did not exercise it. See clause 7(4) of the draft Bill and para 6.173 and following below.

[120] Consultation Paper, paras 8.90 to 8.97.

[121] Farrer & Co LLP.

way linked, on breach, to the value of the land; nor are we aware of similar limitations in other jurisdictions upon the damages available for breach of positive obligations.

6.163   Damages for breach of a land obligation should follow contractual principles, both in terms of the measure of damages – the cost of putting matters right[122] – and in terms of the rules of remoteness. It is hard to see that in practice there would be a great deal of difference, if any, between a contractual and a tortious measure of damages;[123] but it is important that the rules of remoteness applied be contractual.

6.164   In the tort of nuisance, the basis of liability for damages is causation; anything caused by the wrong is encompassed in the calculation of liability, however unlikely the consequence was.[124] In contract, liability is for losses flowing naturally from the breach (and therefore objectively foreseeable) or for anything actually known to the parties at the time of the contract. This is a less dramatic basis for liability. If adopted for land obligations it would eliminate liability for loss that would not normally be caused by breach of the obligation in question. For example, failure to mend a fence next to a domestic garden would not normally cause an escape of farm animals but might do so in special and unforeseeable circumstances; we think that such an extended potential liability would not be appropriate for breach of a land obligation.

**6.165   We recommend that on proof of breach a court may, in its discretion grant an injunction, make an order for performance of the obligation, or for payment of damages or of the payment of the amount due under the obligation.**

**6.166   We recommend that contract principles be applied to the calculation of damages for breach of a land obligation.**

6.167   Clause 7(2) and (3) of the draft Bill embodies these recommendations.[125]

---

[122] E Peel, *Treitel, The Law of Contract* (12th ed 2007) para 20-001 and following: a claim for damages is one for compensation in money for the fact that the claimant has not received the performance for which he bargained, based on loss to the claimant rather than gain to the defendant.

[123] There is currently a body of law concerning damages for positive covenants, even though they do not give rise to interests in land. H McGregor, *McGregor on Damages* (18th ed 2009) para 22-040 and following, explains that damages for breach of positive covenants are awarded on the basis of loss in value to the dominant land or on the basis of the cost of the dominant owner doing the work, and the court's choice is heavily influenced by whether or not the dominant owner actually plans to do the work. In terms of the measure of damages, consideration of *Leakey v National Trust* [1978] QB 849 indicates that damages awarded under either contract or tort law would have been the same, namely the cost of repairs.

[124] H McGregor, *McGregor on Damages* (18th ed 2009) para 6-011, indicates that this remains the case for the land torts despite the foreseeability principle introduced for negligence by *Overseas Tankship (UK) Ltd v Morts Dock & Engineering Co Ltd (The Wagon Mound)* [1961] AC 388.

[125] The availability of these remedies for breach does not, of course, affect the court's jurisdiction to make declarations, as to which see the Civil Procedure Rules, r 40.20 and para 7.39 and following below.

6.168　We have noted that when a person parts with possession of the estate to which a land obligation is attached, then he or she is no longer liable for breaches of it. However, what if that person parts with the land after a breach has occurred? The answer depends upon whether the breach is continuous or not.

6.169　If the breach is not continuous (for example failing to comply with an obligation to do something on a specific date) then that liability crystallises at the moment that the land obligation is breached and the owner is therefore liable. A subsequent parting with possession makes no difference to that, and liability remains for the whole of the limitation period. However, an incoming owner would not be liable for that specific breach. If the breach is continuous (for example failing to keep a fence maintained to a particular standard at all times), and the breach continues when one person parts with possession and another takes it, then both the incoming owner and the outgoing owner will be liable. This is a matter of general law and needs no specific provision in the draft Bill.

6.170　Finally, there must be a limitation period for liability for breach of a land obligation. We take the view that section 8 of the Limitation Act 1980 would, in the absence of any other provision, impose a twelve-year period at least where land obligations are imposed by deed; but to avoid doubt and for the sake of consistency we recommend express provision.

**6.171　We recommend that the limitation period for liability for breach of a land obligation shall be twelve years.**

6.172　Paragraph 12 of schedule 3 to the draft Bill puts this into effect by adding a provision to the Limitation Act 1980.

### Self-help

6.173　We have recommended that it be possible for the parties to a land obligation to add ancillary provisions, such as provision for the dominant owner to enter the servient land and carry out the work required by a positive obligation, if the servient owner had failed to do it.[126] The owner of the land burdened by an obligation to mend a fence, say, might be obliged to allow the dominant owner to enter his or her land, on notice, and inspect the work done, and to carry out the work himself or herself in certain defined circumstances. We recommend no separate statutory provision about self-help, and we do not think that it would be appropriate to provide for a self-help remedy in all cases. This will be for the parties and their advisers to consider and to draft in terms that suit the individual circumstances.[127]

---

[126] See paras 6.33 to 6.36 above.

[127] There is a general right to enter land to abate a nuisance, in cases where the problem is so clear and easily remediable that there is no possible need to resort to the courts: see *Clerk and Lindsell on Torts* (20th ed 2010) para 30-26 and following; there will be some cases where failure to comply with a positive land obligation does constitute a nuisance and where that remedy will be available – for example, an obligation to maintain a retaining wall. We note also the provision of RSC Order 45, r 8, which enables the court to permit self-help where a mandatory injunction is not complied with; this too will be relevant to land obligations on occasions.

6.174    However, we need to recommend provisions that will apply if an obligation is drafted in terms that allow self-help.

6.175    First, we think that the dominant owner should not be obliged to carry out the work himself or herself even if there is provision for self-help, and that damages should not be reduced if the dominant owner chooses not to do so. But where the dominant owner has that right and chooses to exercise it, then of course the costs of the work are recoverable from the servient owner who should have carried out the work. If there are more than one servient owners involved, liability for that payment should be joint and several. But it should arise only insofar as the cost is reasonable and the work done to a reasonable standard. This is similar to the provision we recommended for reciprocal payment obligations, and again is intended to guard against abuse.[128]

6.176    **We recommend that where there is provision for self-help by the dominant owner in the terms of the land obligation, the fact that the dominant owner chooses not to exercise that right should not reduce damages payable by the servient owner for breach of the obligation.**

6.177    **We recommend that where the dominant owner is entitled to exercise self-help and does so, the costs of the work should be recoverable from the servient owner who should have carried out the work, but only insofar as the cost is reasonable and the work done to a reasonable standard. Liability for such a payment should be joint and several where more than one servient owner is subject to the same obligation.**

6.178    Clauses 7(4) and 8 of the draft Bill puts those recommendations into effect.

### LAND OBLIGATIONS AND THE CROWN

6.179    It is intended that Crown land[129] shall be able to benefit from and be burdened by land obligations. Crown land can currently benefit from and be burdened by restrictive covenants, and the position so far as positive obligations are concerned should be the same.[130] The draft Bill contains a blank clause 13. This is intended to indicate that, on implementation of our recommendations concerning land obligations, consideration will have to be given to the way in which the Queen will grant, or enter into, them. Currently the Keeper of the Privy Purse enters into restrictive covenants on behalf of the Queen; but there is no statutory authority for this.

6.180    A special issue arises in relation to land that is burdened with a positive obligation and escheats. Escheat is a feature of the feudal system of land ownership: all land is held of the Crown.[131] If an estate in land determines, the Crown continues

---

[128]  See paras 6.156 and 6.157 above.

[129]  By which is meant, in this context, land held by the Queen in her personal capacity and as Duke of Lancaster, the Duke of Cornwall, and the Crown Estates.

[130]  Paragraphs 1 and 2 of schedule 3 to the draft Bill make provision for the Duchies to be able to expend capital in the performance of a land obligation.

[131]  This term derives from the complexity of feudal landholding, where land was granted by the King to X, who made a further grant to Y. X in that case was known as the "mesne lord"; if Y's land escheated, it escheated to X.

"to be the owner of the land, freed from the estate previously carved out of the Crown's interest in the land".[132] The escheat is not completed until the Crown takes possession or exercises control over the property or takes proceedings for its recovery.[133]

6.181　The Administration of Estates Act 1925 abolished a number of instances of escheat; as a result, escheat of land on the termination of a freehold estate is now limited to three situations:[134]

(1)　Where a landowner's trustee in bankruptcy or liquidator exercises the statutory power to disclaim the freehold estate under section 315 or section 178 of the Insolvency Act 1986.

(2)　On dissolution of a company, its property will vest in the Crown in the person of the Treasury Solicitor as *bona vacantia*. The Crown has a statutory right to disclaim the property under the Companies Act 2006, sections 1013 and 1014. If it does so, for example because the property is onerous, any freehold land will escheat to the Crown, which will not incur liability for it unless it takes possession or exercises control over the property. This means that the Crown can avoid being liable for the property.

(3)　Where the Crown has made a grant of a freehold subject to restrictions as to the user of the land, enforceable by a right of entry which has been exercised.[135]

6.182　Under the current law, escheat will not determine a subordinate interest in the escheated land. It is clear from the decision in *Scmlla Properties Ltd v Gesso Properties (BVI) Ltd*,[136] which concerned disclaimer of a freehold by a liquidator, and earlier cases cited in that decision, that a mortgage or legal charge and a lease will continue to burden land which has escheated.

6.183　In view of the current law concerning subordinate interests on escheat, the burden of a positive land obligation will not terminate on the escheat of a freehold estate to the Crown Estates or one of the Duchies. It will continue to burden the land in the same way that a lease or mortgage will. But the Crown will not be liable on the obligation unless it enters into possession or takes control of the land and thus completes the escheat.[137] If a new freehold estate is granted out of

---

[132] F A Enever, *Bona Vacantia under the Law of England* (1927) pp 15 and 16, quoted in *Scmlla Properties Ltd v Gesso Properties (BVI) Ltd* [1995] BCC 793, 800 by Stanley Burnton QC, sitting as a deputy High Court judge.

[133] Land Registration for the Twenty-First Century (2001) Law Com No 271, para 11.21, citing *Blackstone's Commentaries*, vol 2, p 245. See also *Halsbury's Laws of England*, vol 12(1), para 234.

[134] *Megarry and Wade*, para 2-023.

[135] The nature of escheat and the situations when it arises are discussed in more detail in our earlier report, Land Registration for the Twenty-First Century (2001) Law Com No 271, paras 11.20 to 11.25.

[136] [1995] BCC 793.

[137] *Halsbury's Laws of England*, vol 12(1), para 234.

the land, the burdens will attach to that and the new owner will be liable on the obligations.

6.184 It is not possible to deduce from the current law whether the benefit of a positive land obligation will survive escheat. A land obligation can be imposed on the basis that the estate burdened by it has the benefit of a reciprocal payment obligation; and it will be important for the draft Bill to ensure that where the Crown is bound by a positive obligation as a result of escheat, in a case where it has taken possession or control of the land, it also has the benefit of any reciprocal payment.

**6.185 We recommend that where land that is burdened or benefited by a positive land obligation (including an obligation to make an apportionment payment) escheats, the Crown shall not be bound by that obligation, or entitled to enforce it (as the case may be), unless it takes possession or control of the land.**

6.186 Clause 12 of the draft Bill accomplishes this.[138]

6.187 The same issues do not arise in the context of easements which burden land which has escheated. The remedies for interference with an easement lie in the tort of nuisance, for which the Crown cannot be liable.[139]

[138] Paragraphs 1(3)(c) and 2(3)(c) of schedule 1 to the draft Bill make corresponding provision for the disregarding, in calculating an apportionment payment, of land in relation to which the Crown is relieved of liability by clause 12.

[139] Crown Proceedings Act 1947, s 40(4).

# PART 7
# THE JURISDICTION OF THE LANDS CHAMBER OF THE UPPER TRIBUNAL

## INTRODUCTION

7.1    An essential feature of property rights is their durability; they remain attached to land, whether as a benefit or as a burden, despite changes in ownership and the passage of time. They can be released by agreement; but it is also important for the law to provide other ways for them to be modified or removed, eventually and when they have outlived their usefulness, lest land be sterilised or rendered unmarketable. For easements and profits this is achieved by proving that they have been abandoned; but for restrictive covenants a different avenue is provided, namely the jurisdiction of the Lands Chamber to modify and discharge restrictions under section 84 of the Law of Property Act 1925.[1]

7.2    In this final Part we recommend extensions to the Lands Chamber's jurisdiction, and in particular the introduction of provisions that necessarily go along with the introduction of land obligations. Before we explain our recommendations we provide some background to section 84 in its current form; and we consider the provisional proposals that we made in the Consultation Paper and discuss the reactions of consultees, which have shaped our final recommendations.

### The background to section 84

7.3    In the nineteenth century, and well into the twentieth, land was sold off from large estates so as to facilitate urban expansion, but frequently subject to extensive restrictive covenants. Those covenants had an important social function in the era before public planning control and often served to preserve the amenity of an area, controlling building and land use and ensuring consistent development.[2] In many cases restrictive covenants preserved green spaces, and continue to do so. However, social needs change over time; there are instances where a restrictive covenant is no longer conferring a benefit. Landowners and developers may wish to discharge, or at least modify, covenants on the basis that they are no longer serving a useful purpose but their presence on the title to the land is impeding a change of use or a development. The Lands Chamber's jurisdiction is important both in facilitating development of land and in preserving amenity that is still regarded as important.

7.4    Section 84 enables the Lands Chamber to discharge or modify restrictive covenants on the grounds – to paraphrase roughly – that they are no longer useful. The full grounds are set out in section 84(1), and supplemented by subsections (1A) to (1C); those additional subsections were added in January 1970[3] and implemented the Law Commission's recommendations in *Transfer of*

---

[1]    Referred to simply as "section 84" for the remainder of this Part.

[2]    For further discussion of the social functions of the restrictive covenant, see *Gray and Gray*, paras 3.4.2 to 3.4.5.

[3]    Law of Property Act 1969, s 31(2).

*Land: Report on Restrictive Covenants*.[4] The intention at that time was to make it easier to discharge and modify covenants.

7.5    The provisions of the statute are supplemented in practice by the Tribunal Procedure (Upper Tribunal) (Lands Chamber) Rules 2010,[5] which regulate the procedure in the Lands Chamber. Formerly this was the Lands Tribunal, and its new title arises from its entry into the new tribunal structure in June 2009.[6] Section 84 also gives the court a jurisdiction to make declarations about the meaning or validity of a restrictive covenant; and while some of its numerous subsections are relevant only to the tribunal jurisdiction, others refer both to the court and to the tribunal. These two very different subjects – the tribunal jurisdiction and that of the court – do not sit happily within the same, unusually long, section.

**The proposals in the Consultation Paper**

7.6    The Consultation Paper made a number of provisional proposals.

7.7    First, we proposed some changes in the section 84(1) grounds, so as to clarify them and also to bring them more explicitly into line with the way that they are currently interpreted by the Lands Chamber. We adopted language used in decisions of the Chamber[7] in proposing that in exercising its jurisdiction it should seek to give effect to the purpose for which the restriction was imposed.[8] We proposed amended grounds for modification and discharge,[9] subject to an overall test of reasonableness.[10]

7.8    Second, we provisionally proposed that the Lands Chamber's jurisdiction to modify and discharge be extended to easements, profits and land obligations.[11]

7.9    Third, we proposed the addition of new grounds to be used only in the context of the modification and discharge of positive land obligations.[12] Positive obligations are likely to be rather more onerous than most restrictive covenants, since all that is needed to comply with the latter is inaction; a positive obligation is likely to involve expenditure, and may require modification or discharge on grounds rather different from those that are relevant to restrictive covenants, as we go on to discuss below.

---

[4]    (1967) Law Com No 11, p 21 (Proposition No 9).

[5]    SI 2010 No 2600. These new rules came into force in November 2010 and supersede the Lands Tribunal Rules 1996 SI 1996 No 1022.

[6]    See the Transfer of Tribunal Functions (Lands Tribunal and Miscellaneous Amendments) Order 2009 SI 2009 No 1307.

[7]    See, for example, *Re Truman, Hanbury, Buxton & Co Ltd's Application* [1956] 1 QB 261; *Shephard v Turner* [2006] EWCA Civ 8, [2006] 2 P & CR 28 at [41].

[8]    Consultation Paper, para 14.70(1).

[9]    Consultation Paper, paras 14.71 and 14.72.

[10]   Consultation Paper, para 14.70(2).

[11]   Consultation Paper, para 14.41; see also para 14.82 and 14.83 of the Consultation Paper.

[12]   Consultation Paper, paras 14.93 and following; see also para 14.83 of the Consultation Paper.

7.10 Fourth, we made some supplementary proposals in connection with entitlement to apply, stays of proceedings, and the use of grounds in the alternative.[13]

7.11 We also asked for consultees' views on the provisions of section 84 that relate to compensation;[14] and we discussed briefly, without making provisional proposals, the possibility of extending to the Lands Chamber itself the jurisdiction to make declarations conferred on the court by section 84(2).

**Consultees' responses**

7.12 Of those four groups of proposals, consultees favoured all but the first. In particular, there was widespread support for the proposal that the Lands Chamber's jurisdiction to discharge or modify interests should be extended to easements, profits and land obligations. In addition, a number of consultees pointed out the inconvenience of the Lands Chamber's current inability to make declarations under section 84(2), which often imposes delay and additional expense when proceedings in the Lands Chamber have to be stayed in order for a court application to be heard, the matter rehearsed afresh before the court, and a declaration made. The bulk of this Part of our Report is taken up with the discussion of our recommendations for reform, which we have now grouped under three heads:

    (1)    our recommendations for the extension of the jurisdiction of the Lands Chamber, to enable it to order the discharge and modification of easements, profits and land obligations in freehold and leasehold land;

    (2)    our recommendation for the extension of the jurisdiction of the Lands Chamber to enable it to make declarations; and

    (3)    our recommendations in relation to the grounds for the modification and discharge of interests in land and in particular of positive land obligations.

7.13 However, before we embark on those three groups of recommendations we pause to discuss three issues on which we make no recommendations for reform.

***The amendment of the grounds for discharge and modification of restrictions?***

7.14 The Consultation Paper made proposals for the amendment of the grounds for modification and discharge of restrictive covenants. A number of consultees felt strongly that these should not be changed, so as to ensure that no adjustment is made to the delicate balance that section 84 embodies, between the interests of developers, and those who hold the benefit of restrictive covenants. This is a very emotive and controversial issue. Our intention had not been to change the law as it is applied by the Lands Chamber, merely to achieve transparency. Consultees' comments persuaded us that we should recommend no change to the wording of the grounds for discharge of restrictive covenants, and that those same grounds should be applicable for the future to restrictive land obligations. That means that

[13] Consultation Paper, paras 14,74, 14.101 and 14.106.

[14] Consultation Paper, para 14.15.

we make no recommendations that will make it easier, or harder, to modify or discharge restrictive covenants. For more detail on consultees' responses, and for insight into some of the very difficult issues raised here, the reader is referred to the Analysis of Responses.[15]

### *The basis for compensation?*

7.15    Another issue on which consultation responses made it difficult to recommend reform was the possibility of amendment to the basis of compensation set out in section 84(1), on which we made no provisional proposals but asked for consultees' views.[16] Our request prompted a number of responses, strongly advocating reform[17] but expressing diametrically opposed views as to what a reformed provision should say, and that has made it impracticable to make a recommendation.[18]

7.16    The current provisions are found in section 84(1), which provides for the payment to any person entitled to the benefit of the restriction, of either, but not both, of the following:

(1)    a sum to make up for any loss or disadvantage suffered by that person in consequence of the discharge or modification; or

(2)    a sum to make up for any effect which the restriction had, at the time when it was imposed, in reducing the consideration then received for the land affected by it.

7.17    Both these alternative limbs have come in for criticism. The first limb apparently gives straightforward damages to the dominant owner, to compensate for the loss resulting from the release of the burden on the burdened land. But does that mean the loss in value of the dominant land as a result of the disappearance of the benefit of the restriction (or other interest)? Or the loss of the chance to bargain for the release, which is therefore going to have something to do with the uplift in value of the servient land and the profit expected from development? The latter may well be far higher than the former.

7.18    Most consultees were adamant that it should reflect the former. The covenant was not imposed to give X a ransom value but to enhance his land, so that is the loss he should get back. The Chancery Bar Association suggested that "any compensation should be plainly based on diminution in value only". But significant opposition to that view was raised by a number of consultees, including the Royal Institution of Chartered Surveyors. It felt that a restrictive covenant may be imposed in order to preserve for the dominant owner the chance to extract further value from the land when the covenant is released, and

---

[15]    See the Analysis of Responses, paras 14.26 to 14.46, and see paras 7.52 and following below.

[16]    Consultation Paper, para 14.15.

[17]    The Conveyancing and Land Law Committee of the Law Society considered the present compensation rules to be "confusing" while the Chancery Bar Association thought them "clearly unsatisfactory".

[18]    See the Analysis of Responses, paras 14.1 to 14.13.

that the basis of compensation should reflect that. We prefer the view of the Chancery Bar Association; the jurisdiction to discharge or modify restrictions is not intended to preserve bargains but to release land from burdens that are no longer useful.[19] Additional and future consideration for a sale should be secured by a charge or by an overage agreement.

7.19 Turning to the second limb, the thinking behind the provision is that X sold part of his land to Y and imposed a restriction on it. X therefore received less for the land than he would otherwise have received. So when he loses the benefit of the restriction he loses twice – so this limb compensates him for that initial loss.

7.20 This provision gives rise to difficulties because it may be very difficult to look back in time and assess just how much less X received for the land because of the presence of the restriction than he would otherwise have received. Moreover, there is no provision for index-linking the payment made under the second limb. Consultees differed widely in their views about reform of this limb, with some calling for abolition, and some advocating provision for the payment of interest on this element of the compensation.

7.21 The reader is referred to the Analysis of Responses (paragraphs 14.1 to 14.13) for a full discussion of the issues arising from the compensation provisions. The difficulty that we would face in recommending reform is that there is no consensus among consultees on either the first or second limbs. We made no provisional proposal in the Consultation Paper for the reform of the compensation provisions, and we think that consultees' responses reveal the need for further work in this specialist area, which our project was not intended to address. We think that it is particularly important to make recommendations here which command consensus, without making inevitably controversial proposals about compensation.

### An entitlement for benefited owners to apply?

7.22 The third issue on which we make no recommendation is our proposal in the Consultation Paper that entitlement to apply for discharge or modification of an interest should no longer be confined to people burdened by the interest but should be extended to benefited owners.[20]

7.23 We made that proposal on the basis that there might well be circumstances where the person with the benefit of an easement, for example, would find it useful to have its route changed or where the details of a land obligation might usefully be amended. However, we have decided not to pursue that proposal, having considered how very closely the current grounds for discharge and modification are tailored to applications by the burdened party. A completely fresh set of grounds would be needed in order to extend a right to apply to benefited owners. We were also concerned that applications by benefited owners might well involve an increased burden on the other party or parties involved. That raises very difficult issues of balance between different interests, and we came to

---

[19] See *Winter v Traditional & Contemporary Contracts Ltd* [2007] EWCA Civ 1088, [2008] 1 EGLR 80 and *Re Skupinski* [2004] EWLands 34 2003, [2005] RVR 269.

[20] Consultation Paper, para 14.106.

the conclusion that the Lands Chamber's jurisdiction should not be extended in this way.[21]

## OUR RECOMMENDATIONS AND THE DRAFT BILL

7.24 Before we go on to discuss the three groups of recommendations that we now make, we comment on one further issue that was brought to our attention, not only by consultees but also by the President of the Lands Chamber, namely the difficulty of reading and navigating section 84. We commented above that it is unusually long (the text is set out at Appendix E) and that the interrelationship of some of its provisions is not clear. One of the concerns expressed in the Consultation Paper was the accessibility of the legislation, and so we want to address that.

7.25 In drafting our Bill we have had regard to the need for clarity and accessibility. Section 84 is represented in the draft Bill by clauses 29 to 39 and schedule 2, which reproduce the terms of section 84 but re-arrange them, with the addition only of the provisions that we go on to recommend here. We say no more in this Part about those provisions of the draft Bill that simply replicate the wording of section 84; our recommendations here relate only to the new provisions. The draft Bill changes nothing of the section 84 provisions save for those required by the changes we recommend here. The Explanatory Notes to the draft Bill make clear the derivation of the various provisions.

7.26 We now turn to our recommendations for reform.

### Extending the jurisdiction of the Lands Chamber by bringing more interests within its scope

7.27 Section 84(1) defines applicants as:

> ... any person interested in any freehold land affected by any restriction arising under covenant or otherwise as to the user thereof or the building thereon ... .

This wording establishes who can apply to the Lands Chamber under this section, and the type of interest that can be addressed by it.[22] "Interested in" includes parties with any interest in qualifying land such as mortgagees, option holders and even purchasers under uncompleted or conditional contracts.[23] "Freehold land" is extended by section 84(12), which allows leases granted for a minimum of 40 years of which at least 25 have expired to be treated "in like manner" to a freehold, allowing them to fall under section 84(1).

7.28 Although section 84 is generally referred to as a provision about restrictive covenants, it clearly extends wider than restrictive covenants, to "any restriction

---

[21] With one exception, which we note at para 7.67 below. As to the question at Consultation Paper, para 14.106, see the Analysis of Responses, paras 14.136 to 14.151.

[22] See generally: A Francis, *Restrictive Covenants and Freehold Land* (3rd ed 2009) ch 16 and G L Newsom, *Preston and Newsom: Restrictive Covenants Affecting Freehold Land* (9th ed 1998) ch 10.

[23] A Francis, *Restrictive Covenants and Freehold Land* (3rd ed 2009) para 16.45.

under covenant or otherwise".[24] Conversely, it may be that some restrictive covenants are outside its scope; it is not clear whether this is so, nor whether that is what the draftsman, or Parliament, intended.[25]

7.29   We need to look at three possible extensions of the scope of the jurisdiction of the Lands Chamber for the future: to easements and profits, to land obligations, and to a wider range of leasehold titles.

7.30   We pointed out in the Consultation Paper that there have been calls for some years now for the extension of the Lands Chamber's jurisdiction so as to enable it to make orders for the discharge and modification of easements. This was a recommendation of the Law Reform Committee, in its Fourteenth Report,[26] as well as a proposal made in the 1971 Law Commission Working Paper on Appurtenant Rights.[27] The lack of such an extended jurisdiction has been the subject of adverse comment by the courts.[28] We noted that a number of other countries have introduced such a jurisdiction, whether for their courts or for a tribunal.[29]

7.31   We rejected, in the Consultation Paper, the idea found in the American Restatement,[30] that the owner of land burdened by an easement may unilaterally change its location or dimensions if the change is necessary to permit the normal use or development of the land. This, we felt, would be unsafe and likely to lead to a wide range of disputes. We proposed instead that the Lands Chamber's jurisdiction be extended to easements, and also to profits since we saw no reason to distinguish profits in this context.[31]

---

[24]   The extended reach of the power of discharge and modification is reflected by subsection (11), which excepts from the power under subsection (1) restrictions imposed under various statutory powers. An example of a power to impose restrictions which is covered by the exception in subsection (11) is the Law of Property Act 1922, s 137 (provision for the protection of royal parks and gardens).

[25]   A Francis, *Restrictive Covenants and Freehold Land* (3rd ed 2009) para 16.57 notes that some covenants may not fall within the section 84 jurisdiction, giving the example of covenants not to sell below a certain price.

[26]   The Acquisition of Easements and Profits by Prescription (1966) Cmnd 3100, para 97.

[27]   The 1971 Working Paper, para 121.

[28]   For example, *Greenwich Healthcare NHS Trust v London and Quadrant Housing Trust* [1998] 1 WLR 1749, 1755 concerned the realignment of a right of way. Lightman J noted that, "there is (unfortunately) no statutory equivalent in case of easements to the jurisdiction vested by statute in the Lands Tribunal in case of restrictive covenants to modify the covenant to enable servient land to be put to a proper use".

[29]   These include Northern Ireland (Property (Northern Ireland) Order 1978, Part II), Scotland (Title Conditions (Scotland) Act 2003, Part 9) and the Republic of Ireland (Land and Conveyancing Law Reform Act 2009, s 50), as well as some of the Australian jurisdictions (Law of Property Act 2000, s 177 (NT), Conveyancing and Law of Property Act 1884, s 84C (Tas), Conveyancing Act 1919, s 89 (NSW)) and New Zealand (Property Law Act 2007, s 317).

[30]   The American Law Institute, *Restatement of the Law Third: Property (Servitudes)* (2000) § 4.8.

[31]   Consultation Paper, paras 14.41(1) and (2).

7.32 Consultees supported that change,[32] and we recommend it below. However, our recommendation extends only to easements and profits created after implementation of reform; to extend the jurisdiction to interests already in existence would risk contravening Article 1 of the First Protocol to the European Convention on Human Rights and Fundamental Freedoms. That is because the benefit of an easement or profit currently includes the freedom to bargain for its release (even if it is obsolete) and, either to refuse a release[33] or to demand a price for its release which could exceed the amount likely to be recovered as compensation by order of the tribunal. So to bring existing easements and profits within the scope of reform would be, in effect, to strip value out of existing property rights. Our recommendation refers therefore only to interests to be created in the future; so far as existing interests are concerned, the reform we recommend in relation to the requirements for proof of abandonment will make the establishment of abandonment somewhat easier.[34]

7.33 So far as land obligations are concerned, we have to consider separately restrictive and positive obligations. Restrictive land obligations will, if our recommendations are accepted, take the place of restrictive covenants for the future (although of course there will be no change in the status or legal effect of existing restrictive covenants). The Lands Chamber's jurisdiction to discharge or modify restrictive land obligations should be exactly the same as that applicable currently to restrictive covenants, since restrictive land obligations will perform the same function as restrictive covenants.

7.34 Positive land obligations are, as we have commented, potentially more onerous than restrictive ones, and we have taken it as essential that if positive obligations are to be able to bind land, it must be possible to apply for them to be discharged or modified.[35] Consultees agreed, and we so recommend.

**7.35 We recommend that the jurisdiction of the Lands Chamber of the Upper Tribunal be extended so as to enable it to make orders for the modification or discharge of:**

    **(1) easements and profits created after reform; and**

    **(2) land obligations.**

7.36 Clause 30 in the draft Bill embodies this recommendation.

7.37 The third extension we have to look at is the range of leases encompassed by section 84. We commented in the Consultation Paper that the restriction of the scope of section 84 to leases of 40 years or more where at least 25 years have expired seems arbitrary and unduly restrictive. Consultees agreed that that limitation is unnecessary.[36] We make the corresponding recommendation; but so

---

[32] See the Analysis of Responses, paras 14.14 to 14.25.

[33] For whatever reason, for example to prevent a development.

[34] See para 3.230 above.

[35] See para 5.21 above.

[36] See the Analysis of Responses, paras 14.136 to 14.151.

as to avoid retrospectivity (as we have done for easements and profits) we retain the current restriction for leases granted prior to reform. Clause 38(1) puts that into effect.

**7.38** **We recommend that the jurisdiction of the Lands Chamber of the Upper Tribunal should, following reform, be extended to include leasehold land of any term.**

### Extending the jurisdiction of the Lands Chamber to enable it to make declarations

7.39    Section 84(2) enables the court to make declarations, "on the application of any person interested", as to whether or not land is burdened by "a restriction imposed by any instrument"[37] and as to the construction of any such instrument and, therefore, the nature, extent and enforceability of the restriction. This power is additional to the power of the court to make binding declarations in relation to restrictive covenants under the Civil Procedure Rules, rule 40.20, and is broader in that it operates *in rem*, that is, it binds the land and so is good against everyone interested in it, rather than just against the parties to the proceedings.

7.40    Section 84(2) does not specify any particular court. It seems that application is generally made to the High Court;[38] but section 21 of the County Courts Act 1984 gives the county courts jurisdiction to hear and determine actions relating to title to land, and we take the view that the section 84(2) jurisdiction is equally exercisable by the county courts.[39]

7.41    This is an important jurisdiction. Proceedings brought in the Lands Chamber may be unable to be concluded because of uncertainty about the nature or validity of the right in question; this uncertainty can only be resolved by a declaration. A declaration may also be sought by someone claiming to have the benefit of a restriction, but who has not been admitted by the Lands Chamber pursuant to section 84(3A); there is no appeal against such a decision but in practice the matter is pursued by an application for a declaration that the scope of the restriction is such that the would-be objector has the benefit of it.[40]

---

[37]    A Francis, Restrictive Covenants and Freehold Land (3rd ed 2009) para 15.10 notes that the scope of s 84(2) extends to restrictions entered into under statutory authority even though they are excluded from the scope of s 84(1).

[38]    A Francis, *Restrictive Covenants and Freehold Land* (3rd ed 2009) para 15-14, refers only to the Chancery Division.

[39]    Draft Bill, cl 39 accordingly makes reference to both High Court and county courts.

[40]    Rule 35 of the Tribunal Procedure (Upper Tribunal) (Lands Chamber) Rules 2010 provides that the proceedings in the Lands Chamber must be stayed pending such an application; where the declaration is required for other reasons the stay is no longer mandatory as it was under rule 6 of the Lands Tribunal Rules 1996.

7.42    It is important for the provisions of section 84(2) to be extended to easements and profits created after reform, and to land obligations, and we so recommend below. In the case of easements, some adjustment is needed to the current wording of section 84(2), which refers closely to the provisions and construction of an "instrument". However, easements (but not profits) will continue to be able to arise by prescription and implication, and the jurisdiction should encompass them all.

7.43    The court's jurisdiction under section 84(2) is not without its problems. Where a declaration is wanted, proceedings must be diverted into court by an application under section 84(2). They proceed under a different roof, therefore, until a declaration is made, and then revert to the Lands Chamber; inevitably, this causes delay and expense. There is some anecdotal evidence that applications for declarations are used as delaying tactics to encourage another party to settle or withdraw.

7.44    We have to ask, therefore, whether the declaration jurisdiction might be given to the Lands Chamber, in addition to the court,[41] so as to avoid the diversion of proceedings in this way.

7.45    Until recently, that has not been an option. Although the President of the Lands Tribunal has always been a judge with expertise in property law, most of its full-time members were surveyors.

7.46    We did raise this point briefly in the Consultation Paper[42] but did not ask a question about it, and we took the view at that stage that the extension of the declaration jurisdiction would not be practicable because too few judges with experience of making declarations sat in the Lands Tribunal (as it then was).

7.47    Nevertheless a number of consultees pointed out the inconvenience and expense entailed by the present position.[43] Andrew Francis,[44] responding to the Consultation Paper, put it thus:

> I see no reason why the jurisdiction to deal with all issues in one forum should not be widened so that the newly constituted Lands Tribunal (in the new Lands Chamber) can deal with both declarations and injunctions as well as modifying or discharging the covenant in the application.

7.48    We now think that there is reason to recommend reform because the position within the Lands Chamber differs from that which applied to the Lands Tribunal. All judges including High Court judges are also now judges of the Upper

---

[41]   We do not suggest that the Court's jurisdiction should be limited to force applications for declarations to proceed by way of the Lands Chamber route. There are occasions where it may be necessary to obtain a declaration alongside the resolution of other matters that can only be heard in Court.

[42]   Consultation Paper, para 14.100.

[43]   See the Analysis of Responses, paras 14.118 to 14.135.

[44]   Barrister, Serle Court Chambers.

Tribunal.[45] The judges currently assigned to the Lands Chamber include a Chancery Division judge and a number of circuit judges who also sit as High Court judges. So the legal expertise within the Lands Chamber is greater and there is the ability to call both on judges currently assigned to the Chamber and on other judges with such expertise as may be needed. In particular the availability of High Court judges should be noted. It makes no sense for proceedings in the Lands Chamber to be adjourned and an application made to the court for a declaration, which might actually come before the judge who was hearing the Lands Chamber application.

7.49 **We recommend that the jurisdiction to make declarations, currently embodied in section 84(2) of the Law of Property Act 1925, be extended to encompass easements created (expressly or otherwise) after reform, profits created after reform, and land obligations; and we recommend that that jurisdiction be exercisable by the Lands Chamber of the Upper Tribunal, as well as by the court when the need for a declaration arises in the course of an application under clause 30 of the draft Bill.**

7.50 That recommendation is put into effect by clause 29(1) of the draft Bill. The practical effect of the reform would be as follows:

(1) if a party would like to have a declaration made in the course of proceedings in the Lands Chamber, he or she could choose between going to court and having the Lands Chamber make the declaration. An application to the court would be costly and time-consuming; it is therefore likely that all parties would choose for the Lands Chamber to make the declaration;

(2) if the desire for a declaration arises from a section 84(3A) decision – reproduced in clause 33 – any party could ask the Lands Chamber to make the declaration, in which case the Lands Chamber – which would have heard the evidence already – would simply express its decision in the form of a declaration. Alternatively any party could apply to the court for a declaration. In either case there might be an appeal against the decision made. The Upper Tribunal's rules would make it clear when and how such an application might be made, for example, within a certain period of the adverse decision, as under the current rule 35(7).

7.51 **We recommend that the Tribunal Procedure (Upper Tribunal) (Lands Chamber) Rules 2010 be amended so as to make the rules necessary to regulate that extended jurisdiction.[46]**

**The grounds for the discharge and modification of interests in land**

7.52 Under this head we discuss: the existing grounds for modification and discharge and their application to new interests, the introduction of new grounds relating to

---

45 Tribunals, Courts and Enforcement Act 2007, s 6.

46 The 2010 rules, together with the recommendations we make, render unnecessary the provision we proposed in the Consultation Paper, para 14.101, relating to the stay of the Lands Chamber's proceeding pending application to the court for a declaration. See the Analysis of Responses, paras 14.114 to 14.135.

positive obligations and apportionment arrangements, the Lands Chamber's power to add new provisions to existing interests, and the use of alternative grounds against different objectors.

### The existing grounds and their extension to the new interests

7.53 Section 84(1) and subsections (1A) to (1C) set out the current grounds for the modification and discharge of restrictions. To summarise, a restriction can be modified or discharged if the Lands Chamber is satisfied that:

(1) it ought to be deemed to be obsolete because of changes in the character of the property or the neighbourhood or other circumstances;[47]

(2) it impedes some reasonable use of the land and either does not give those entitled to the benefit of it any practical benefits of substantial value or advantage to them, or is contrary to the public interest;[48]

(3) everyone of full age and capacity entitled to the benefit of the restriction has agreed, expressly or impliedly, to its modification or discharge;[49] or

(4) the proposed discharge or modification will not injure those entitled to the benefit of the restriction.[50]

7.54 We explained above that we have reached the conclusion that the existing grounds for the discharge and modification of restrictions should not be changed, and that easements, profits and land obligations should be governed by these grounds too.

7.55 **We recommend that the grounds for modification and discharge of restrictions, currently contained in section 84 of the Law of Property Act 1925, be applied to the modification and discharge of easements, profits and land obligations.**

7.56 In the draft Bill, grounds for discharge are set out in schedule 2; we say more below about the detail of the provisions of that schedule.[51] For now, we have to ask whether any additional provisions are needed in the light of the extension of the Lands Chamber's jurisdiction to future easements and profits, and to positive land obligations.

---

[47] LPA 1925, s 84(1)(a).

[48] LPA 1925, s 84(1)(aa) and s 84(1A).

[49] LPA 1925, s 84(1)(b).

[50] LPA 1925, s 84(1)(c).

[51] See paras 7.84 to 7.89 below.

7.57    We asked consultees if they thought that additional grounds are required for easements and profits. None were suggested,[52] and we do not recommend any, although we have to say more, below, about some of the detail of the orders that may be made when an easement or profit is modified.[53]

7.58    However, the jurisdiction to modify and discharge easements and profits will be a new one, and unfamiliar to Lands Chamber judges. Discharge may well be more straightforward than modification, because the latter may involve some creative measures such as the change of the route of an easement. One consultee told us about a case where an easement from a factory to a road had followed a circuitous route around a number of streets and corners; later the buildings between the factory and the road were all demolished and it would have been far better for the route of the easement to pass straight over the servient land rather than following the lines of streets that were no longer there. The jurisdiction to modify should be able to deal with cases like that.

7.59    The jurisdiction to modify easements and profits in this way is new, and some guidance may be helpful and we make the following recommendation with that in view.

**7.60    We recommend that the Lands Chamber of the Upper Tribunal should only modify an easement or profit if it is satisfied that the modified interest will not be materially less convenient to the benefited owner and will be no more burdensome to the land affected.**

### Additional grounds and powers relating to positive obligations

7.61    We do not recommend any additional grounds for the modification and discharge of restrictive land obligations. These will be functionally identical to restrictive covenants and there is no reason for there to be any different grounds for their modification or discharge.

7.62    Positive land obligations are a different matter. One of the reasons why the law has not been quick to extend the scope of property rights to positive obligations is the fear that land will become sterile through being bound by obligations that are difficult to get rid of. An obligation that was initially reasonable and moderate may become unduly onerous because of a change in the price of materials or a change in the character of a neighbourhood, or perhaps because one or more of the properties involved in a development has been demolished or even because of some extreme event such as coastal erosion. These sorts of happenings are a considerable risk, potentially, to neighbouring landowners whose interests are linked by positive land obligations. It is therefore generally agreed that if it is to be possible to bind land with positive obligations, it must be possible to get rid of them or to modify them on reasonably flexible grounds.

---

[52]    See our question at Consultation Paper, para 14.95 and the Analysis of Responses, paras 14.107 to 14.113.

[53]    We have not discovered additional grounds used in other statutes for the modification of easements and profits; the Australian states and New Zealand all have provisions derived from section 84 encompassing the discharge and modification of easements, none of which has additional grounds designed for easements.

7.63    We made two provisional proposals in the Consultation Paper for additional grounds relevant to positive land obligations. One follows directly from the comments we have just made about changing circumstances, and would enable a positive obligation to be discharged or modified because performance of it has become impracticable or disproportionately expensive when compared with the benefit that it confers. Consultees agreed with that proposal;[54] we continue to regard it as extremely important and indeed as a provision without which the introduction of proprietary positive obligations could not be recommended.

7.64    The other provisional proposal related to reciprocal payment obligations. It will be clear that we envisage that wide use will be made of reciprocal payment obligations; X enters into a land obligation to repair the boundary between his land and Y's, and Y enters into a reciprocal payment obligation to pay half the cost. Similar arrangements will be able to be made with a shared road.

7.65    There will therefore be occasions when the modification of a positive land obligation will mean that it is necessary, in the interests of fairness, to make a consequential modification to a reciprocal payment obligation, and indeed when a reciprocal payment obligation is modified or discharged with the result that it is necessary to discharge the corresponding obligation. But it may be that application is made to modify or discharge only one of the linked obligations.

7.66    For example, Y may apply for the terms of his payment obligation to be modified so that he no longer has to fund the use of a material which has become unreasonably expensive (in circumstances where the job could be done adequately with something different). If his application succeeded, then depending upon the precise terms of X's obligation it is likely to be appropriate for the Lands Chamber to have power, whether or not application was made, to order the corresponding modification to X's obligation.[55]

7.67    We made a proposal in the Consultation Paper about the linking of the discharge or modification of reciprocal payment obligations and the corresponding positive obligation,[56] and consultees agreed with our proposal. In recommending a provision along the lines we have just described, we also make a recommendation that encompasses a more complex situation, where more than one reciprocal payment obligation was set up to contribute to the cost of carrying out a positive obligation. In such a case, it might be that the release of one of the properties burdened by the payment obligation[57] would leave a shortfall, which could only be met by the adjustment of the other reciprocal payment obligations.

---

[54]    Consultation Paper, para 14.93 and Analysis of Responses, paras 14.78 to 14.106.

[55]    A similar situation might arise where the application was to modify the performance obligation; but in that case the reciprocal payment obligation might not need modification, since payment can only be demanded for the work actually done: see the draft Bill, cl 9(2).

[56]    Consultation Paper, para 14.94; see the Analysis of Responses, paras 14.81 to 14.106.

[57]    There might be any number of good reasons for the release; the dramatic example is where the burdened property actually disappears due to coastal erosion. For more practical examples see the Analysis of Responses, paras 14.101 to 14.106.

So we have made provision for that eventuality.[58] We set out a worked example in the Analysis of Responses.[59]

7.68 So the special grounds for modification and discharge that we recommend for positive land obligations are as follows:

**7.69 We recommend that the Lands Chamber of the Upper Tribunal should have the power to modify or discharge a positive land obligation if, as a result of changes in circumstances, performance of the obligation has ceased to be reasonably practicable or has become unreasonably expensive when compared with the benefit that it confers.**

**7.70 We recommend that the Lands Chamber of the Upper Tribunal should have the power, whenever a positive obligation is discharged or modified, also to discharge or modify a reciprocal payment obligation owed in respect of that covenant, and *vice versa*.**

**7.71 We recommend that where the Lands Chamber of the Upper Tribunal makes an order which modifies or discharges a reciprocal payment obligation, it may on the application of the person subject to the related obligation ("the performance obligation") also modify another reciprocal payment related to the performance obligation, if without such an order the burden of the costs of complying with the performance obligation will not be appropriately distributed.**

7.72 These additional grounds relating to positive obligations are to be found in paragraph 8 of schedule 2 to the draft Bill and in clause 32(5), (6) and (7).

### *An additional provision for apportionment arrangements*

7.73 We explained in Part 6 the need to make provision for the apportionment of responsibility for compliance with positive obligations when the land burdened by such an obligation is sub-divided. The servient owners must remain jointly and severally liable to the dominant owner, so that he or she can pursue any or all the servient owners for the whole obligation; but between themselves the servient owners must be able to look to a rule that determines how they share responsibility. There are two possibilities: either the liability is apportioned by area under the default rule,[60] or the parties enter into an agreement for apportionment which will function as a positive land obligation (generally vis-à-vis both servient owners; but such arrangements might also oblige just one of them to be liable to the other for the whole payment).

---

[58] Again, the point is to enable the Lands Chamber to make an order even if no application had been made in a situation where several obligations are linked. All those concerned would in any event be given notice of the proceedings, but they could not be forced to participate. This is the only circumstance in which an application to discharge or modify a positive obligation (in this case a reciprocal payment obligation) can be made by the benefited, rather than the burdened, party. See para 7.71 below.

[59] See the Analysis of Responses, paras 14.102 to 14.106.

[60] Draft Bill, sch 1.

7.74 However, in some instances the default apportionment rule will be inappropriate, yet the servient owners may be unable to agree an alternative apportionment. Likewise, an apportionment agreement that was initially appropriate may cease to be so, as a result of a change in circumstances. So it is important that the Lands Chamber should be able to change apportionment arrangements, whether arising under the default rule or from an express agreement, on the application of any or all parties to it and in a way that binds all the relevant servient owners.

7.75 **We recommend that the Lands Chamber of the Upper Tribunal should be able to make an order modifying or discharging an obligation to make an apportionment payment if the payment as it stands obliges someone to make payments that are substantially out of proportion to the benefit conferred on that person.**

7.76 This recommendation is embodied in clause 35 of the draft Bill, which enables the Lands Chamber to adjust the default apportionment rule in an individual case, and by paragraph 9 of schedule 2 to the draft Bill which enables the Lands Chamber to modify an apportionment agreement.

### *A power to add new provisions*

7.77 Section 84(1C) declares that the Lands Chamber's power to modify restrictions includes a power to add new restrictions if the applicant accepts that; and, of course, that the Lands Chamber may refuse to make the order requested unless the new restriction is added. The subsection is declaratory; when it was added to section 84 it made no change but merely clarified the law.

7.78 What it does is to spell out the idea of "modification", which must include some re-shaping of the interest under consideration but is not to include any new burden unless the applicant agrees. Underlying this is the idea that the original restriction remains in place, although its content is altered. The effect is that the priority of the additional restriction will be the same as that of the original one; the same people will be bound by it and will benefit from it. The shell of the original restriction remains intact but its content has changed.[61]

7.79 The modification of land obligations, positive and negative, must follow the same thinking, and we made provisional proposals to that effect in the Consultation Paper.[62] We distinguished the sort of new provisions that might be imposed in the case of restrictive covenants and those that might be imposed in the case of land obligations; in the latter case we took the view that it might in narrowly defined circumstances be appropriate to dispense with consent to the imposition of a new land obligation. In the main, consultees agreed; but the proposal about dispensing with consent met with significant resistance and we have not pursued it.[63]

---

[61] G L Newsom, *Preston and Newsom: Restrictive Covenants Affecting Freehold Land* (9th ed 1998) para 10-42.

[62] Consultation Paper, paras 14.82 and 14.83.

[63] See the Analysis of Responses, paras 14.62 to 14.77.

**7.80** **We recommend that the power of the Lands Chamber of the Upper Tribunal to modify a land obligation should include power to add new provisions to the interest, if the change appears to the Chamber to be reasonable and the applicant does not object; equally, the Lands Chamber may refuse to modify an interest unless an additional provision is accepted by the applicant.**

7.81 This is reflected in clause 32(1) of the draft Bill; the clause incorporates the existing law relating to restrictions and applies it equally to land obligations.

7.82 Our provisional proposal in the Consultation Paper also related to easements and profits. Modification in the context of these interests has a somewhat different flavour; while the assumption underlying section 84(1C) is that a restriction is being relaxed, and that remains the thinking behind clause 32(1), the idea of modification does not have very ready application to the modification of easements and profits. Moreover, it may be impossible to say whether a modification of an easement or profit amounts to a modified interest or to a new interest. If the route of a right of way is changed, at what point is the change so great that it amounts to the substitution of a new easement? So we make a further recommendation in relation to the modification of easements and profits, which is reflected in clause 32(2) of the draft Bill, in order to ensure that this ambiguity does not cause difficulty.

**7.83** **We recommend that the power of the Lands Chamber of the Upper Tribunal to modify easements and profits should include power to provide for the interest to have effect as a different kind of easement or profit, if the change appears to the Chamber to be reasonable and the applicant does not object; equally, the Lands Chamber may refuse to modify an easement or profit unless such a change is accepted by the applicant.**

### Establishing alternative grounds for discharge and modification

7.84 Section 84 sets out four different grounds for the modification and discharge of restrictions. We have retained these in the draft Bill and have recommended that they be applicable to all the interests that fall within the scope of the Lands Chamber's jurisdiction. The grounds are now to be found in schedule 2 to the draft Bill.

7.85 What is perhaps not instantly clear from section 84 is whether the same ground must be established against all the objectors to an application. Clearly a restriction either is or is not deemed to be obsolete (section 84(1)(a)), and if the Lands Chamber is satisfied of that ground then that holds good against all possible objectors. Equally, either all those entitled to the benefit, of full age and capacity, have agreed or they have not. But it does not seem obvious that it should be impossible for the Lands Chamber to discharge or modify an interest where some of those entitled have agreed while the rest (who have not agreed) will not be injured by the order sought (section 84(1)(c)).

7.86    In the Consultation Paper we made a provisional proposal to the effect that it should be possible to establish different grounds against different objectors, and consultees agreed.[64]

**7.87    We recommend that where different grounds for modification or discharge of an interest are established against different persons who hold the benefit of the interest, that should be sufficient for the Lands Chamber of the Upper Tribunal to make an order.**

7.88    Schedule 2 of the draft Bill manages this by separating out two grounds that are not specific to different objectors; it may be that the interest is obsolete (paragraph 1) or that all those concerned who are of full age and capacity have agreed (paragraph 2). The rest of the grounds applicable to all the interests within the Lands Chamber's jurisdiction, including the one relating to consent, are made available as alternatives (paragraphs 3 to 6).

7.89    Part 2 of schedule 2 sets outs grounds relevant to positive land obligations, and the issue about the use of alternative grounds does not arise in this context because the grounds refer to the burdened land or owner rather than to the potential objectors.

---

[64]    Consultation Paper, para 14.74. Some consultees felt that we were proposing that it should not be necessary to establish grounds against *all* objectors, but that was not our proposal; aside from that misunderstanding, consultees agreed with our proposal; see the Analysis of Responses, paras 14.47 to 14.58.

# PART 8
# LIST OF RECOMMENDATIONS

## PART 3: REFORM OF THE LAW OF EASEMENTS AND PROFITS

8.1 We recommend that profits should, for the future, be able to be created only by express grant or reservation or by statute.

**[paragraph 3.9]**

8.2 We recommend that in determining whether an easement should be implied, it should not be material whether the easement would take effect by grant or by reservation.

**[paragraph 3.30]**

8.3 We recommend that an easement shall be implied as a term of a disposition where it is necessary for the reasonable use of the land at that date, bearing in mind:

(1) the use of the land at the time of the grant;

(2) the presence on the servient land of any relevant physical features;

(3) any intention for the future use of the land, known to both parties at the time of the grant;

(4) so far as relevant, the available routes for the easement sought; and

(5) the potential interference with the servient land or inconvenience to the servient owner.

**[paragraph 3.45]**

8.4 We recommend that section 62 of the Law of Property Act 1925 shall no longer operate to transform precarious benefits into legal easements or profits on a conveyance of land.

**[paragraph 3.64]**

8.5 We recommend that section 62 of the Law of Property Act 1925 should continue to be able to convert easements, but not profits, from leasehold to freehold interests.

**[paragraph 3.69]**

8.6 We recommend that the current law of prescription should be abolished, and replaced with a new statutory scheme for the prescriptive acquisition of easements.

**[paragraph 3.113]**

8.7    We recommend that:

    (1)    an easement will arise by prescription on completion of 20 years' continuous qualifying use;

    (2)    qualifying use shall be use without force, without stealth and without permission; and

    (3)    qualifying use shall not be use which is contrary to the criminal law, unless such use can be rendered lawful by the dispensation of the servient owner.

**[paragraph 3.123]**

8.8    We recommend that qualifying use must be carried out by, and against, a freeholder.

**[paragraph 3.150]**

8.9    We recommend that rights to light created under the new scheme shall be subject to any local usage or custom to which they are currently subject.

**[paragraph 3.161]**

8.10    We recommend that use of land cannot be qualifying use, for the purposes of prescription, at any time when the land is in the freehold ownership of a person or body who is not competent to grant an easement over it.

**[paragraph 3.168]**

8.11    We recommend that use of land which is let shall not amount to qualifying use at any time when the servient freehold owner does not have power to prevent the use while the lease continues, or does not know about it and could not reasonably have discovered it, unless

    (1)    the use began before the lease was granted; and

    (2)    at the time when the lease was granted the landlord knew about the use or could reasonably have discovered it.

**[paragraph 3.172]**

8.12    We recommend that it shall not be possible to prescribe for a right to light, under the new scheme, against Crown land.

**[paragraph 3.177]**

8.13    We recommend that the new statutory scheme for prescription that we recommend shall apply to use that commenced before the implementation of reform, subject to the recommendation that follows.

**[paragraph 3.185]**

8.14 We recommend that the Prescription Act 1832 shall continue in force for one year after the implementation of reform, in order to enable potential claimants who, at the date of implementation, are in a position to take advantage of sections 1, 2 or 3 of that Act or are within one year of being able to do so to make their claim.

**[paragraph 3.186]**

8.15 We recommend that a right to use another's land in a way that prevents that other from making any reasonable use of it will not for that reason fail to be an easement.

**[paragraph 3.209]**

8.16 We recommend that where an easement or profit has not been used for a continuous period of 20 years, there should be a rebuttable presumption that it has been abandoned.

**[paragraph 3.230]**

8.17 We recommend:

(1) that the decision in *Wall v Collins,* that an easement that benefits a lease survives the termination of the leasehold estate by merger with the freehold, be reversed by statute but

(2) that statute should provide a mechanism to enable the reversioner, on merger and surrender, (or the tenant, where there is a surrender and re-grant) to elect to keep the benefit of interests appurtenant to the lease surrendered or merged.

**[paragraph 3.255]**

8.18 We recommend that Land Registry make rules to enable an election to be made in cases where title to the relevant estate is registered, or where application is made to register that estate because the transaction concerned is a registrable disposition.

**[paragraph 3.259]**

8.19 We recommend that where title to the relevant estate is unregistered, the election should be made by endorsement on the document that evidences the title of the person who made the election.

**[paragraph 3.261]**

## PART 4: REFORMS FOR REGISTERED TITLES

8.20 We recommend that statute should state, for the avoidance of doubt, that section 58(1) has no effect in relation to an entry made in pursuance of an instrument that purports to create an easement that does not accommodate and serve the dominant land.

**[paragraph 4.17]**

8.21    We recommend that provided that title to the benefited and burdened land is registered, the fact that they are in common ownership and possession shall not prevent the creation or existence of easements or profits.

**[paragraph 4.44]**

8.22    We recommend that the express variation or release of a registered appurtenant interest shall be a registrable disposition pursuant to section 27 of the Land Registration Act 2002.

**[paragraph 4.57]**

8.23    We recommend that Land Registry investigate the feasibility of making provision for short-form easements in Land Registration Rules and, if provision is thought feasible, that it draft and consult upon the necessary Rules.

**[paragraph 4.64]**

## PART 5: COVENANTS: THE CASE FOR REFORM

8.24    We recommend that the owner of an estate in land shall be able to create positive and negative obligations that will be able to take effect (subject to the formal requirements for the creation of legal interests) as legal interests appurtenant to another estate in land, and therefore as registrable interests pursuant to the Land Registration Act 2002, provided that:

(1)    the benefit of the obligation touches and concerns the benefited land;

(2)    the obligation is either:

(a)    an obligation not to do something on the burdened land;

(b)    an obligation to do something on the burdened land or on the boundary (or any structure or feature that is treated as marking or lying on the boundary) of the burdened and benefited land; or

(c)    an obligation to make a payment in return for the performance of an obligation of the kind mentioned in paragraph (b); and

(3)    the obligation is not made between lessor and lessee and relating to the demised premises.

**[paragraph 5.69]**

8.25    We recommend that for the future, covenants made by the owner of an estate in land and that satisfy the conditions set out above shall take effect, not as promises and not in accordance with the current law relating to restrictive covenants, but as legal interests in the burdened land, appurtenant to the benefited estate in land.

**[paragraph 5.70]**

8.26 We recommend that following the implementation of reform it should no longer be possible to create freehold covenants enforceable under *Tulk v Moxhay*.

**[paragraph 5.89]**

8.27 We recommend that, for the future, an obligation to fence must take effect as a land obligation and not as an easement.

**[paragraph 5.94]**

**PART 6: A NEW LEGAL INTEREST IN LAND**

8.28 We recommend that it shall be possible to create obligations ancillary to the legal interests recommended above, and that such obligations shall also be able to take effect as legal interests in land.

**[paragraph 6.36]**

8.29 We recommend that where title to the burdened land is unregistered, the burden of a land obligation be registrable as a land charge under the Land Charges Act 1972, and if not registered should be void against a purchaser of the burdened land or of any interest in that land.

**[paragraph 6.57]**

8.30 We recommend that land obligations, whether restrictive or positive, should be incapable of creation by implication or prescription, and that section 62 of the Law of Property Act 1925 should not operate so as to create a land obligation or to convert one from a leasehold to a freehold interest.

**[paragraph 6.62]**

8.31 We recommend that where land burdened by a land obligation is registered voluntarily, and the obligation is not noted in the charges register because it was not registered as a land charge, this shall not amount to a mistake on the register for the purposes of schedule 8 to the Land Registration Act 2002.

**[paragraph 6.73]**

8.32 We recommend that statute should state, for the avoidance of doubt, that section 58(1) of the Land Registration Act 2002 has no effect in relation to an entry made in pursuance of an instrument that purports to create a land obligation that does not touch and concern the dominant land.

**[paragraph 6.78]**

8.33 We recommend that provided that title to the benefited and burdened land is registered, the fact that they are in common ownership and possession shall not prevent the creation or existence of land obligations.

**[paragraph 6.83]**

8.34    We recommend that Land Registry investigate the feasibility of making provision for short-form land obligations in Land Registration Rules and, if provision is thought feasible, that it draft and consult upon the necessary rules.

**[paragraph 6.89]**

8.35    We recommend that the benefit of a land obligation shall be appurtenant to the estate in land for the benefit of which it is imposed and shall therefore be transmitted with that estate and to any estates (but not to interests) derived out of it.

**[paragraph 6.98]**

8.36    We recommend that where more than one estate has the benefit of a reciprocal payment obligation, only the proprietor of an estate who has incurred the relevant expenditure in carrying out the linked obligation shall be entitled to recover the payment (and if more than one, in proportion to their expenditure).

**[paragraph 6.99]**

8.37    We recommend that the burden of a restrictive land obligation should be transmitted to all estates and interests derived out of the burdened estate, and to all occupiers of the burdened land, save for:

(1)     the owner of an estate or interest that has priority to the land obligation (and an occupier authorised by such an owner); and

(2)     a mortgagee of the burdened land who is not in possession of it.

**[paragraph 6.104]**

8.38    We recommend that the burden of a positive land obligation be transmitted:

(1)     to estates derived out of a burdened estate which confer a right to immediate possession of the burdened land, in accordance with the normal priority rules, save that the burden of a positive obligation shall not pass to a lease for seven years or less; and

(2)     to mortgagees when they come into possession of a burdened estate.

**[paragraph 6.115]**

8.39    We recommend that where a landlord and a tenant are both burdened by a positive land obligation, the landlord shall be liable to the tenant if the tenant suffers loss as a result of the landlord's breach of the obligation unless the parties expressly provide otherwise in the relevant lease.

**[paragraph 6.116]**

8.40    We recommend that where property burdened by a positive obligation is divided, the resulting estates should be jointly and severally liable on the obligation, but that liability between those estates should be apportioned in the proportions which, in the absence of express apportionment, will be based upon the areas which their respective parts bear to the area of the burdened property.

**[paragraph 6.126]**

8.41    We recommend that where land burdened by a positive obligation is divided, and the parties (that is, the various servient owners) agree between themselves the extent to which both (or all) are liable to perform the obligation, the obligations arising under that agreement shall be land obligations.

**[paragraph 6.131]**

8.42    We recommend that both an adverse possessor of land, who has not made a successful application to be registered as proprietor to that land, and an adverse possessor of unregistered land who has had his or her own title registered, should be subject to the land obligations that bound the estate of the dispossessed proprietor.

**[paragraph 6.144]**

8.43    We recommend that breach of a land obligation shall be enforceable by action.

**[paragraph 6.148]**

8.44    We recommend that a person who is bound by a negative land obligation breaches it by doing something which it prohibits, or by permitting or suffering someone else to do so; and that a person who is bound by a positive obligation breaches it if the obligation is not performed.

**[paragraph 6.154]**

8.45    We recommend no amount should be payable under a reciprocal payment obligation in respect of work not carried out to a reasonable standard; and that in determining the amount payable under such an obligation, only costs which are reasonably incurred in performing the obligation for which payment is made are to be taken into account.

**[paragraph 6.157]**

8.46    We recommend that on proof of breach a court may, in its discretion grant an injunction, make an order for performance of the obligation, or for payment of damages or of the payment of the amount due under the obligation.

**[paragraph 6.165]**

8.47    We recommend that contract principles be applied to the calculation of damages for breach of a land obligation.

**[paragraph 6.166]**

8.48    We recommend that the limitation period for liability for breach of a land obligation shall be twelve years.

**[paragraph 6.171]**

8.49    We recommend that where there is provision for self-help by the dominant owner in the terms of the land obligation, the fact that the dominant owner chooses not to exercise that right should not reduce damages payable by the servient owner for breach of the obligation.

**[paragraph 6.176]**

8.50    We recommend that where the dominant owner is entitled to exercise self-help and does so, the costs of the work should be recoverable from the servient owner who should have carried out the work, but only insofar as the cost is reasonable and the work done to a reasonable standard. Liability for such a payment should be joint and several where more than one servient owner is subject to the same obligation.

**[paragraph 6.177]**

8.51    We recommend that where land that is burdened or benefited by a positive land obligation (including an obligation to make an apportionment payment) escheats, the Crown shall not be bound by that obligation, or entitled to enforce it (as the case may be), unless it takes possession or control of the land.

**[paragraph 6.185]**

## PART 7: THE JURISDICTION OF THE LANDS CHAMBER OF THE UPPER TRIBUNAL

8.52    We recommend that the jurisdiction of the Lands Chamber of the Upper Tribunal be extended so as to enable it to make orders for the modification or discharge of:

(1)     easements and profits created after reform; and

(2)     land obligations.

**[paragraph 7.35]**

8.53    We recommend that the jurisdiction of the Lands Chamber of the Upper Tribunal should, following reform, be extended to include leasehold land of any term.

**[paragraph 7.38]**

8.54    We recommend that the jurisdiction to make declarations, currently embodied in section 84(2) of the Law of Property Act 1925, be extended to encompass easements created (expressly or otherwise) after reform, profits created after reform, and land obligations; and we recommend that that jurisdiction be exercisable by the Lands Chamber of the Upper Tribunal, as well as by the court when the need for a declaration arises in the course of an application under clause 30 of the draft Bill.

**[paragraph 7.49]**

8.55    We recommend that the Tribunal Procedure (Upper Tribunal) (Lands Chamber) Rules 2010 be amended so as to make the rules necessary to regulate that extended jurisdiction.

**[paragraph 7.51]**

8.56    We recommend that the grounds for modification and discharge of restrictions, currently contained in section 84 of the Law of Property Act 1925, be applied to the modification and discharge of easements, profits and land obligations.

**[paragraph 7.55]**

8.57    We recommend that the Lands Chamber of the Upper Tribunal should only modify an easement or profit if it is satisfied that the modified interest will not be materially less convenient to the benefited owner and will be no more burdensome to the land affected.

**[paragraph 7.60]**

8.58    We recommend that the Lands Chamber of the Upper Tribunal should have the power to modify or discharge a positive land obligation if, as a result of changes in circumstances, performance of the obligation has ceased to be reasonably practicable or has become unreasonably expensive when compared with the benefit that it confers.

**[paragraph 7.69]**

8.59    We recommend that the Lands Chamber of the Upper Tribunal should have the power, whenever a positive obligation is discharged or modified, also to discharge or modify a reciprocal payment obligation owed in respect of that covenant, and *vice versa*.

**[paragraph 7.70]**

8.60    We recommend that where the Lands Chamber of the Upper Tribunal makes an order which modifies or discharges a reciprocal payment obligation, it may on the application of the person subject to the related obligation ("the performance obligation") also modify another reciprocal payment related to the performance obligation, if without such an order the burden of the costs of complying with the performance obligation will not be appropriately distributed.

**[paragraph 7.71]**

8.61    We recommend that the Lands Chamber of the Upper Tribunal should be able to make an order modifying or discharging an obligation to make an apportionment payment if the payment as it stands obliges someone to make payments that are substantially out of proportion to the benefit conferred on that person.

**[paragraph 7.75]**

8.62    We recommend that the power of the Lands Chamber of the Upper Tribunal to modify a land obligation should include power to add new provisions to the interest, if the change appears to the Chamber to be reasonable and the applicant does not object; equally, the Lands Chamber may refuse to modify an interest unless an additional provision is accepted by the applicant.

**[paragraph 7.80]**

8.63 We recommend that the power of the Lands Chamber of the Upper Tribunal to modify easements and profits should include power to provide for the interest to have effect as a different kind of easement or profit, if the change appears to the Chamber to be reasonable and the applicant does not object; equally, the Lands Chamber may refuse to modify an easement or profit unless such a change is accepted by the applicant.

**[paragraph 7.83]**

8.64 We recommend that where different grounds for modification or discharge of an interest are established against different persons who hold the benefit of the interest, that should be sufficient for the Lands Chamber of the Upper Tribunal to make an order.

**[paragraph 7.87]**

(*Signed*)  JAMES MUNBY, *Chairman*
ELIZABETH COOKE
DAVID HERTZELL
DAVID ORMEROD
FRANCES PATTERSON

MARK ORMEROD, *Chief Executive*
20 May 2011

# APPENDIX A
# DRAFT BILL AND EXPLANATORY NOTES

# Law of Property Bill

## CONTENTS

### PART 1

### ATTACHING OBLIGATIONS TO LAND

*Imposition of obligations*

1   Power to impose obligations
2   Conversion of future covenants

*Benefit and burden*

3   Benefit of obligations
4   Burden of negative obligations
5   Burden of positive obligations

*Breach and enforcement*

6   Breach of obligations
7   Enforcement of obligations
8   Recovery of costs of self-help

*Liability under reciprocal payment obligations*

9   Limitation of liability
10   Liability to more than one estate owner

*Special rules*

11   Allocation between co-obligees of responsibility for performance
12   Obligations relating to land which defaults to the Crown
13   [Application of Part to the Crown]

*Interpretation*

14   Construction of statutory references to interests, or rights, in or over land
15   Interpretation of Part

PART 2

EASEMENTS, PROFITS AND OBLIGATIONS UNDER SECTION 1

*Prescription*

16   Acquisition of easements by long use
17   "Qualifying use" for the purposes of section 16
18   Easements and profits: repeal of existing law

*Implication*

19   Certain rights not to be capable of creation by implication
20   Implied grant or reservation of easements
21   Restriction of effect of section 62 Law of Property Act 1925

*Effect of unity of ownership and possession*

22   Creation and extinction of obligations under section 1: general law
23   Creation and extinction of rights appurtenant to registered land

*Subject-matter of easements*

24   Abolition of ouster principle
25   No new easements of fencing

*Miscellaneous*

26   Effect of determination of leasehold estate on appurtenant rights
27   Non-use of easements and profits: presumption of abandonment
28   Variation and release of appurtenant rights: registered land

PART 3

POWERS WITH RESPECT TO INTERESTS ETC AFFECTING LAND

29   Declarations about certain interests affecting land
30   Discharge and modification of certain interests affecting land
31   Matters relevant to power under section 30
32   Supplementary powers
33   Proceedings under section 30
34   Staying of proceedings pending application under section 30
35   Displacement of default allocation rules
36   Making of orders without production of instrument
37   Effect of orders
38   Transition
39   Interpretation of Part

PART 4

GENERAL

40   Crown application
41   Minor and consequential amendments and repeals

42    Saving for certain profits
43    Short title, commencement and extent

———————————

Schedule 1 — Responsibility for performance of positive obligations: default
            allocation rules
Schedule 2 — Grounds for making orders under section 30
     Part 1 — General grounds
     Part 2 — Grounds specific to positive obligations
Schedule 3 — Minor and consequential amendments
Schedule 4 — Repeals

DRAFT

OF A

# B I L L

TO

Make provision about attaching obligations to land; to make provision about easements, profits a prendre and obligations attached to land; to restate section 84 of the Law of Property Act 1925, with modifications; and for connected purposes.

**B** E IT ENACTED by the Queen's most Excellent Majesty, by and with the advice and consent of the Lords Spiritual and Temporal, and Commons, in this present Parliament assembled, and by the authority of the same, as follows: —

## PART 1

### ATTACHING OBLIGATIONS TO LAND

*Imposition of obligations*

**1 Power to impose obligations**

(1) The owner of an estate in land may burden the land in which the estate subsists    5
with a qualifying obligation.

(2) The power to impose an obligation under subsection (1) may be exercised
only —
     (a) for the benefit of an estate in land, and
     (b) if the benefit of the obligation touches and concerns the land in which    10
the benefited estate subsists.

(3) Subject to subsection (4), the following are qualifying obligations for the
purposes of this section —
     (a) an obligation not to do something on the land burdened by the
obligation;    15
     (b) an obligation to do something —
         (i) on the land burdened by the obligation, or

        (ii)   in relation to any structure or feature that marks, or lies on, or is treated as marking, or lying on, the boundary of the land burdened by the obligation and the land in which the benefited estate subsists;

    (c)   an obligation to make a reciprocal payment;     *5*

    (d)   an obligation under an apportionment arrangement with respect to a positive obligation imposed under subsection (1).

(4)   An obligation is not a qualifying obligation for the purposes of this section if—

    (a)   the parties to the obligation are the lessor and lessee under a lease, and

    (b)   the obligation relates to the demised premises under the lease.     *10*

(5)   The reference in subsection (3)(c) to a reciprocal payment is to a payment of costs incurred in the performance of an obligation imposed under subsection (1) which—

    (a)   is owed to the person liable to make the payment, and

    (b)   is of a kind mentioned in subsection (3)(b).     *15*

(6)   The power under subsection (1) includes power to impose an obligation ancillary to the performance of a qualifying obligation; and any obligation imposed by virtue of this subsection is to be regarded as taking effect as part of the obligation to the performance of which it is ancillary.

**2    Conversion of future covenants**     *20*

(1)   This section applies to a covenant made on or after the date on which section 1 comes into force if—

    (a)   the covenantor is the owner of an estate in land,

    (b)   the obligation under the covenant is of a kind which is capable of being imposed under section 1 on the land in which the covenantor's estate    *25* subsists,

    (c)   the benefit of the covenant touches and concerns land in which the covenantee has an estate, and

    (d)   the covenant is not expressed to be personal to the covenantor or covenantee.     *30*

(2)   A covenant to which this section applies is to be treated as not being the making by the covenantor of a promise but as an exercise by the covenantor of the power conferred by section 1, under which the land in which the covenantor's estate subsists is burdened with the covenanted obligation for the benefit of the covenantee's estate.     *35*

*Benefit and burden*

**3    Benefit of obligations**

(1)   The benefit of an obligation imposed under section 1 is appurtenant to the estate in land for the benefit of which the obligation is imposed.

(2)   As an appurtenant right, the benefit of such an obligation is, in particular,    *40* capable of passing (expressly or by operation of law) to the owner of a freehold or leasehold estate in the benefited land, or any part of it, which—

    (a)   is created or acquired after the imposition of the obligation, and

    (b)   derives from the benefited estate.

**4    Burden of negative obligations**

(1)    A negative obligation imposed under section 1 binds the owner of the burdened estate and, subject to subsections (2) and (3) —

    (a)    the owner of any other estate or interest in the burdened land, and

    (b)    any occupier of the burdened land.                                             5

(2)    Subsection (1)(a) does not apply to the owner of an estate or interest which has priority over the interest constituted by the negative obligation.

(3)    Subsection (1)(b) does not apply to a person whose occupation is authorised by the owner of an estate or interest which has priority over the interest constituted by the negative obligation.                                           10

**5    Burden of positive obligations**

(1)    A positive obligation imposed under section 1 binds —

    (a)    the owner of the burdened estate, and

    (b)    subject to subsection (2), the owner of any other estate or interest which confers a right to immediate possession of the burdened land.         15

(2)    Subsection (1)(b) does not apply to —

    (a)    the owner of an estate or interest which has priority over the interest constituted by the positive obligation, or

    (b)    the owner of a leasehold estate granted for a period of seven years or less from the date of the grant.                                              20

(3)    The reference in subsection (1) to a right to immediate possession of the burdened land includes the right to receive any rents and profits of the land.

(4)    In subsection (3), "rent" has the same meaning as in the Law of Property Act 1925.

*Breach and enforcement*                                                            25

**6    Breach of obligations**

(1)    A person bound by a negative obligation imposed under section 1 breaches the obligation by —

    (a)    doing something which it prohibits, or

    (b)    permitting or suffering another person to do such a thing.              30

(2)    A person bound by a positive obligation imposed under section 1 breaches the obligation if it is not performed.

(3)    However, a person bound by an obligation imposed under section 1 only because of ownership of a charge is not capable of breaching the obligation unless the right to possession under the charge is being exercised.         35

(4)    If non-performance of a positive obligation imposed under section 1 results in breach of the obligation by more than one person, the liability of those in breach is joint and several.

(5)    In this section, "charge" means any mortgage, charge or lien for securing money or money's worth.                                                          40

**7   Enforcement of obligations**

(1)   An obligation imposed under section 1 is enforceable by action.

(2)   In proceedings for the enforcement of an obligation imposed under section 1 the available remedies are—

    (a)   injunction,

    (b)   specific performance,

    (c)   damages, and

    (d)   order for payment of an amount due under the obligation.

(3)   Contract principles apply to damages for breach of an obligation imposed under section 1.

(4)   If damages are awarded to any person for breach of an obligation imposed under section 1 which requires the carrying out of works, the amount of damages is not to be reduced on the ground that the works are ones which that person could lawfully have carried out.

**8   Recovery of costs of self-help**

(1)   Subsection (2) applies if a person entitled to the benefit of a positive obligation imposed under section 1 lawfully carries out works which the obligation requires to be carried out.

(2)   If the works are carried out to a reasonable standard, the reasonable cost of carrying them out, less any contribution due from the person by whom they are carried out, is a debt due to that person from the person subject to the positive obligation.

(3)   If more than one person is subject to the positive obligation, the liability under subsection (2) is joint and several.

(4)   The reference in subsection (2) to any contribution due from the person by whom the works are carried out is to any amount which that person would have been required to pay under a reciprocal payment obligation had the works been carried out in accordance with the positive obligation.

*Liability under reciprocal payment obligations*

**9   Limitation of liability**

(1)   No amount is payable under a reciprocal payment obligation in respect of works not carried out to a reasonable standard.

(2)   In determining the amount payable under a reciprocal payment obligation, only costs which are reasonably incurred in performing the related obligation are to be taken into account.

**10   Liability to more than one estate owner**

(1)   This section applies if—

    (a)   an obligation imposed under section 1 is a reciprocal payment obligation, and

    (b)   the benefit of the reciprocal payment obligation is appurtenant to more than one estate in land.

(2)    The owner of an estate in land to which the reciprocal payment obligation is appurtenant may only recover an amount due under the obligation if that person has incurred costs in the performance of the related obligation which gives rise to the liability under the reciprocal payment obligation.

(3)    If more than one estate owner is entitled to recover an amount due under the reciprocal payment obligation, each may recover only an appropriate proportion of the amount due.

(4)    In subsection (3), "appropriate proportion" means A/B where—

    A is the amount of costs which the estate owner has reasonably incurred in the performance of the related obligation which gives rise to the liability under the reciprocal payment obligation, and

    B is the total amount of costs reasonably incurred in that performance of the related obligation.

*Special rules*

**11    Allocation between co-obligees of responsibility for performance**

Schedule 1 (which provides default rules for the allocation of responsibility for performance of positive obligations between co-obligees) has effect.

**12    Obligations relating to land which defaults to the Crown**

(1)    This section applies if land vests in the Crown by virtue of any rule of law which operates independently of the acts or the intentions of the Crown.

(2)    If the land is affected by a positive obligation imposed under section 1, then until such time, if any, as the Crown, or any person acting for the Crown, has taken possession or control of the land or entered into occupation of it, the Crown—

    (a)    is not bound by the obligation, and

    (b)    is not liable to share responsibility under paragraph 1 or 2 of Schedule 1 for its performance.

(3)    If—

    (a)    the land vests in the Crown as a result of the termination of an estate in land, and

    (b)    immediately before the termination of the estate, there was appurtenant to it the benefit of an obligation imposed under section 1,

the benefit of the obligation survives the termination of the estate, but is not enforceable by the Crown until such time, if any, as the Crown, or any person acting for the Crown, has taken possession or control of the land or entered into occupation of it.

**13    [Application of Part to the Crown]**

*Interpretation*

### 14      Construction of statutory references to interests, or rights, in or over land

(1)      Any reference in an existing enactment to interests, or rights, in or over land, unless expressed to be limited to interests or rights of a particular kind, is to be read as including obligations imposed under section 1.                                  5

(2)      Any reference in an existing enactment to incumbrances affecting land, unless expressed to be limited to incumbrances of a particular kind, is to be read as including obligations imposed under section 1.

(3)      References in this section to an existing enactment are to an enactment contained in—                                                                              10
         (a)      an Act passed before the date on which this Act is passed, or
         (b)      an instrument made under an Act before that date.

### 15      Interpretation of Part

In this Part—
         "apportionment arrangement", in relation to a positive obligation           15
         imposed under section 1, means an arrangement about the allocation of responsibility for performance of the obligation;
         "burdened estate", in relation to an obligation imposed under section 1, means the estate in land by virtue of the ownership of which the obligation was imposed;                                                              20
         "burdened land", in relation to an obligation imposed under section 1, means the land, or any part of the land, burdened by the obligation at the time of imposition;
         "negative", in relation to an obligation imposed under section 1, means of a kind mentioned in subsection (3)(a) of that section;                              25
         "positive", in relation to an obligation imposed under section 1, means of a kind mentioned in subsection (3)(b), (c) or (d) of that section;
         "reciprocal payment obligation" means an obligation of a kind mentioned in section 1(3)(c) (as to which see section 1(5));
         "related obligation", in relation to a reciprocal payment obligation, means    30
         the obligation whose performance gives rise to liability to pay an amount under the reciprocal payment obligation.

## PART 2

EASEMENTS, PROFITS AND OBLIGATIONS UNDER SECTION 1

*Prescription*                                                                  35

### 16      Acquisition of easements by long use

(1)      Qualifying use of land for a continuous period of 20 years has effect to create an easement in relation to that use.

(2)      An easement created by virtue of this section is—
         (a)      for an interest equivalent to an estate in fee simple absolute in    40
         possession, and

    (b)   appurtenant to the fee simple in the dominant tenement.

(3)   When an easement is created by virtue of this section, it binds the owner of any interest then subsisting in the servient tenement.

(4)   Rights to light created by virtue of this section are subject to any local usage or custom to which rights to light acquired by prescription at common law or under the doctrine of lost modern grant are subject.    *5*

(5)   This section has effect in relation to use before, as well as in relation to use on or after, the date on which this section comes into force, but only if the use before that date is part of a period of use which includes that date.

**17    "Qualifying use" for the purposes of section 16**    *10*

(1)   Subject to subsections (2) to (6), use is qualifying use for the purposes of section 16 if—
    (a)   it is of a kind in relation to which a right could be granted as an easement, and
    (b)   it takes place without force, without stealth and without permission.    *15*

(2)   Use is not qualifying use for the purposes of section 16 if it takes place at a time when there is —
    (a)   unity of possession in relation to the dominant and servient tenements, or
    (b)   unity of ownership of the fee simple in those tenements.    *20*

(3)   Use is not qualifying use for the purposes of section 16 if it takes place at a time when the person in whom the fee simple in the servient tenement is vested is not competent to grant an easement in relation to that use for an interest equivalent to a fee simple absolute in possession.

(4)   Subject to subsection (5), use which takes place when the servient tenement is  *25* let is not qualifying use for the purposes of section 16 if—
    (a)   the person in whom the fee simple in the servient tenement is vested does not have power to prevent the use while the lease continues, or
    (b)   the use takes place at a time when it has not come to the knowledge of, and could not reasonably have been discovered by, that person.    *30*

(5)   Subsection (4) does not apply if—
    (a)   the use began before the lease was granted, and
    (b)   when the lease was granted, the person in whom the fee simple in the servient tenement was vested knew about the use or could reasonably have discovered it.    *35*

(6)   Use is not qualifying use for the purposes of this section if—
    (a)   it is use for the purpose of access of light, and
    (b)   the land which is the subject of the use is land in which there is a Crown or Duchy interest.

(7)   In subsection (6), "Crown or Duchy interest" means any interest—    *40*
    (a)   belonging to Her Majesty or the Duchy of Cornwall, or
    (b)   belonging to a Government department or held in trust for the purposes of a Government department.

(8)   In any proceedings, it is for a person who relies on the application of any of subsections (2) to (6) to prove the facts relevant to its application.

## 18   Easements and profits: repeal of existing law

(1)   The existing law of prescription ceases to have effect in relation to use on or after the date on which this section comes into force.                                5

(2)   Notwithstanding subsection (1), if on the coming into force of this section a person—

    (a)   is in a position to take advantage of section 1, 2 or 3 of the Prescription Act 1832, or

    (b)   is within a year of being able to do so,                                      10

then, for the purposes of enabling that person to take advantage of that section, the existing law of prescription continues in force in relation to use before the first anniversary of the date on which this section comes into force.

(3)   References in this section to the existing law of prescription are to—

    (a)   the rules of law relating to the acquisition of easements and profits a        15
prendre by prescription at common law or under the doctrine of lost modern grant, and

    (b)   the Prescription Act 1832.

*Implication*

## 19   Certain rights not to be capable of creation by implication                         20

(1)   On the grant of an estate in land, the following are not to be taken to be granted or reserved without express provision to that effect—

    (a)   an obligation under section 1, and

    (b)   a profit a prendre.

(2)   This section has effect in relation to any grant made on or after the date on        25
which this section comes into force, except one made in pursuance of an agreement entered into, or court order made, before that date.

## 20   Implied grant or reservation of easements

(1)   The grant of an estate in land—

    (a)   includes any easement over land retained by the grantor that is            30
necessary for the reasonable use of the land which is the subject-matter of the grant, and

    (b)   is subject to the reservation of any easement over the land which is the subject-matter of the grant that is necessary for the reasonable use of land retained by the grantor.                                                        35

(2)   In deciding for the purposes of subsection (1) whether a particular easement is necessary for the reasonable use of land, the matters to which it is relevant to have regard include—

    (a)   the use of the dominant and servient land at the time of the grant,

    (b)   the presence on the servient land of any relevant physical features,         40

    (c)   any intended future use of the dominant land known, at the time of the grant, to the grantor and grantee,

(d)    so far as relevant, the routes available for the easement, and

(e)    the extent to which the easement would or might interfere with the servient land or inconvenience the servient owner.

(3)    Subsection (1) does not apply —

(a)    in the case of a grant made by means of a conveyance, if the conveyance so provides;    *5*

(b)    in the case of a grant consisting of the creation of a lease by parol, if the parties to the lease have so agreed.

(4)    This section is to be the only basis for implying the grant or reservation of easements; accordingly the rules of law that previously applied for that purpose are abolished.    *10*

(5)    This section has effect in relation to any grant made on or after the date on which this section comes into force, except one made in pursuance of an agreement entered into, or court order made, before that date.

**21    Restriction of effect of section 62 Law of Property Act 1925**    *15*

(1)    The words implied by section 62 of the Law of Property 1925 (general words implied in conveyances) are not to have effect —

(a)    to create an easement, a profit a prendre or an obligation under section 1, or

(b)    to convert from a leasehold to a freehold interest —    *20*

(i)    a profit a prendre, or

(ii)    an obligation imposed under section 1.

(2)    This section has effect in relation to any conveyance made on or after the date on which this section comes into force, except one made in pursuance of an agreement entered into, or court order made, before that date.    *25*

*Effect of unity of ownership and possession*

**22    Creation and extinction of obligations under section 1: general law**

The rule of law under which unity of ownership and possession of dominant and servient tenements prevents the creation, and causes the extinction, of appurtenant rights applies in relation to —    *30*

(a)    exercise of the power conferred by section 1, and

(b)    obligations imposed under that section.

**23    Creation and extinction of rights appurtenant to registered land**

(1)    The Land Registration Act 2002 is amended as follows.

(2)    After section 27 insert —    *35*

*"Exercise of certain powers despite unity of ownership and possession*

**27A    Creation of appurtenant rights for benefit of registered estate in land**

(1)    Owner's powers in relation to a registered estate in land may be exercised for the purpose of creating a qualifying interest for the benefit

of a registered estate in land, notwithstanding unity of ownership and possession of dominant and servient tenements.

(2) The following are qualifying interests for the purposes of subsection (1)—

    (a) an easement,

    (b) a profit a prendre, and

    (c) an obligation under section 1 of the Law of Property Act 2011.

(3) For the purposes of this Act, creation of an interest by virtue of subsection (1) is a disposition which is required to be completed by registration.

(4) In its application to a disposition under this section, the power conferred by section 25(1) includes power to disapply section 52(1) of the Law of Property Act 1925 (conveyances to be by deed).

(5) A disposition under this section does not have effect until the registration requirements under paragraph 7 of Schedule 2 are met in relation to it.

(6) Section 27(1) does not apply to a disposition under this section."

(3) After section 116 insert—

**"116A Unity of ownership and possession and extinction of appurtenant rights**

(1) The existence of unity of ownership and possession of dominant and servient tenements does not have effect to extinguish an interest which subsists for the benefit of a registered estate in land.

(2) Subsection (1) applies in relation to interests whenever created or acquired.

(3) In its application to the release of an interest in relation to which subsection (1) has effect, the power conferred by section 25(1) includes power to disapply section 52(1) of the Law of Property Act 1925 (conveyances to be by deed)."

*Subject-matter of easements*

## 24 Abolition of ouster principle

(1) Use of land is not prevented from being of a kind which may be the subject of an easement by reason only of the fact that it prevents the person in possession of the land from making any reasonable use of it.

(2) This section has effect in relation to the creation of easements on or after the date on which this section comes into force.

## 25 No new easements of fencing

It ceases to be possible to create or acquire an easement of fencing.

*Miscellaneous*

## 26 Effect of determination of leasehold estate on appurtenant rights

(1) Subject to subsections (2) and (3), determination of a leasehold estate in land has effect to extinguish an interest of any of the following kinds that subsists for the benefit of the estate —

    (a) an easement,

    (b) a profit a prendre, and

    (c) an obligation imposed under section 1.

(2) If a leasehold estate determines because of —

    (a) merger, or

    (b) surrender, otherwise than in connection with the grant of a new lease to the lessee,

subsection (1) does not apply in relation to an interest which the owner of the estate in land immediately expectant on the determination of the leasehold estate ("the superior estate") elects, on the occasion of the merger or surrender, to save for the benefit of the superior estate.

(3) If a leasehold estate determines because of surrender in connection with the grant of a new lease to the lessee, subsection (1) does not apply in relation to an interest which the lessee elects, on the occasion of the surrender, to save for the benefit of the new lease.

(4) The power of election under subsection (2) or (3) is not exercisable by a person whose lease is created by parol.

(5) The power of election under subsection (2) or (3) is exercisable in accordance with land registration rules if —

    (a) in a subsection (2) case, title to the superior estate is registered, and

    (b) in a subsection (3) case, the grant of the new lease is a registrable disposition.

(6) If subsection (5) does not apply, the power of election under subsection (2) or (3) is exercisable by endorsing notice of election on a document evidencing the title of the person by whom the election is made to the land to which the determined leasehold estate related.

(7) An interest saved under subsection (2) or (3) is appurtenant to the estate in land for the benefit of which it is saved.

(8) In subsection (2), references to merger do not include merger as a result of disclaimer.

(9) In this section, "land registration rules", "registered" and "registrable disposition" have the same meaning as in the Land Registration Act 2002.

## 27 Non-use of easements and profits: presumption of abandonment

The fact that the right conferred by an easement or profit a prendre has not been exercised for a continuous period of 20 years or more shall be evidence of an intention on the part of the owner to abandon the easement or profit, until the contrary is proved.

**28 Variation and release of appurtenant rights: registered land**

(1) The Land Registration Act 2002 is amended as follows.

(2) In section 27(2) (dispositions of a registered estate required to be completed by registration) for "and" at the end of paragraph (e) substitute—

> "(ea) where the registered estate subsists for the benefit of another registered estate, its express release, and".          5

(3) Before section 115 insert—

**"114A Variation of appurtenant rights**

(1) The variation of an appurtenant right which affects, or subsists for the benefit of, a registered estate has effect as the grant of a new right in place of the existing right, which is accordingly released.          10

(2) Section 27(2)(d) and (ea) apply to grant and release by virtue of subsection (1) as if they were express.

(3) The reference in subsection (1) to an appurtenant right is to—

> (a) an easement,          15
> (b) a profit a prendre, other than a profit a prendre in gross, or
> (c) an obligation imposed under section 1 of the Law of Property Act 2011."

(4) In Schedule 2 (registrable dispositions: registration requirements) after paragraph 7 insert—          20

*"Release of registered appurtenant right*

> 7A In the case of the release of a registered estate which subsists for the benefit of another registered estate, the registered estate released, and any notice entered in the register in respect of it, must be removed from the register."          25

## PART 3

### POWERS WITH RESPECT TO INTERESTS ETC AFFECTING LAND

**29 Declarations about certain interests affecting land**

(1) The court may on the application of any person interested declare whether or not in a particular case freehold or leasehold land is, or would in a given event          30
be, affected by any of the following—

> (a) a restriction imposed by an instrument,
> (b) an obligation imposed under section 1,
> (c) an easement created on or after the date on which this section comes into force, and          35
> (d) a profit a prendre created on or after that date.

(2) The court may on the application of any person interested declare what, upon the true construction of an instrument purporting—

> (a) to impose a restriction,
> (b) to impose an obligation under section 1, or          40

    (c)    to create an easement or profit a prendre on or after the date on which this section comes into force,

is the nature and extent of the restriction, obligation, easement or profit imposed or created and whether it is, or would in a given event be, enforceable and, if so, by whom.

(3) The court may on the application of any person interested declare what is the nature and extent of an easement created by virtue of section 16 or section 20 and whether it is, or would in a given event be, enforceable and, if so, by whom.

(4) The powers under subsections (1) to (3) are also exercisable by the Upper Tribunal, but only on an application made in the course of proceedings under section 30.

## 30 Discharge and modification of certain interests affecting land

(1) The Upper Tribunal may, on the application of a person interested in any freehold or leasehold land affected by an interest to which this section applies, by order discharge or modify the interest if any of the grounds in Schedule 2 applies.

(2) Subject to subsections (3) to (5), the interests to which this section applies are—
    (a)    a restriction as to the use of, or building on, land which—
        (i)    is imposed under section 1, or
        (ii)    arises under covenant or otherwise,
    (b)    a positive obligation imposed under section 1,
    (c)    an easement created on or after the date on which this Part comes into force, and
    (d)    a profit a prendre created on or after that date.

(3) This section does not apply to an interest imposed or created on the occasion of a disposition made gratuitously or for a nominal consideration for public purposes.

(4) This section does not apply to—
    (a)    an interest imposed or created under any statutory power for the protection of any Royal Park or Garden, or
    (b)    an interest of a like character imposed or created on the occasion of any enfranchisement effected before the commencement of the Law of Property Act 1925 in any manor vested in Her Majesty in right of the Crown or the Duchy of Lancaster.

(5) Subject to subsections (6) and (7), this section does not apply to an interest imposed or created—
    (a)    for naval, military or air force purposes, or
    (b)    for civil aviation purposes under the powers of the Air Navigation Act 1920, section 19 or 23 of the Civil Aviation Act 1949 or section 30 or 41 of the Civil Aviation Act 1982.

(6) Subsection (5)(a), so far as relating to interests imposed or created otherwise than in connection with the use of any land as an aerodrome, applies only so long as the interest is enforceable by or on behalf of the Crown.

(7) Subsection (5)(a), so far as relating to interests imposed or created in connection with the use of any land as an aerodrome, and subsection (5)(b)

apply only so long as the interest is enforceable by or on behalf of the Crown or any public or international authority.

(8) This section is without prejudice to any concurrent jurisdiction of the court.

## 31 Matters relevant to power under section 30

(1) In determining—
   (a) whether paragraph 4 of Schedule 2 (interest impeding reasonable use) applies, and
   (b) whether to exercise the power under section 30,
   the Upper Tribunal must take into account such of the matters mentioned in subsection (2) as appear to it to be relevant in the circumstances of the case, and any other material circumstances.

(2) The matters referred to are—
   (a) the development plan,
   (b) any declared or ascertainable pattern for the grant or refusal of planning permissions in the relevant areas, and
   (c) the period at which, and context in which, the interest was imposed or created.

(3) The Upper Tribunal may only modify an easement or profit a prendre if satisfied that, as modified, the interest—
   (a) will not be materially less convenient to the person entitled to it, and
   (b) will not be more burdensome to the land affected.

## 32 Supplementary powers

(1) The power under section 30 to modify a restriction, or a positive obligation imposed under section 1, includes power to provide for the interest to have effect with the addition of such further provisions as—
   (a) appear to the Upper Tribunal to be reasonable in view of any relaxation of the existing provisions, and
   (b) are accepted by the applicant.

(2) The power under section 30 to modify an easement or profit a prendre includes power to provide for the interest to have effect as a different kind of easement or profit if the change—
   (a) appears to the Upper Tribunal to be reasonable in the circumstances, and
   (b) is accepted by the applicant.

(3) The Upper Tribunal may refuse to modify an interest if the applicant refuses to accept a proposed addition under subsection (1) or change under subsection (2).

(4) An order under section 30 which affects the benefit of an interest may direct the applicant to pay to any person entitled to the benefit of the interest such sum by way of consideration as the Upper Tribunal thinks it just to award under one (but not both) of the following heads—
   (a) a sum to make up for any loss or disadvantage suffered by the person in consequence of the order;

     (b)    a sum to make up for any effect which the interest had, at the time when it was imposed or created, in reducing the consideration then received for the land affected by it.

(5)    If positive obligations imposed under section 1 are linked, an order under section 30 discharging or modifying one of them may include provision discharging or modifying the other.

(6)    For the purposes of subsection (5) positive obligations are linked if one is a reciprocal payment obligation and the other is the related obligation.

(7)    If the Upper Tribunal makes an order under section 30 which discharges or modifies a reciprocal payment obligation, it may, on the application of a person subject to the related obligation, include in the order provision modifying another reciprocal payment obligation if—

     (a)    the costs to which the reciprocal payment obligations relate are the same, and

     (b)    the Upper Tribunal is satisfied that, unless the other reciprocal payment obligation is modified, the burden of those costs will not be appropriately distributed.

(8)    In this section, "reciprocal payment obligation" and "related obligation" have the same meaning as in Part 1.

## 33    Proceedings under section 30

(1)    On an application under section 30, the Upper Tribunal must give any necessary directions as to the persons who are, or are not, to be admitted to oppose the application, as appearing, or not appearing, to be entitled to the benefit of the interest.

(2)    No appeal lies against a direction under subsection (1).

(3)    Before making an order under section 30, the Upper Tribunal must—

     (a)    direct such enquiries to be made of any government department or local authority as it thinks fit (if any), and

     (b)    direct such notices to be given to such of the persons who appear to be entitled to the benefit of the interest intended to be discharged or modified as it thinks fit (if any).

(4)    Notices for the purposes of subsection (3)(b) may be by advertisement or otherwise as the Upper Tribunal thinks fit.

(5)    In considering what directions to give under subsection (3), the Upper Tribunal is to have regard to any enquiries, notices or other proceedings previously made, given or taken.

(6)    Tribunal Procedure Rules must make provision enabling or requiring proceedings on an application under section 30 in which any such question as is referred to in section 29(1), (2) or (3) arises to be suspended to enable the decision of the court on the question to be obtained by means of an application under that provision or otherwise as those rules, or rules of court, may provide.

## 34    Staying of proceedings pending application under section 30

A person against whom proceedings by action or otherwise are taken to enforce an interest to which section 30 applies may in such proceedings apply to the court for an order giving leave to make an application under that section and staying the proceedings in the meantime.

## 35    Displacement of default allocation rules

(1)    If, on the application of any person interested, the Upper Tribunal is satisfied that the effect of paragraph 1(1) or 2(1) of Schedule 1 in relation to the allocation    5
between estate owners of responsibility for performance of a positive obligation imposed under section 1 is not appropriate, it may by order provide for responsibility for the performance of the obligation to be allocated between the estate owners in such manner as it thinks fit.

(2)    An obligation under an order under subsection (1) has effect —    10
  (a)    as if arising under an arrangement about the allocation of responsibility for performance entered into with respect to the positive obligation by the estate owners to whom the order relates, and
  (b)    as if imposed under section 1.

(3)    The arrangement mentioned in subsection (2)(a) is deemed to be made by    15
deed.

## 36    Making of orders without production of instrument

An order under section 29 or 30 may be made notwithstanding that any instrument which is alleged to impose or create the interest to which the order relates may not have been produced to the court or the Upper Tribunal, and the    20
court or the Upper Tribunal may act on such evidence of that instrument as it may think sufficient.

## 37    Effect of orders

(1)    An order under section 29 or 30 which affects the benefit of an interest is binding on all persons then entitled, or thereafter capable of becoming entitled,    25
to the benefit of the interest.

(2)    An order under section 29 or 30 which affects the burden of an interest is binding on all persons then subject, or thereafter capable of becoming subject, to the burden of the interest.

(3)    Subsections (1) and (2) apply regardless of whether a person —    30
  (a)    is ascertained or of full age or capacity, or
  (b)    is a party to the proceedings or has been served with notice.

## 38    Transition

(1)    Nothing in this Part applies to a restriction under a lease granted before the date on which this Part comes into force if —    35
  (a)    the lease was granted for a term of 40 years or less,
  (b)    the lease was granted for a term of more than 40 years and less than 25 years of the term have expired, or
  (c)    the lease is a mining lease within the meaning of the Law of Property Act 1925.    40

(2)    Nothing in this Part has effect in relation to proceedings begun under section 84 of the Law of Property Act 1925.

**39    Interpretation of Part**

In this Part—

"the court" means the High Court or the county court;

"instrument" does not include a statute, unless the statute creates a settlement;

"positive", in relation to an obligation imposed under section 1, means of a kind mentioned in subsection (3)(b), (c) or (d) of that section.

PART 4

GENERAL

**40    Crown application**

This Act binds the Crown.

**41    Minor and consequential amendments and repeals**

(1)    Schedule 3 (which makes minor and consequential amendments) has effect.

(2)    The enactments specified in Schedule 4 are repealed to the extent specified there.

**42    Saving for certain profits**

Nothing in this Act applies to profits a prendre which are rights in common for the purposes of the Commons Act 2006.

**43    Short title, commencement and extent**

(1)    This Act may be cited as the Law of Property Act 2011.

(2)    This Act comes into force on such day as the Lord Chancellor may by order made by statutory instrument appoint, and different days may be so appointed for different purposes.

(3)    This Act extends to England and Wales only.

# SCHEDULES

## SCHEDULE 1                                                    Section 11

RESPONSIBILITY FOR PERFORMANCE OF POSITIVE OBLIGATIONS: DEFAULT ALLOCATION
RULES

*Default apportionment in case of division of estates*                          5

1    (1)  If the burdened estate in relation to a positive obligation imposed under
          section 1 has been divided, then, as between the owners of the estates in land
          resulting from the division, responsibility for performance of the positive
          obligation is to be shared in the proportions that the areas of their respective
          interests in the burdened land bear to the area of the burdened land as a         10
          whole.

     (2)  Sub-paragraph (1) does not apply —
          (a)  to an estate owner whose interest has priority over the interest
               constituted by the positive obligation, or
          (b)  as between estate owners between whom there is in force an                    15
               apportionment arrangement with respect to the positive obligation.

     (3)  In calculating the area of the burdened land for the purposes of this
          paragraph, there is to be disregarded —
          (a)  the area of any land in which the interest of such an estate owner as
               is mentioned in sub-paragraph (2)(a) subsists,                               20
          (b)  the area of any land in relation to which the positive obligation has
               ceased to be enforceable as a result of discharge by the Upper
               Tribunal or compulsory acquisition,
          (c)  the area of any land in relation to which the positive obligation is
               overridden by virtue of a statutory provision authorising             25
               interference with adverse rights, and
          (d)  the area of any land in relation to which liability to share
               responsibility under sub-paragraph (1) is suspended because of
               section 12.

2    (1)  If a lease granted subject to an existing positive obligation imposed under        30
          section 1 has been divided, then, as between the owners of the estates in land
          resulting from the division, responsibility for performance of the positive
          obligation is to be shared in the proportions that the areas of their respective
          interests in the land which was the subject of the lease before division bear
          to the area of that land as a whole.                                              35

     (2)  Sub-paragraph (1) does not apply —
          (a)  to an estate owner whose interest has priority over the interest
               constituted by the positive obligation, or

       (b)    as between estate owners between whom there is in force an apportionment arrangement with respect to the positive obligation.

    (3)  In calculating the area of the land which was the subject of the lease before division, there is to be disregarded—

       (a)    the area of any land in which the interest of such an estate owner as is mentioned in sub-paragraph (2)(a) subsists,     *5*

       (b)    the area of any land in relation to which the positive obligation has ceased to be enforceable as a result of discharge by the Upper Tribunal or compulsory acquisition,

       (c)    the area of any land in relation to which the positive obligation is   *10* overridden by virtue of a statutory provision authorising interference with adverse rights, and

       (d)    the area of any land in relation to which liability to share responsibility under sub-paragraph (1) is suspended because of section 12.     *15*

*Default apportionment between lessor and lessee*

3    (1)  If a positive obligation imposed under section 1 binds the lessor and lessee under a lease, then, as between themselves, the lessor is to be responsible for performance of the obligation.

    (2)  Sub-paragraph (1) does not apply if there is in force between the lessor and   *20* lessee an apportionment arrangement with respect to the positive obligation.

*Supplementary*

4      For the purposes of this Schedule, there is an apportionment arrangement with respect to a positive obligation imposed under section 1 in force   *25* between estate owners if one owes the other an obligation with respect to responsibility for performance of the positive obligation.

SCHEDULE 2             Section 30

GROUNDS FOR MAKING ORDERS UNDER SECTION 30

PART 1           *30*

GENERAL GROUNDS

*Interest obsolete*

1      The Upper Tribunal may make an order under section 30 if it is satisfied that the interest ought to be deemed obsolete because of—

       (a)    changes in the character of the property or neighbourhood, or   *35*

       (b)    other circumstances which the Upper Tribunal considers material.

*Discharge or modification agreed*

2      The Upper Tribunal may make an order under section 30 if it is satisfied that the persons of full age and capacity entitled to the benefit of the interest have

207

by their actions or omissions expressly or impliedly agreed to the proposed discharge or modification.

*Satisfaction of one or more conditions in relation to each person entitled to benefit of interest*

3       The Upper Tribunal may make an order under section 30 if, in relation to each of the persons entitled to the benefit of the interest, it is satisfied that     5
paragraph 4, 5 or 6 applies.

4       This paragraph applies in relation to a person entitled to the benefit of the interest if the Upper Tribunal is satisfied—

   (a)    that the continued existence of the interest would impede some reasonable use of the land for public or private purposes, or, as the     10
          case may be, would do so unless modified,

   (b)    that in impeding the use the interest—

       (i)    does not secure to the person any practical benefits of substantial value or advantage, or

       (ii)   is contrary to the public interest, and     15

   (c)    that money will be an adequate compensation for any loss or disadvantage (if any) which the person will suffer from the proposed discharge or modification.

5       This paragraph applies in relation to a person entitled to the benefit of the interest if the Upper Tribunal is satisfied that the person has by action or     20
omission expressly or impliedly agreed to the proposed discharge or modification.

6       This paragraph applies in relation to a person entitled to the benefit of the interest if the Upper Tribunal is satisfied that the proposed discharge or modification will not injure the person.     25

PART 2

GROUNDS SPECIFIC TO POSITIVE OBLIGATIONS

*Application of Part*

7       This Part applies only to positive obligations imposed under section 1.

*General*     30

8   (1)  The Upper Tribunal may make an order under section 30 in respect of an obligation to which this Part applies if it is satisfied that, as a result of a change of circumstances, performance of the obligation—

   (a)    has ceased to be reasonably practicable, or

   (b)    has become disproportionately expensive relative to the benefit     35
          conferred by performance.

   (2)  The reference in sub-paragraph (1) to a change of circumstances does not include a change of personal circumstances.

*Obligations under apportionment arrangements*

9       The Upper Tribunal may make an order under section 30 in respect of an     40
obligation to which this Part applies if—

*Law of Property Bill*
*Schedule 2 — Grounds for making orders under section 30*
*Part 2 — Grounds specific to positive obligations*

21

> (a) it is an obligation under an arrangement about the allocation of responsibility for performance of a positive obligation imposed under section 1, and
>
> (b) the Upper Tribunal is satisfied that the burden of the obligation under the arrangement is substantially out of proportion to the benefit which the person subject to it derives from performance of the positive obligation.

SCHEDULE 3

Section 41(1)

MINOR AND CONSEQUENTIAL AMENDMENTS

*Duchy of Lancaster Act 1817 (c. 93)*

1 (1) The purposes for which money may be applied under section 25 of the Duchy of Lancaster Act 1817 include the performance of a positive obligation imposed under section 1 of this Act affecting land belonging to Her Majesty in right of the Duchy of Lancaster.

  (2) The reference in sub-paragraph (1) to a positive obligation imposed under section 1 is to an obligation of a kind mentioned in subsection (3)(b), (c) or (d) of that section.

*Duchy of Cornwall Management Act 1863 (c. 49)*

2 (1) The purposes for which money may be advanced and applied under section 8 of the Duchy of Cornwall Management Act 1863 include the performance of a positive obligation imposed under section 1 of this Act affecting land belonging to the Duchy of Cornwall.

  (2) The provisions of that section about money advanced for improvements apply to money advanced for the purpose mentioned in sub-paragraph (1).

  (3) The reference in sub-paragraph (1) to a positive obligation imposed under section 1 is to an obligation of a kind mentioned in subsection (3)(b), (c) or (d) of that section.

*Green Belt (London and Home Counties) Act 1938 (1&2 Geo. 6 c. xciii)*

3 In section 22(2) of the Green Belt (London and Home Counties) Act 1938 —
  (a) for "Section 84 of the Law of Property Act 1925" substitute "Section 30 of the Law of Property Act 2011", and
  (b) for "restrictive covenants" substitute "certain interests affecting land".

*National Trust Act 1939 (2&3 Geo. 6 c. lxxxvi)*

4 In section 5(3) of the National Trust Act 1939, for "Section 84 of the Law of Property Act 1925" substitute "Section 30 of the Law of Property Act 2011".

*Requisitioned Land and War Works Act 1945 (c. 43)*

5 In section 38(3) of the Requisitioned Land and War Works Act 1945 —

(a) for "Section eighty-four of the Law of Property Act 1925" substitute "Section 30 of the Law of Property Act 2011",

(b) for "restrictive covenants" substitute "certain interests affecting land",

(c) for "restriction", in both places where it occurs, substitute "interest", 5

(d) for "subsection (11) of the said section eighty-four" substitute "section 30(5) of the Law of Property Act 2011", and

(e) for "restrictions" substitute "interests".

*Forestry Act 1967 (c. 10)*

6    In section 5(2)(b) of the Forestry Act 1967 —                                    10

(a) for "section 84 of the Law of Property Act 1925" substitute "section 30 of the Law of Property Act 2011", and

(b) for "restrictive covenants" substitute "certain interests affecting land".

*Leasehold Reform Act 1967 (c. 10)*                                                   15

7    In paragraph 1(5) of Schedule 4 to the Leasehold Reform Act 1967 —

(a) for "Section 84 of the Law of Property Act 1925" substitute "Section 30 of the Law of Property Act 2011", and

(b) for "restrictive covenants" substitute "certain interests affecting land".                                                                                 20

*Countryside Act 1968 (c. 10)*

8    In section 15(4) of the Countryside Act 1968 —

(a) for "Section 84 of the Law of Property Act 1925" substitute "Section 30 of the Law of Property Act 2011", and

(b) for "restrictive covenants" substitute "certain interests affecting land".       25

*National Trust Act 1971 (c. vi)*

9    In section 27 of the National Trust Act 1971 —

(a) for "Section 84 of the Law of Property Act 1925" substitute "Section 30 of the Law of Property Act 2011", and                                            30

(b) for "restrictive covenants" substitute "certain interests".

*Land Charges Act 1972 (c. 61)*

10   (1) The Land Charges Act 1972 is amended as follows.

(2) In section 2, after subsection (7) insert —

"(7A)  A Class G land charge is an obligation imposed under section 1 of the 35 Law of Property Act 2011 (power of estate owner to burden land with obligations)."

(3) In section 4(8), after "Class F" insert "and a land charge of Class G".

*Ancient Monuments and Archaeological Areas Act 1979 (c. 46)*

11      In section 17(7) of the Ancient Monuments and Archaeological Areas Act
         1979—
         (a)   for "Section 84 of the Law of Property Act 1925 (c 20)" substitute
               "Section 30 of the Law of Property Act 2011", and                          5
         (b)   for "restrictive covenants" substitute "certain interests affecting
               land".

*Limitation Act 1980 (c. 58)*

12      After section 19 of the Limitation Act 1980 insert—

                          *"Obligations attached to land*                                  10

         **19ZA Time limit for actions for breach of obligation attached to land**

                 No action in respect of breach of an obligation imposed under section
                 1 of the Law of Property Act 2011 (power to attach obligations to
                 land) shall be brought after the expiration of 12 years from the date
                 on which the cause of action accrued."                                    15

*Pastoral Measure 1983 (No. 1)*

13      In section 62(3) of the Pastoral Measure 1983—
         (a)   for the words from "Section 84" to "1925" substitute "Section 30 of the
               Law of Property Act 2011",
         (b)   for "restrictions" substitute "certain interests".                          20

*Town and Country Planning Act 1990 (c. 46)*

14      In section 106A(10) of the Town and Country Planning Act 1990—
         (a)   for "Section 84 of the Law of Property Act 1925" substitute "Section
               30 of the Law of Property Act 2011", and
         (b)   for "restrictive covenants" substitute "certain interests".                 25

*Care of Churches and Ecclesiastical Jurisdiction Measure 1991 (No. 1)*

15      In section 22(7) of the Care of Churches and Ecclesiastical Jurisdiction
         Measure 1991—
         (a)   for the words from "Section 84" to "1925" substitute "Section 30 of the
               Law of Property Act 2011", and                                              30
         (b)   for "restrictions" substitute "certain interests".

*Land Registration Act 2002*

16      (1)  The Land Registration Act 2002 is amended as follows.

         (2)  After section 58(2) insert—

                 "(3)  Subsection (1) is not to be taken to apply in relation to an entry made   35
                       in pursuance of an instrument which purports to create a right for the
                       benefit of a registered estate, but which—

        (a)   fails to impose an obligation under section 1 of the Law of Property Act 2011 because the benefit of the obligation does not touch and concern the land in which the registered estate subsists, or

        (b)   fails to create an easement because the right does not accommodate and serve that land."     *5*

(3)  In Schedule 8, after paragraph 2 insert—

*"Obligations attached to land*

    2A      No indemnity is payable under this Schedule on account of failure on first registration of title to include an entry in respect of the   *10* burden of an obligation imposed under section 1 of the Law of Property Act 2011 if at the time of the application for first registration the obligation was registrable, but not registered, as a land charge under the Land Charges Act 1972."

(4)  In Schedule 10, at the end of Part 1 insert—     *15*

*"Elections under section 26(2) or (3) of LPA 2011*

    4A      Rules may make provision about the exercise of the power of election under section 26(2) or (3) of the Law of Property Act 2011 (election to save appurtenant interest on merger or surrender of leasehold estate in land) in circumstances in which subsection (5)   *20* of that subsection applies (title to superior estate registered or grant of new lease a registrable disposition)."

## SCHEDULE 4                                Section 41(2)

### REPEALS

| Short title and chapter | Extent of repeal | |
|---|---|---|
| Prescription Act 1832 (2 & 3 Will. 4 c. 71) | The whole Act. | *25* |
| Law of Property Act 1925 (15 & 16 Geo. 5 c. 20) | Section 84. | |
| Rights of Light Act 1959 (7&8 Eliz. 2 c. 56) | In section 3(1), the words "(by virtue of the Prescription Act 1832, or otherwise)". Section 4(2). | *30* |
| Law of Property Act 1969 (c. 59) | Section 28(1) to (6), (9) and (11). Schedule 3. | |
| Civil Aviation Act 1982 (c. 16) | In Schedule 15, paragraph 1. | *35* |
| Title Conditions (Scotland) Act 2003 (asp 9) | In Schedule 14, paragraph 8. | |

# EXPLANATORY NOTES

## INTRODUCTION

A.1 The draft Bill implements the recommendations made by the Law Commission in its Report: Making Land Work: Easements, Covenants and Profits à Prendre, published in 2011.

A.2 The Law Commission's work was concerned with certain rights over land in England and Wales: not ownership rights, but the rights that an individual may have over someone else's land, and in particular easements, covenants and profits à prendre (called simply "profits" in the rest of these notes).

### Easements

A.3 Easements can be described generally as rights to do something on land that belongs to someone else; for example, a private right of way or a right to run a drain across a neighbour's land. Easements are rights that one landowner has over another's land; the holder of the right is known as the 'dominant owner" and his or her land is known as the "benefited" or "dominant" land; the land over which the right is exercised is known as the "servient" or "burdened" land, and the owner of that land is known as the "servient owner". The easement is said to be "appurtenant" to the benefited land.

A.4 Some easements cannot be described as rights to do something on another's land; they are the "negative easements", so called because they give one landowner a right to prevent a neighbour from doing something on the neighbour's own land. The negative easements are rights of support (enabling X to prevent Y from removing earth or a structure on Y's land that supports X's land), rights to light (enabling X to prevent Y from obstructing light through an aperture), or rights to air or water in defined channels.

### Profits

A.5 Profits are rights to take something from someone else's land; fishing rights are an obvious example, as are grazing rights. Profits are often attached to land, as easements are; but they may also be held independently, so that there is a dominant owner but no dominant land.

A.6 Profits may be either "several" or "in common"; a several profit excludes the dominant owner while a profit in common does not. Excluded from the scope of the draft Bill are rights which are "profits in common" for the purposes of the Commons Act 2006 (see clause 42). It is therefore mainly concerned with several profits, but also profits in common held for a term of years or from year to year, which do not fall within the definition of "rights of common" for the purposes of the Commons Act 2006. Some grazing agreements fall within this category.

A.7 Easements and profits are generally created expressly, as part of a sale or lease of part of property; they can also be acquired by implication (where the law reads into a transfer or other document the creation of an easement) and prescription. Once validly created (and subject to registration requirements, discussed below), the easement will be "appurtenant" to the benefited land; that is, it will benefit all subsequent owners of that land without the need for it to be expressly assigned to them.

A.8 Easements and profits are, in technical terms, interests in land that are capable of being legal interests under the Law of Property Act 1925; that means that they are among the rights that can be registered, so that Land Registry guarantees their validity and there is a public record both of the benefited land and of the burdened land.

**Covenants**

A.9 Covenants are contractual promises, whereby one landowner covenants with another to do or not do certain activities on their land in the future. A covenant that prevents an activity on land (for example, a covenant to use land only for residential purposes, which therefore prevents business use) is known as a restrictive or negative covenant. Where certain technical requirements are met, a restrictive covenant can bind not only the person who made the promise but also future owners of the land, pursuant to the rule in *Tulk v Moxhay* (1848) 2 Ph 774. Positive covenants, by contrast, are obligations to do something on land, and they cannot bind future owners in the way that negative covenants can; so it is impossible to use covenants to attach positive obligations to land.

A.10 Restrictive covenants are often created on a sale of part (as when a new housing or business estate is created). Unlike easements and profits they cannot arise by implication or prescription.

A.11 Another way in which restrictive covenants are different from easements and profits is that they are not legal interests in land. So they cannot be registered and Land Registry does not guarantee their validity. That means that there is no public record of the land that benefits from a restrictive covenant. However, the burden of a restrictive covenant can be noted on the register of title to the burdened land, and indeed must be noted if it is to bind later owners of the land.

A.12 The Law Commission's project, and this draft Bill, are not concerned with leasehold covenants, that is, covenants made between landlord and tenant and relating only to the leasehold property.

**THE LAW OF PROPERTY DRAFT BILL**

A.13 Part 1 of the draft Bill contains provisions that make it possible to create both restrictive and positive obligations as legal interests in land. This means that, for the future, an obligation to do or not to do something on land can be created, and can be registered, and guaranteed by Land Registry, so that the benefit and burden of the obligation will pass to future owners of the benefited and burdened land.

A.14 The draft Bill makes provision for the transmission of benefit and burden in special cases (for example, where land is leased or mortgaged); and for the allocation of responsibility where land is sub-divided. It makes provision for the enforcement of obligations, and for remedies for their breach.

A.15    The obligations created pursuant to clause 1 of the draft Bill – referred to in these notes as "land obligations" – will, for the future, replace restrictive covenants, in the sense that it will no longer be possible to create restrictive covenants that bind land pursuant to the rules currently in operation. Clause 2 prevents this by ensuring that future covenants take effect – where the requirements of clause 1 are satisfied – as land obligations. But the restrictive covenants that are already in existence at the date of reform will continue to exist, and their status and enforceability will be unaffected by the reform.

A.16    Part 2 of the draft Bill puts into effect a number of Law Commission recommendations for the law relating to easements and profits, including reforms of the law relating to prescription and implication. The draft Bill replaces the three methods that exist under the current law for the acquisition of these rights by long use, known as prescription, with a single statutory regime applying to easements only (so that it will no longer be possible to acquire profits by prescription). It also makes provision for a new basis for the implication of easements, in place of the numerous different principles found currently in the case law.

A.17    Part 3 of the draft Bill relates to the Lands Chamber of the Upper Tribunal, which currently has jurisdiction, pursuant to section 84 of the Law of Property Act 1925, to discharge or modify restrictive covenants that are obsolete or have outlived their usefulness. But it cannot make declarations (that is, legally binding statements about the extent or enforceability of rights in land); so if in the course of proceedings under section 84 a question arises as to the validity or construction of a restriction, the proceedings must be adjourned while the parties resort to the court to seek a declaration.

A.18    Part 3 does three things:

(1)    It extends the Upper Tribunal's jurisdiction so as to enable it to discharge or modify land obligations, and easements and profits created after the implementation of the draft Bill.

(2)    It enables the Upper Tribunal to make declarations in the course of proceedings following an application for discharge or modification of an interest.

(3)    It re-states the remaining provisions of section 84 of the Law of Property Act 1925.

**COMMENTARY ON CLAUSES**

**PART 1**

**ATTACHING OBLIGATIONS TO LAND**

### Clause 1: power to impose obligations

A.19    Clause 1 of the draft Bill makes it possible to create an obligation that burdens one plot of land and benefits another, so that the obligation takes effect as an interest attached to the benefited land. The Law Commission has referred to such obligations as "land obligations".

A.20    Clause 1(1) achieves this by extending the powers of an estate owner (that is, a freeholder or leaseholder) to enable him or her to burden his or her land with certain types of obligation (known as "qualifying obligations").

A.21    Clause 1(2) states that the estate owner may do so only if two conditions are met:

(1)    The obligation must be for the benefit of an estate in land, rather than merely for the benefit of an individual.

(2)    The obligation must "touch and concern" the benefited (or dominant) land. That means that it must benefit the land, rather than its owner personally. For example, an obligation to maintain a boundary, or not to build on neighbouring land, benefits the land by making it more convenient or secure; an obligation to pay to the owner of neighbouring land part of the profits realised in developing the land, or to buy goods from his or her shop, benefits the owner but has no effect upon the land itself and does not meet the touch and concern requirement.

A.22    Clause 1(3) sets out the four different types of qualifying obligation; only an obligation that falls into one of these categories can be created as a land obligation.

A.23    The first category (clause 1(3)(a)) is an obligation not to do something on the burdened (or servient) land; for example an obligation not to use the land for business purposes, not to grow certain crops, or not to keep certain animals on the land. These obligations are referred to in the draft Bill as "negative obligations" (see the definitions in clause 15).

A.24    The remaining three categories of qualifying obligation are defined (by clause 15) as positive obligations, namely:

(1)    Clause 1(3)(b): an obligation to do something on the burdened land, or on the boundary between the benefited and burdened land. So an obligation to keep a line of trees on the land below a certain height would qualify, or an obligation to maintain a fence; an obligation to mow the grass on a neighbour's land would not qualify (even though it would pass the "touch and concern" test).

(2)     Clause 1(3)(c): an obligation to make a reciprocal payment. This is explained in clause 1(5) as an obligation to pay the cost of another person's performance of a positive obligation. For example, the freeholder of Whiteacre might be subject to a positive obligation to maintain a driveway used also by the owner of Blackacre, with Blackacre being subject to an obligation to make a reciprocal payment of half the cost of that maintenance.

(3)     Clause 1(3)(d): an apportionment arrangement. Apportionment arrangements are defined by clause 15 as arrangements about the allocation of responsibility for the performance of a positive obligation. Such arrangements may be made when the land burdened by an obligation is divided up; clause 11 and schedule 1 provide rules for the sharing of responsibility where, say, land burdened by a fencing obligation is divided because part of it is sold. But the two burdened owners are free to make an apportionment arrangement if those default rules do not provide an appropriate allocation, and the arrangement they make will be a land obligation pursuant to this provision.

A.25     Clause 1(4) qualifies the clause by removing from its scope obligations between lessor and lessee that relate to the leased property. Such obligations remain leasehold covenants and will not amount to land obligations.

A.26     Clause 1(6) adds one further type of land obligation, namely an obligation ancillary to the performance of a qualifying obligation. An ancillary obligation is one that may not by itself fall into one of the categories in clause 1(3) but relates to the way in which it is performed – for example, the way that work is done, or the way that payment is made or the timing of payment, or an obligation to allow the dominant owner to enter and inspect work, or to do it himself or herself (and see clause 8 as to the recovery of costs of self-help). Ancillary obligations must meet the requirements of clause 1(2).

A.27     A land obligation created pursuant to clause 1 amounts to a right in or over land, because it gives the dominant owner the right to have something done or not done by the owner for the time being of the servient land; it is therefore capable of taking effect as a legal interest in land under section 1(2)(a) of the Law of Property Act 1925 (being a "right or privilege in or over land"), provided that the conditions in that provision are met and the well-established formalities for the creation of a legal interest are observed. So to be a legal interest in land the land obligation must be granted for "for an interest equivalent to an estate in fee simple absolute in possession or for a term of years absolute" (section 1(2)(a) of the Law of Property Act 1925), it must be made by deed (section 52 of the Law of Property Act 1925) and if the burdened land is registered the relevant registration requirements must be met (section 27 of the Land Registration Act 2002).

A.28     Compliance with registration requirements will also be required to ensure that the interest binds future owners of the burdened land; that means that if the burdened land is unregistered it must be protected by registration as a land charge (see paragraph 10 of schedule 3 below), and where the burdened land is registered it must be protected by notice on the register of the burdened land.

**Clause 2: conversion of future covenants**

A.29 The effect of clause 2 is that, for the future, obligations expressed as covenants (that is, as contractual promises) will take effect as land obligations (and not as covenants) provided that:

(1) the promisor owns an estate in land;

(2) the obligation is capable of being imposed under clause 1;

(3) the benefit of the covenant touches and concerns land in which the person to whom it is made has an estate; and

(4) the covenant is not expressed to be personal to either party.

A.30 Accordingly, if a transfer of land contains wording to the effect that the transferee covenants with the transferor not to use the land for business purposes, that will take effect as a negative land obligation – unless the transfer also states that the obligation is personal to either party. A covenant in a transfer to make an overage payment to the transferor, on the other hand, does not touch and concern the benefited land and so will not take effect as a land obligation.

A.31 As a result of this clause, covenants created after the draft Bill is enacted will be enforceable against future owners of the servient land, not as a result of the rule in *Tulk v Moxhay* (1848) 2 Ph 774, but because they are land obligations; the rule in *Tulk v Moxhay* (1848) 2 Ph 774, and other rules specific to restrictive covenants, will continue to be relevant to existing covenants but will have no application to covenants created post-commencement where the covenanted obligation falls within the scope of clause 1.

**Clause 3: benefit of obligations**

A.32 The objective of creating obligations in the form of interests in land is to ensure that they remain effective when land changes hands, in the sense that the benefit of the obligation passes to future owners of the dominant land, and the burden of the obligation continues to bind the servient land and its owners for the future.

A.33 There are general rules for the transmission of the benefit and burden of interests in land which will apply to land obligations except insofar as they are modified in the draft Bill.

A.34 Clause 3 states that the benefit of a land obligation attaches to the estate for the benefit of which it is created. Accordingly, it passes to future owners of that estate, as a whole or in part, and to estates derived out of it (unless it is expressly released); but it can last no longer than the estate to which the benefit is attached (but see also clause 26).

A.35 For example, A holds a 99-year lease of Blackacre; he grants to his neighbour, B, who holds a 50-year lease of Whiteacre, a land obligation that burdens Blackacre with an obligation to maintain the boundary wall between their properties. That obligation is made by a leaseholder, but it is not made between landlord and tenant, and so it is a land obligation (and is not excluded by clause 1(4)). It is appurtenant to B's leasehold estate and so will cease to exist when the term of B's lease expires (subject to clause 26). If B assigns the lease to C, C will have

218

the benefit of the obligation. If C assigns the lease of part of the demised premises to D, D and C will both be able to enforce the obligation; if it is an obligation to make a reciprocal payment obligation, clause 10 will determine how much each is entitled to receive.

A.36     Provision also has to be made for the transmission of the burden of land obligations when land changes hands; clauses 4 and 5 set out the rules for the transmission of the burden of negative and positive obligations, respectively.

**Clause 4: burden of negative obligations**

A.37     Clause 4 relates to negative obligations. Clause 4(1) provides that they are to bind the owner of the burdened estate, the owner of any other estate or interest in the burdened land, and any occupier of the burdened land.

A.38     So where land is subject to an obligation not to build upon it above a certain height, for example, that obligation prevents building above a certain height by anyone who owns the land or part of it, or has a lease of all or part of it, or who has another interest such as a charge over the land or is simply occupying it – whether with or without the permission of the owner. Accordingly, anyone in adverse possession of the burdened land is also bound by the obligation.

A.39     The exception to the provisions of clause 4(1) is that a negative obligation does not bind anyone who holds an estate or interest in the burdened land that has priority over the obligation – either because the interest was created and (where necessary) registered prior to the imposition of the obligation, or because the interest took effect at a time when the obligation was not protected by registration.

**Clause 5: burden of positive obligations**

A.40     Clause 5 relates to positive obligations. The range of persons bound by these is narrower than the range of persons bound by negative obligations. Clause 5(1) provides that they are:

(1)     the owner of the burdened estate; and

(2)     the owner of any other estate or interest that confers a right to immediate possession of the burdened land. Clause 5(3) extends the meaning of "immediate possession" to include anyone entitled to receive rent from the land.

A.41     Clause 5(2) qualifies that by adding that the following are not bound by a positive obligation:

(1)     the owner of an estate or interest that has priority over the obligation (see the comments above on clause 4(1)); and

(2)     the owner of a lease granted for a term of seven years or less.

A.42     Accordingly, where the freehold of Whiteacre is burdened with an obligation to mend the fence, and the freeholder (A) lets half of the land to X for 99 years, and declares a trust of the rest of the land for the benefit of Y for Y's lifetime with remainder to Z, then A, X and Y share the burden of the obligation. Z does not, because his estate does not give him the right to immediate possession of the land. Y is bound because, although he holds an equitable interest rather than a legal estate, that interest gives him a right to immediate possession. If T sub-lets the land to T2 for a term of ten years, T2 is also bound by the obligation, but T remains bound also because he is entitled to the rent, if any, owed by T2. However, if T2's term is for, say, five years, he is not bound by the obligation.

### Clause 6: breach of obligations

A.43 Clause 6(1) and clause 6(2) set out what amounts to a breach of negative and positive obligations, respectively.

A.44 Clause 6(3) exempts from liability for breach a mortgagee (or anyone holding a charge or lien over the land – see clause 6(5)) who is not exercising its right to possession of the land.

A.45 Clause 6(4) states that where a number of persons are bound by the same obligation, they are jointly and severally liable to the benefited owner for its breach, which means that they can all be called upon to perform the obligation. (Note that as between themselves, their liability is governed by clause 11 and schedule 1 in the absence of an apportionment arrangement.)

### Clause 7: enforcement of obligations

A.46 Clause 7(1) establishes a cause of action for breach of a land obligation; that means that a remedy for its breach can be obtained from the court.

A.47 The available remedies for a breach of an obligation are set out in clause 7(2).

A.48 One of those remedies is damages; clause 7(3) places a limit on the extent of the damages that may be ordered by stating that contract principles are to be applied to damages for breach of a land obligation. As a result, liability is for losses flowing naturally from the breach, or for anything known to the parties to be a consequence of breach at the time the obligation was imposed; that is a less extensive basis of liability than would be the case if tort principles were applied, since in the law of tort all the damage caused by the wrong is included in the calculation of liability.

A.49 Clause 7(4) ensures that damages for breach of an obligation to carry out works are not liable to be reduced because a person entitled to the benefit of the obligation has the right, under the terms of the obligation, to carry out the works himself or herself but chooses not to do so.

### Clause 8: recovery of costs of self-help

A.50 Clause 8 relates to obligations that entitle the benefited owner to carry out work or perform the obligation himself or herself; such a right might be included among the obligations ancillary to an obligation to maintain a boundary, for example. The right is known as a right to self-help, and may be a more practical course of action than litigation in cases where the servient owner has not performed the obligation. The clause enables a benefited owner who has exercised that right to recover the costs of the work as a debt from the burdened owner. If there is more than one burdened owner, they are jointly and severally liable for that debt (clause 8(3)).

A.51    A positive obligation may be linked with a reciprocal payment obligation. So the owner with the benefit of an obligation to maintain a boundary might be under a reciprocal obligation to pay half the cost. If that owner does the maintenance work himself or herself, clause 8(4) provides that the amount he or she can recover is the cost of the work less the reciprocal payment that he or she would have made if the work had been done by the neighbour who was primarily obliged to do it.

**Clause 9: limitation of liability**

A.52    Clause 9 limits the liability of an owner burdened by a reciprocal payment obligation, by providing that payment is due only in respect of work done to a reasonable standard and only in respect of costs reasonably incurred in performing the obligation.

**Clause 10: liability to more than one estate owner**

A.53    It was noted above (see paragraphs A.34 and A.35) that there will be circumstances where the benefit of an obligation is held by more than one owner of land. Where that obligation is negative, the dividing of the benefit has no effect upon the way in which the obligation is performed; nor does it in the case of positive obligations to do something, since what the burdened owner is obliged to do remains the same. However, where the obligation is a reciprocal payment obligation, the burdened owner has to know whom to pay, and indeed how much to pay to each of the benefited owners if more than one is entitled to payment. Clause 10 resolves this by providing that a benefited owner is entitled to the reciprocal payment only if he or she has incurred expense in the performance of the obligation to which the payment is reciprocal (clause 10(2)); and if more than one landowner is entitled to payment, they are entitled in proportion to what each has reasonably spent (clause 10(4)).

**Clause 11: allocation between co-obligees of responsibility for performance**

A.54    Clause 11 introduces schedule 1 which makes provision for the case where more than one person has the burden of a positive obligation and no apportionment arrangement is in force.

**Clause 12: obligations relating to land which defaults to the Crown**

A.55    Clause 12 is concerned with the situation where land defaults to the Crown, a situation known as "escheat". This is what happens when an estate in land comes to an end in three situations:

(1)    Where a landowner's trustee in bankruptcy or liquidator exercises the statutory power to disclaim the land under section 178 or 315 of the Insolvency Act 1986.

(2)    On dissolution of a company, its property will vest in the Crown in the person of the Treasury Solicitor as *bona vacantia*. The Crown has a statutory right to disclaim the property under the Companies Act 2006, sections 1013 and 1014. If it does so, for example because the property is onerous, the land will escheat to the Crown.

(3)     Where the Crown has made a grant of a freehold subject to restrictions as to the user of the land, enforceable by a right of entry which has been exercised.

A.56    "The Crown" in the context of escheat means the Crown Estates, the Duchy of Lancaster and the Duchy of Cornwall; land in these circumstances escheats to one of these three bodies depending upon its location.

A.57    Clause 12 provides that while the land burdened by a positive obligation is vested in the Crown as a result of escheat, the Crown is not bound by the obligation, nor by the apportionment rules under schedule 1 if they are relevant, unless the Crown has taken possession or control of the land or has occupied it (clause 12(2)). Similarly, if the land has the benefit of a positive obligation the Crown cannot enforce that obligation unless it has taken possession or control of the land or has occupied it (clause 12(3)).

### Clause 13: [application of part to the Crown]

A.58    Clause 13 has been left blank so as to enable the amendment of the draft Bill, before it is introduced into Parliament, to make provision for appropriate arrangements for the Queen to enter into, or be bound by, land obligations.

### Clause 14: construction of statutory references to interests, or rights, in or over land

A.59    Land obligations will take effect as interests in land, and will be capable of being legal interests (see paragraph A.27 above), clause 14 ensures that existing statutory references to rights in land or to encumbrances affecting land are construed (unless they are expressly limited to a particular kind of interest) so as to include land obligations for the future. An example is section 237 of the Town and Country Planning Act 1990, which refers to "any easement, liberty, privilege, right or advantage annexed to land and adversely affecting other land"; that wording will include land obligations.

### Clause 15: interpretation of Part

A.60    Clause 15 sets out definitions of terms for the purposes of Part 1 of the draft Bill.

## PART 2

## EASEMENTS, PROFITS AND OBLIGATIONS UNDER SECTION 1

### Clause 16: acquisition of easements by long use

A.61    Clause 16 creates a new statutory scheme for the acquisition of easements by long use, known as prescription.

A.62    There are three existing methods of prescription: common law prescription, which is very rare because it involves proof that the prescriptive use has continued since 1189; the method known as "lost modern grant", whereby proof of 20 years' prescriptive use gives rise to a presumption that a grant was made; and claims made under the Prescription Act 1832, which itself provides a number of different periods and qualifications.

A.63    Because the existing methods of prescription are abolished by clause 18, for both easements and profits, the scheme set out in clause 16 will become the only method of prescription; and it will not be possible, for the future, to acquire a profit by prescription.

A.64    Clause 16(1) sets out what is required for prescription: "qualifying use" of land for a continuous period of 20 years. "Qualifying use" is defined by clause 17. The 20-year period, familiar from the current law, must be unbroken; there must be no interruptions.

A.65    Clause 16(2) replicates the rule in the current law that an easement acquired by prescription can only be attached to a freehold, and only for the equivalent of a fee simple (or freehold interest). This has the effect that, as in the current law, if a leaseholder uses, say, a path over his neighbour's land for twenty years, and the conditions for qualifying use are met, that use gives rise to an easement appurtenant to the fee simple (that is, the freehold) in the leased land.

A.66    Clause 16(3) makes it clear that once acquired, a prescriptive easement binds the owners of all the interests in the dominant land.

A.67    Clause 16(4) preserves "local usage or custom" which may in some areas affect the acquisition of an easement of light. There have been a number of local customs with this effect in the past; the only one of which anything is clearly known today is the Custom of London, which applies in relation to the buildings in a defined area within the boundary of the City of London. It gives freehold building owners the right to build or rebuild on their ancient foundations to any height regardless of whether this will result in any loss of light to neighbouring properties. It can therefore operate to prevent or qualify the prescriptive acquisition of rights to light; but it cannot prevent acquisition under the Prescription Act 1832 because it is expressly overridden by the words of that statute.

A.68    Clause 16(4) makes the new statutory scheme for prescription subject to local custom; accordingly, in those areas where the Custom of London applies, it will continue to have the same effect in relation to claims under the new scheme as it had in respect of prescriptive claims at common law and under the "lost modern grant" doctrine prior to reform.

A.69    Clause 16(5) deals with transitional situations, and has the effect that where the prescription period includes the date of the enactment of the draft Bill, the new scheme applies (but see clause 18(2)).

**Clause 17: "qualifying use" for the purposes of section 16**

A.70    Clause 17 defines qualifying use, for the purposes of clause 16; in other words, it sets out the characteristics that the use must have in order to give rise to an easement.

A.71    Qualifying use must be a use of land that could be done by virtue of an easement (clause 17(1)(a)), for example, driving down a road or sending water through a drain; contrast enjoying a view across a neighbour's land, or receiving piano lessons from the neighbour in his house, neither of which can subsist as an easement. Qualifying use must take place "without force, without stealth and without permission" (clause 17(1)(b)); these are familiar requirements from the current law. So riding a horse along a neighbour's drive will not be qualifying use if it involves removing barriers (since it must not be done "by force"), nor if it is done only under cover of darkness (since it must not be done "by stealth"), nor if the neighbour has invited the rider or approved the use of the drive (since it must be "without permission").

A.72 Use of land is not qualifying use if it is done at a time when the dominant and servient land are in the possession of the same person or if the same person owns the fee simple (that is, the freehold) in both (clause 17(2)); nor is it qualifying use at any time when the fee simple owner of the servient land does not have power to grant the easement to be claimed (clause 17(3)). An example of such an owner would be a statutory body with limited powers to deal with the land.

A.73 Clause 17(4) and (5) are relevant to the situation when the servient land is let. An easement that is acquired by prescription binds the freeholder, as well as any leasehold estates in the land (clause 16); and when land is not subject to a lease the qualifying use will be obvious to the freeholder because it must not be by force nor by stealth (clause 17(1)). But when the land is let the freeholder may have no knowledge of the use, however openly it is exercised; and the freeholder will in any event have no power to prevent the use unless that power is reserved to him or her in the lease, because the leaseholder will have exclusive possession of the land. Accordingly clause 17(4) provides that use is not qualifying use if it takes place at a time when the land is let and the freeholder cannot prevent it because of the existence of the lease, or does not know about it and could not reasonably have discovered it. That is not the case if the use began before the land was let if, at the point when the lease began, the freeholder knew about it or could not reasonably have discovered it (clause 17(5)); in that event, use while the land is let *will* be qualifying use despite clause 17(4).

A.74 Clause 17(6) prevents prescription for a right to light over land in which there is a Crown or Duchy interest, as defined by clause 17(7).

A.75 Clause 17(8) relates to the burden of proof. A claimant for a prescriptive easement must prove that he or she has exercised 20 years' qualifying use in accordance with the definition in clause 17(1)). But it is for the servient owner to prove that use was not qualifying because of any of the matters set out in subsections (2) to (4) and (6) of the clause (and for the claimant to prove that clause 17(5) applies). Thus, for example, the claimant does not have to prove that the freeholder had capacity to grant the easement, nor that there was no time when the dominant and servient land were in common ownership.

**Clause 18: easements and profits: repeal of existing law**

A.76 Clause 18 abolishes the existing methods of prescription: common law prescription, "lost modern grant", and the Prescription Act 1832. All these methods cease to be effective in relation to claims based in whole or part on use on or after the date of commencement (clause 18(1)); as explained in the context of clause 16(5), such claims must be made under the new law.

A.77    There is one exception. Section 4 of the Prescription Act 1832 contains rules relating to interruptions of the use during the prescription period, with the effect that interruptions to use for a period of less than a year do not have the effect of stopping the prescriptive use. That means that once a claimant has carried out prescriptive use for 19 years and one day, interruption cannot put an end to his or her claim. In order to prevent the loss of this privilege to claimants who have very nearly completed what is required for a prescriptive easement claimed under the 1832 Act, clause 18(2) provides that for those who are able to claim an easement under sections 1, 2 or 3 of the 1832 Act, or are within a year of being able to do so, the Prescription Act 1832 will continue in force for one more year. However, in order to claim an easement under the 1832 Act the claimant must either bring a court action or apply for registration; if no action is taken within that year the new law takes over.

### Clause 19: certain rights not to be capable of creation by implication

A.78    Currently the law can imply the creation of an easement or profit in a transaction under any of a number of different principles, despite there being no express creation of an interest.

A.79    Clause 19 provides that profits and land obligations cannot be created by implication following the commencement of the clause, save (in the case of profits) for any transaction carried out pursuant to a contract or court order made before commencement.

A.80    The clause refers not to a transaction but to a "grant", following the provisions of section 51 of the Law of Property Act 1925 which states (under the heading "conveyances and other instruments") that "all lands and interests therein lie in grant". Therefore the word "grant" encompasses both the grant of a lease and the conveyance or transfer of part of a freehold or leasehold estate.

### Clause 20: implied grant or reservation of easements

A.81    Clause 20 introduces a statutory scheme for the implication of easements; it is to be the sole basis for implication, whether by grant or by reservation – that is, whether for the benefit of the transferee (for example) of part of land, or for the benefit of the transferor of part. The existing methods of implication are therefore abolished (clause 20(4)), save for any transaction carried out pursuant to a contract or court order made before commencement. As in clause 19, the word "grant" is used to encompass all relevant transaction types.

A.82    The new basis for implication is that a conveyance or transfer, or a lease, is to include, for the benefit of the grantor or grantee, any easements that are necessary for the reasonable use of the land retained or granted. "Necessary for reasonable use" is not a term of art drawn from existing law, and does not replicate the narrow test of necessity found in the current law.

A.83    In deciding what is necessary for the reasonable use of the land, the factors to be considered include those set out in subsection (2) of clause 20. Attention is thereby drawn to:

(1)    the use of the dominant and servient land at the time of the transaction;

(2)     any relevant physical features of the servient land (which might be relevant, for example, to an easement of support);

(3)     any intended future use of the dominant land known to both parties at the time of the transaction (which might therefore make a particular easement necessary to enable a particular use);

(4)     the available routes for an easement insofar as relevant (this factor would point towards a drainage easement using an existing drain, for example); and

(5)     the extent of any inconvenience to the servient owner or interference with the servient land.

A.84    The implication of easements can be expressly excluded, whether in the written document or by agreement between the parties in the case of an oral lease (clause 20(3)).

**Clause 21: restriction of effect of section 62 Law of Property Act 1925**

A.85    Clause 21 restricts the effect of section 62 of the Law of Property Act 1925. That section sets out a number of matters that a conveyance (defined broadly by section 205 of the Law of Property Act 1925) is to be taken to include. It has a wide effect; regardless of the intention of the parties in the absence of contrary provision; in certain circumstances it creates new easements and profits, as well as "upgrading" them from leasehold to freehold interests in cases where a lessee acquires the freehold of the demised premises.

A.86    For the future, section 62 cannot create, or "upgrade", either profits or land obligations, and it cannot create new easements (clause 21(1)); it can still, however, operate to upgrade easements.

A.87    Clause 21 does not affect a transaction carried out pursuant to a contract or court order made before commencement.

**Clause 22: creation and extinction of obligations under section 1: general law**

A.88    Clause 22 relates to the rule colloquially known as the "unity of seisin" rule, which is that an easement or profit cannot be created when the same person owns and has possession of the dominant and servient land, and also that an easement or profit will come to an end when the dominant and servient land fall into common ownership and possession.

A.89    Clause 22 applies the unity of seisin rule to land obligations; but this is subject to clause 23.

**Clause 23: creation and extinction of rights appurtenant to registered land**

A.90    Clause 23 amends the Land Registration Act 2002 so as to disapply the unity of seisin rule in certain circumstances. It does so by the addition of two new sections to the 2002 Act.

A.91    First, a new section 27A is inserted into the 2002 Act. Its effect is to extend owner's powers in relation to land the title to which is registered so as to enable the owner to create easements, profits and land obligations notwithstanding unity of seisin (section 27A(1), (2)). Such creation must be completed by registration (section 27A(3)), and has no effect (at law or in equity) until the registration requirements are fulfilled (section 27A(5). The general rule in section 27(1) of the 2002 Act (which is simply that a disposition does not operate at law until it is registered) is therefore disapplied to the creation of interest pursuant to this new section (section 27A(6)).

A.92    The creation of interests that benefit and burden different areas of land in the same ownership can thus only take place where the title to all the land involved is registered; and it will be for Land Registry to make rules prescribing how it is to be done. Section 27A(4) extends the rule-making power conferred upon Land Registry by section 25 of the 2002 Act, enabling the relevant rules to disapply section 52 of the Law of Property Act 1925 and so to provide that the creation of interests in this way does not require the use of a deed.

A.93    Second, a new section 116A is added to the 2002 Act, providing that the unity of seisin rule does not operate to extinguish easements, land obligations and profits in cases where title to the benefited land is registered. Accordingly, where a registered proprietor whose estate has the benefit of an easement acquires the servient land, the easement is not extinguished. The landowner may, however, wish to bring the easement to an end (for example, if he or she has no intention of disposing of the servient land), in which case the interest may be expressly released. Land Registration Rules will prescribe how this is to be done, and again the rule-making power conferred upon Land Registry by section 25 of the 2002 Act is extended, enabling the relevant rules to disapply section 52 of the Law of Property Act 1925 and so to provide that the release of interests in this way does not require the use of a deed.

### Clause 24: abolition of ouster principle

A.94    The ouster principle is the rule that there cannot be an easement that prevents the servient owner from making any reasonable use of his or her land. Clause 24 abolishes that principle for easements created after commencement, thereby confirming the validity of a number of arrangements that tend to involve extensive use of the land affected by the easement – in particular, parking easements. *Copeland v Greenhalf* [1952] Ch 488 is thereby overruled.

### Clause 25: no new easements of fencing

A.95    In general an easement should not involve the servient owner in work or expenditure. An exception to that rule is the possibility of an easement of fencing. Clause 25 makes it impossible to create or acquire (for example, by prescription) an easement of fencing; such arrangements, for the future, can be made by using positive land obligations.

### Clause 26: effect of determination of leasehold estate upon appurtenant rights

A.96    It was noted above that the benefit or the burden of an easement, profit, or a land obligation can be attached to a freehold or leasehold estate. Clause 26 confirms

227

that when any of those rights benefits a leasehold estate, on the ending of the lease (whether on the expiry of its term or for another reason such as forfeiture or surrender) the rights that benefited it end too (clause 26(1)).

A.97    The clause therefore overrules the principle in *Wall v Collins* [2007] EWCA Civ 444, [2007] Ch 390. In that case the Court of Appeal held that if a lease merges with the freehold (as a result of the acquisition of the freehold by the tenant), an easement that benefited the lease will thereafter benefit the freehold (albeit only for the term of the lease). However, the practical effect of *Wall v Collins* is able to be replicated where that is wanted, because clause 26(2) provides that where a lease merges with the superior estate (freehold or leasehold), or is surrendered, the holder of the superior estate can elect to preserve for the benefit of the freehold a right that benefited the lease (and see also clause 26(7)).

A.98    Accordingly, if a 25-year lease that benefited from an easement over the neighbour's land is surrendered to the landlord, the landlord may elect to preserve that easement for the benefit of his or her own estate; the leasehold easement will continue, but only until the point when it would have expired by effluxion of time.

A.99    Clause 26(3) provides for the case where a lease is technically surrendered because the grant to the lessee of a longer (or shorter) term takes effect as a deemed surrender and re-grant. In that event the tenant may elect to preserve the easement that benefited the original lease for the new lease. Again, election does not affect the duration of the leasehold easement. If the tenant's estate is extended, the easement will continue for its original term, unless the neighbour is willing to extend it. If the tenant's estate is shortened, the easement will determine with the estate by virtue of clause 26(1).

A.100   The election referred to in clause 26(2) and (3) must be made in accordance with land registration rules where the estate that is to benefit from the right is registered, whether before or as a result of the transaction that gives rise to the election (clause 26(5)). Those rules will specify the form that is to be used and the time by which the election is to be made. Paragraph 16(4) of schedule 3 to the Bill inserts a new paragraph 4A into schedule 10 to the Land Registration Act 2002 giving Land Registry power to make the appropriate rules.

A.101   Where the estate to be benefited remains unregistered (for example, where a lease is surrendered to a freeholder whose title is unregistered), the election is made by endorsement on a document of title to the estate now benefited.

A.102   The election referred to in clause 26(2) and (3) cannot be made in the case of an oral lease (clause 26(4)); nor in a case where the lease merges with the freehold because it is disclaimed by the trustee in bankruptcy of an individual tenant, or by the Treasury Solicitor following the insolvency of a corporate tenant (clause 26(8)).

**Clause 27: non-use of easements and profits: presumption of abandonment**

A.103 Clause 27 provides that if an easement or a profit has not been used for 20 years it shall be presumed to have been abandoned. The presumption is rebuttable, and so it is open to the dominant owner to demonstrate, in proceedings brought by the servient owner, that he or she has not in fact abandoned the right.

**Clause 28: variation and release of appurtenant rights**

A.104 Currently the express release of an easement, for example, is not a registrable disposition. Therefore it takes effect at law without the need for any application to be made to change the register of title. As a result, an easement or profit that has been expressly released will remain on the register and, where title to the benefited land is registered, its validity will remain guaranteed by Land Registry. The details on the register are out of alignment with reality, and the indemnity fund is put at risk.

A.105 The same situation would apply, post-reform, to land obligations in the absence of provision to the contrary.

A.106 Clause 28 provides that the express release of an appurtenant interest – whether an easement, profit or land obligation – is a registrable disposition. It does so by inserting a further paragraph (ea) into section 27(2) of the Land Registration Act 2002. Accordingly, where an interest is appurtenant to a registered estate, its express release will not take effect at law until the register is altered.

A.107 Clause 28 also inserts a new section 114A in the Land Registration Act 2002, so as to provide that the variation of an appurtenant right that affects or benefits a registered estate takes effect as the release of the right and the grant of a new one; for the purposes of section 27(2) of the Land Registration Act 2002 that release and grant are treated as express, and so they are registrable dispositions pursuant to section 27(2).

**PART 3**

**POWERS WITH RESPECT TO INTERESTS ETC AFFECTING LAND**

A.108 Part 3 of the draft Bill is concerned with the jurisdiction of the Lands Chamber of the Upper Tribunal ("the Upper Tribunal" in these notes and in the draft Bill). Currently the Upper Tribunal has jurisdiction, pursuant to section 84 of the Law of Property Act 1925, to make orders discharging or modifying restrictions over land. It therefore hears applications made by those whose land is burdened by restrictive covenants and who seek the discharge or modification of restrictions; the Upper Tribunal's rules (the Tribunal Procedure (Upper Tribunal) (Lands Chamber) Rules 2010) determine its procedure and, in particular, the giving of notice to those with the benefit of the relevant restriction(s) when an application is made.

A.109 Section 84(2) of the Law of Property Act 1925 confers upon the court a jurisdiction to declare (that is, to make a statement that binds the parties and all those interested in the land):

(1) whether a restriction affects freehold land (and some leasehold, by virtue of section 84(12));

(2)     what a restriction means; and

(3)     whether or not a restriction is enforceable.

A.110    That jurisdiction is not currently available to the Upper Tribunal; accordingly, where the need for a declaration arises during proceedings in the Upper Tribunal, those proceedings are normally stayed while an application is made to the court under section 84(2).

A.111    As noted above (see paragraphs A.17 and A.18), Part 3 re-enacts section 84 of the Law of Property Act 1925, and also introduces a number of modifications to extend the Upper Tribunal's jurisdiction under that section. A number of the provisions within Part 3 therefore reproduce the existing provisions of section 84, albeit with reference where relevant to Part 3 of the draft Bill or to orders made under clauses 29 and 30 rather than to section 84 itself, and to the interests to be encompassed for the future within the Upper Tribunal's jurisdiction rather than merely to restrictions. The notes that follow comment only upon the changes to the law effected by clauses 29 to 39; where there is no change save that the provisions of section 84 are reproduced but made to refer to the new jurisdiction the notes simply record the correspondence with the old provisions.

**Clause 29: declarations about certain interests affecting land**

A.112    Clause 29 reproduces, but extends, section 84(2) of the Law of Property Act 1925 (see paragraphs A.108 to A.111 above). The jurisdiction to make declarations is extended to the Upper Tribunal, provided that the application for a declaration is made in the course of proceedings under clause 30; and the subject-matter of declarations is no longer restrictions only, but extends to easements, land obligations and profits. The land involved may be freehold or leasehold (subject to clause 38, below).

A.113    The expression "restrictions imposed by an instrument" in clause 29(1)(a) encompasses all the interests currently within the scope of section 84(2); it would also include restrictive land obligations, but these are in any event included specifically within clause 29(1)(b).

**Clause 30: discharge and modification of certain interests affecting land**

A.114    Clause 30 extends the jurisdiction of the Upper Tribunal so that orders can be made to discharge or modify not only restrictions but also easements, land obligations and profits, burdening freehold or leasehold land (clause 30(1)).

A.115    The grounds on which orders may be made are set out in schedule 2.

A.116    Subsections (3) to (8) of clause 30 correspond to section 84(7), (11) and (11A) of the Law of Property Act 1925; subsection 30(8) derives from the words in brackets at the beginning of section 84(1) of the Law of Property Act 1925.

**Clause 31: matters relevant to power under section 30**

A.117    Subsections (1) and (2) of clause 31 correspond to section 84(1B) of the Law of Property Act 1925, and relate to the matters to be taken into account by the Upper Tribunal in determining whether to exercise its powers under clause 30 or whether paragraph 4 of schedule 2 (impeding reasonable use) applies.

A.118    Clause 31(3) provides that the Upper Tribunal may only modify easements and profits – for example, an application to change the route of a right of way – if the interest as modified will not be materially less convenient to the benefited owner(s), nor more burdensome to the burdened land.

**Clause 32: supplementary powers**

A.119    Clause 32(1) relates to the addition of further provisions to restrictions or to land obligations when such interests are modified; the subsection provides that this may be done if it seems reasonable to the Upper Tribunal to add them in view of any relaxation of the existing provisions of the interest, and if the applicant accepts the addition of one or more further provisions. The subsection adapts the terms of the section 84(1)(c) of the Law of Property Act 1925 by applying them to land obligations as well as to restrictions.

A.120    Clause 32(2) relates to the modification of easements and profits, and enables the Upper Tribunal to make provision for an easement or profit to have effect as a different kind of easement or profit if that seems reasonable to the Upper Tribunal and if the applicant consents. Such a modification might be the substitution of a right of way on foot for a vehicular right of way, for example.

A.121    Clause 32(3) adds that the Upper Tribunal may refuse to modify an interest if the applicant does not consent to an additional provision under clause 32(1) or a change under clause 32(2), as the case may be.

A.122    Clause 32(4) replicates the provisions of section 84(1) of the Law of Property Act 1925 relating to compensation.

A.123    Subsections (5) and (6) of clause 32 relate to "linked obligations"; two obligations are linked if one is a positive land obligation and the other is the reciprocal payment obligation granted in respect of it. Clause 32(5) provides that if the Upper Tribunal makes an order discharging or modifying one of a pair of linked obligations, it may also make an order discharging or modifying the other, whether or not application is made for that. So where the Upper Tribunal has modified a fencing obligation so as to provide for it to be fulfilled using cheaper materials, for example, it may also modify the reciprocal payment obligation if that obligation made explicit reference to payment for the more expensive materials.

A.124    Clause 32(7) relates to the situation where more than one reciprocal payment obligation is linked with a positive land obligation – for example, where several properties are each burdened with an obligation to pay a proportion of the cost of maintaining a shared driveway. Where one of the burdened owners makes an application to have the payment obligation discharged or modified, the Upper Tribunal may, on the application of the person burdened by the linked positive obligation, also make an order modifying the other payment obligations in a case where otherwise the cost of the burden of the costs will be inappropriately distributed.

A.125    An example would be a case where A, B and C each have to pay one quarter of the cost of the maintenance of a driveway by D, where D is bound by an obligation to carry out the maintenance; in such a case the scheme is obviously that the four owners share the drive and pay a quarter of the maintenance costs each. In a case where A successfully applied to have his contribution reduced, it would be possible for D to make an application to have the costs redistributed so that he alone did not have to bear the cost that A no longer had to pay. The Upper Tribunal's rules would ensure that B and C had notice of the application and were able to be heard.

### Clause 33: proceedings under section 30

A.126    Clause 33 makes procedural provisions about the giving of notice, the making of enquiries, corresponding to section 84(3) and (3A) of the Law of Property Act 1925.

### Clause 34: staying of proceedings pending application under section 30

A.127    Clause 34 corresponds to section 84(9) of the Law of Property Act 1925.

### Clause 35: displacement of default allocation rules

A.128    Clause 35(1) enables the Upper Tribunal to make one further type of order, namely an order displacing the default allocation rules provided in schedule 1 to the draft Bill (which regulate the apportionment of responsibility of burdened owners between themselves, in cases where land burdened by a positive obligation has been divided). It may do so if it is satisfied that the rules in schedule 1 are not appropriate for the particular case. An example might be where land burdened by a reciprocal payment obligation is divided in such a way that only one part benefited from the related obligation. In that case it might be decided that it was right for the part that benefited from the related obligation to be responsible, as between the two burdened owners, for the whole payment. Both the burdened owners must remain jointly and severally liable to the landowner with the benefit of the reciprocal payment obligation, absent an express variation agreed with the benefited owner or a successful application to the Upper Tribunal for the modification or discharge of the reciprocal payment obligation itself.

A.129    Clause 35(2) and (3) provides that an order of this kind takes effect as a land obligation and as if made by deed. It will therefore be subject to the same registration requirements as a land obligation.

### Clause 36: making of orders without production of instrument

A.130    Clause 36 corresponds to section 84(6) of the Law of Property Act 1925.

### Clause 37: effect of orders

A.131    Clause 37(1) and (3) derive from section 84(5) of the Law of Property Act 1925, and provide that an order affecting the benefit of an interest binds everyone who becomes entitled to that benefit in the future. Subsection (3) makes similar provision for cases where the Upper Tribunal's order has affected the burden of an interest (as it may do in particular pursuant to clauses 32(1) and (2)).

### Clause 38: transition

A.132    Section 84(12) of the Law of Property Act 1925 provides that section 84 applies to restrictions affecting certain categories of leases (thereby extending the meaning of "freehold" in section 84(1) and (2)). Clause 38 states that nothing in Part 3 of the draft Bill applies to a restriction affecting a lease that was not within the scope of section 84(12) of the Law of Property Act 1925.

**Clause 39: interpretation**

A.133    Clause 39 defines terms for the purposes of Part 3 of the draft Bill.

## PART 4

## GENERAL

**Clause 40: Crown application**

A.134    Clause 40 states that the draft Bill binds the Crown, in order to prevent any claim of Crown immunity in proceedings brought under the draft Bill.

**Clause 41: minor and consequential amendments and repeals**

A.135    Clause 41 gives effect to schedules 3 and 4 to the draft Bill.

**Clause 42: savings for certain profits**

A.136    See paragraph A.6 above.

**Clause 43: short title, commencement and extent**

A.137    Clause 43(3) provides that the draft Bill extends only to England and Wales.

## SCHEDULE 1

A.138    Schedule 1 makes provision for the case where more than one person has the burden of a positive obligation, as will be the case where part of the burdened land is transferred or leased.

A.139    In such a case the burdened owners are jointly and severally liable to the benefited owner (see clause 6(4) above). However, schedule 1 makes provision for their liability between themselves.

A.140    Paragraph 1 provides that where more than one estate owner is burdened by a positive obligation, they are liable between themselves in proportion to the area of the burdened land that they own (paragraph 1(1)), unless an apportionment arrangement is in force between them (paragraph 1(2)(b)); an arrangement that is "in force" is one that currently binds the parties (paragraph 4). So if each owns half, between themselves each pays half of a reciprocal payment obligation, or half the cost of carrying out the work required by the obligation (while remaining jointly and severally liable to the benefited owner). The paragraph makes it clear that it does not apply to any estate owner who is no longer bound by the obligation as a result of the priority rules (for example, land that was transferred to a purchaser at a point when the obligation was not protected on the land register) (paragraph 1(2)(a)).

A.141    The area of land concerned is calculated with reference to its area at the time the obligation was imposed (see the definition of "the burdened estate" in clause 15), less:

    (1)    any land that is no longer burdened by the obligation as a result of the priority rules;

(2) land that has been discharged from the obligation by an order of the Upper Tribunal or as a result of compulsory purchase (paragraph 1(3)(b));

(3) any land in relation to which the positive obligation has been overridden by virtue of a statutory provision (such as, for example, section 237 of the Town and Country Planning Act 1990); and

(4) land that has escheated to the Crown, but which has not been taken into possession or occupied, by it (paragraph 1(3)(c)).

A.142 Paragraph 2 of the schedule makes the same arrangements where a lease is subject to a positive obligation and has been divided, by being assigned in part.

A.143 Paragraph 3 provides that when a lessor and lessee are both bound by a positive obligation, then as between themselves and unless there is an apportionment arrangement that provides otherwise (whether in the lease or otherwise), the lessor is to take responsibility for the obligation.

**SCHEDULE 2**

A.144 Schedule 2 sets out the grounds on which the Upper Tribunal may discharge or modify interests.

**Part 1**

A.145 Part 1 of schedule 2 applies to the discharge or modification of any interest, and paragraphs 1 to 6 reproduce the grounds set out in section 84(1)(a), (aa), (b) and (c) of the Law of Property Act 1925. However, the schedule also changes the relationship between the four grounds, which are presented as exclusive alternatives in section 84 of the 1925 Act. Instead, paragraphs 1 to 6 enable the applicant to prove *either* that the interest is obsolete (paragraph 1) *or* that all those of full age and capacity entitled to the benefit of the interest have consented to its modification or discharge (paragraph 2), *or* that in relation to each of the persons entitled to the benefit of the interest paragraphs 4, 5 or 6 apply. Accordingly, if there are three persons entitled to the benefit and two have consented to its discharge (so that paragraph 5 applies in relation to them) the applicant will be successful if he or she can prove that either paragraph 4 or paragraph 6 is satisfied in relation to the third.

**Part 2**

A.146 Part 2 of schedule 2 relates only to the discharge or modification of positive land obligations. An additional general ground is provided in paragraph 8: a positive obligation may be discharged or modified if the Upper Tribunal is satisfied that as a result of a change of circumstances either it has ceased to be reasonably practicable to perform the obligation, or performance has become disproportionately expensive in relation to the benefit that it confers. An example would be where the cost of the materials prescribed in a fencing obligation had become so expensive that they were no longer felt to be suitable for fencing, in which case the Upper Tribunal might well order the modification of the obligation.

A.147 The changed circumstances referred to in paragraph 8 cannot be personal circumstances; accordingly, a change in the price of materials would be relevant, whereas the fact that the servient owner was unemployed and without means would not.

A.148 Paragraph 9 provides grounds for the modification or discharge of an apportionment arrangement, where the expense of payment has become disproportionate to the benefit conferred upon the servient owner by the positive obligation to which the apportionment arrangement relates.

## SCHEDULE 3

A.149 Schedule 3 makes minor and consequential amendments to a number of enactments, all of them resulting from the availability, for the future, of land obligations.

A.150 Paragraphs 1 and 2 enable the expenditure of capital money by the Duchies of Lancaster and Cornwall in the performance of positive land obligations.

A.151 Paragraphs 3 to 9, 11, and 13 to 15 provide for the substitution of references to clause 30 of the draft Bill in place of references to section 84 of the Law of Property Act 1925, and for changes consequential on the extension of the jurisdiction under that section to easements, profits and land obligations.

A.152 Paragraph 10 amends the Land Charges Act 1972 to provide a land charge, the class G land charge, for the registration of the burden of land obligations where title to the servient land is unregistered. Those not so registered will be void against a purchaser of the burdened land or of any interest in it.

A.153 Paragraph 12 inserts section 19ZA into the Limitation Act 1980; the new section provides that the limitation period for the enforcement of land obligations is to be 12 years.

A.154 Paragraph 16 amends the Land Registration Act 2002. First, section 58 of the 2002 Act is amended by paragraph 16(2) to make it clear that where an entry is made pursuant to an instrument (for example, a transfer of land) that either:

(1) purports to create an easement but in fact fails to do so because the "right" did not accommodate and serve the dominant land, or

(2) purports to create a land obligation but fails to do so because the "right" did not touch and concern the purported dominant land,

then in such cases section 58(1) does not apply and so no legal estate in the "right" supposed to have been created is deemed to be vested in the registered proprietor of that interest.

A.155 Paragraph 16(3) addresses the situation where a mistake is made on first registration of land burdened by a land obligation. It was noted above that a land obligation will be void against a purchaser of the servient land if the latter is unregistered and the land obligation is not registered as a class G land charge. Normally, where land that is burdened by a land obligation comes to have its title registered, the registrar will be aware of the land charge and accordingly will enter a notice in respect of the land obligation on the title to the servient land. However, where no land charge has been registered, due to the inadvertence of the dominant owner, the land obligation may be omitted from the register of title to the servient land. In that event, paragraph 16(3) provides that no indemnity will be payable to the dominant owner in respect of that omission.

A.156    However, that is not the case where the land obligation was created in the course of the disposition that gave rise to the registration of title to the servient land. In that case, section 14(3) of the Land Charges Act 1972 provides that no land charge need be registered in order for the interest to be valid against purchasers. In such a case, the obligation was not "registrable" as a land charge and so paragraph 16(3) does not apply; and the registrar will have full details of the burden of the obligation in the instrument that triggers registration of title to the land.

**SCHEDULE 4**

A.157    Schedule 4 sets out consequential repeals.

# APPENDIX B
# ADVISORY GROUP MEMBERS

Professor David Clarke (Bristol University)

Michael Croker (formerly Land Registry)

Martin Dixon (University of Cambridge)

Andrew Francis (Serle Court Chambers)

Philip Freedman CBE (Mishcon de Reya Solicitors)

Jonathan Gaunt QC (Falcon Chambers)

The Hon Mr Justice Morgan

Emma Slessenger (Allen & Overy)

Geoff Whittaker (Agricultural Law Association)

# APPENDIX C
# SAMPLE REGISTERS

# Land Registry

| Official copy of register of title | Title number DT118424 | Edition date 17.06.2009 |

— This official copy shows the entries in the register of title on 17 June 2009 at 16:22:52.
— This date must be quoted as the "search from date" in any official search application based on this copy.
— The date at the beginning of an entry is the date on which the entry was made in the register.
— Issued on 17 June 2009.
— Under s.67 of the Land Registration Act 2002, this copy is admissible in evidence to the same extent as the original.
— For information about the register of title see Land Registry website www.landregistry.gov.uk or Land Registry Public Guide 1 - *A guide to the information we keep and how you can obtain it.*
— This title is dealt with by Land Registry Weymouth Office.

## A: Property register
This register describes the land and estate comprised in the title.

DORSET : WEYMOUTH AND PORTLAND

1    (22.10.1984) The Freehold land shown edged with red on the plan of the above Title filed at the Registry and being 32 Vincent Street, Weymouth.

2    (07.01.2009) The land edged and numbered in green on the title plan has been removed from this title and registered under the title number or numbers shown in green on the said plan.

3    (07.01.2009) The land  has the benefit of the following covenants contained in the Transfer dated 1 December 2008 referred to in the Charges Register:-

"The transferee covenants with the transferor for the benefit of the retained land:
(a) not to use the transferred land for more than one residential property whose internal gross area shall not exceed two hundred and fifty (250) square  metres.
(b) to erect a 2.5 metre high wall constructed of Despond bricks with retaining piers at 2 metre intervals on a concrete foundation at least 30cm deep along the boundary of the transferred land with the retained land within six months of the date of this transfer, the supporting piers to be situated on the retained land and thereafter to maintain and replace it with an equivalent wall."

## B: Proprietorship register

This register specifies the class of title and identifies the owner. It contains any entries that affect the right of disposal.

### Title absolute

1    (10.10.2001) PROPRIETOR: SANDY DOWN FUELWOOD LLP (LLP Regn. No. OC900612Z) of Morrison House, Burns Road, West Town, Brighton BN1 3TH.

## C: Charges register

This register contains any charges and other matters that affect the land.

1    (07.01.2009) The land is subject to the following rights granted by a Transfer of the land edged and numbered DT504055 in green on the title plan dated 1 December 2008 made between (1) Sandy Down Fuelwood LLP (Transferor) and (2) Lyn Hurst (Transferee):-

"Definitions

"The retained land" means the residue of the land in the title stated in panel 1 after this transfer has been registered;
"The transferred land" means the land in this transfer
"Transferor" and "transferee" include their respective successors in title.

Rights granted for the benefit of the property

The transferor grants to the transferee:
(a) the right to a lay a 200mm diameter pipe on the retained land along the route shown in brown on the plan at a depth of a least 1 metre below the current land surface and thereafter to drain surface water through the pipe from the transferred land together with a right to enter onto the retained land to repair, maintain and replace the pipe upon 48 hours notice except in the case of emergency and in all cases making good all damage caused thereby.
(b) the right limited to an access strip 2 metres wide along the wall referred to in the walling covenant below to enter onto the retained land for the purposes of erection, maintenance and replacement of the wall except in the case of emergency on 48 hours notice.
(c) the right to put such part of the concrete footings as is necessary for the stability of the wall referred to in the walling covenant on the retained land."

NOTE: The title number of the retained land is DT118424. The route shown in brown referred to is shown by a blue broken line on the title plan. The walling covenant referred to is that set out in the Property Register.

## End of register

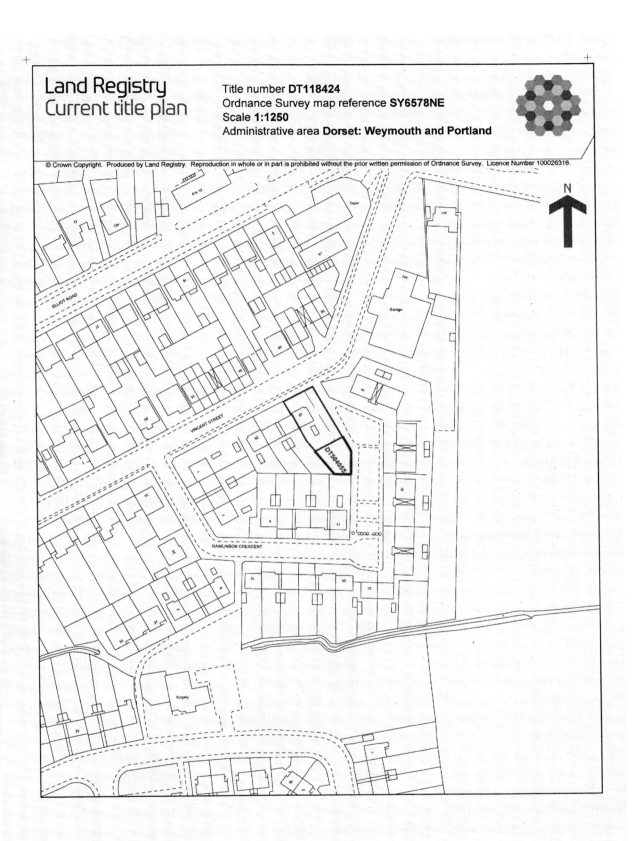

# Land Registry
## Current title plan

Title number **DT118424**
Ordnance Survey map reference **SY6578NE**
Scale **1:1250**
Administrative area **Dorset: Weymouth and Portland**

N

Internal use only

# Land Registry

## Official copy of register of title

**Title number DT504055**   **Edition date 17.06.2009**

- This official copy shows the entries in the register of title on 17 June 2009 at 16:42:23.
- This date must be quoted as the "search from date" in any official search application based on this copy.
- The date at the beginning of an entry is the date on which the entry was made in the register.
- Issued on 17 June 2009.
- Under s.67 of the Land Registration Act 2002, this copy is admissible in evidence to the same extent as the original.
- For information about the register of title see Land Registry website www.landregistry.gov.uk or Land Registry Public Guide *1 - A guide to the information we keep and how you can obtain it.*
- This title is dealt with by Land Registry Weymouth Office.

## A: Property register
This register describes the land and estate comprised in the title.

DORSET : WEYMOUTH AND PORTLAND

1   (22.10.1984) The Freehold land shown edged with red on the plan of the above title filed at the Registry and being land at 32 Vincent Street, Weymouth (DT4 0SG).

2   (07.01.2009) The land has the benefit of the following rights granted by the Transfer dated 1 December 2008 referred to in the Charges Register:-

"Rights granted for the benefit of the property

The transferor grants to the transferee:
(a) the right to lay a 200mm diameter pipe on the retained land along the route shown in brown on the plan at a depth of at least 1 metre below the current land surface through the pipe from the transferred land together with a right to enter onto the retained land to repair, maintain and replace the pipe upon 48 hours notice except in the case of emergency and in all cases making good all damage caused thereby.
(b) the right limited to an access strip 2 metres wide along the wall referred to in the walling covenant below to enter onto the retained land for the purposes of erection, maintenance and replacement of the wall except in the case of emergency on 48 hours notice.
(c) the right to put such part of the concrete footings as is necessary for the stability of the wall referred to in the walling covenant on the retained land.

NOTE: The route coloured brown referred to is shown by a brown broken line on the title plan.

## B: Proprietorship register
This register specifies the class of title and identifies the owner. It contains any entries that affect the right of disposal.

### Title absolute

1    (07.01.2009) PROPRIETOR: LYN HURST of Pannage Cottage, South Oakley, London WC2A 3PH.

2    (07.01.2009) The price stated to have been paid on 1 December 2008 was £150,000.

## C: Charges register
This register contains any charges and other matters that affect the land.

1    (07.01.2009) A Transfer of the land in this title dated 1 December 2008 made between (1) Sandy Down Fuelwood  LLP (Transferor) and (2) Lyn  Hurst (Transferee) contains the following covenants:-

"Definitions
The "retained land" means the residue of the land in this title stated in panel 1 after this transfer has been registered;
"The transferred land" means the land in this transfer
"Transferor" and "transferee" include their respective successors in title.
The transferee covenants with the transferor for the benefit of the retained land:
(a) not to use the transferred land for more than one residential property whose internal gross area shall not exceed two hundred and fifty (250) square metres.
(b) to erect a 2.5 metre high wall constructed of Despond bricks with the retaining piers at 2 metre intervals on a concrete foundation at least 30cm deep along the boundary of the transferred land with the retained land within six months of the date of this transfer, the supporting piers to be situated on the retained land and thereafter to maintain and replace it with an equivalent wall."

NOTE: The title number of the retained land is DT118424.

## End of register

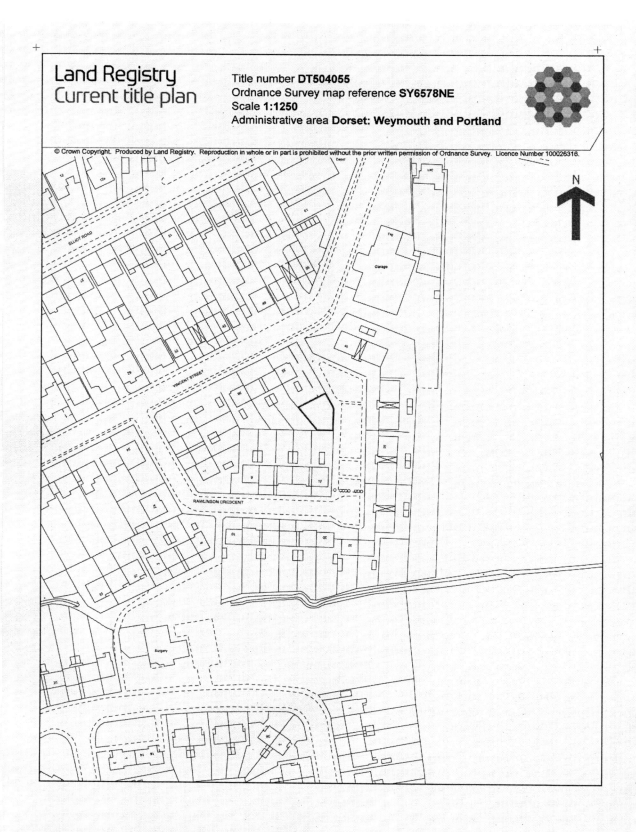

# Internal use only

# APPENDIX D
# A NOTE ON ENFORCEMENT

## THE APPORTIONMENT OF LIABILITY FOR LAND OBLIGATIONS

D.1     In Part 6 we explained that the burden of a land obligation may be fragmented. The burdened land may be sold in part; or it may be leased, in whole or in part. Transmission of the burden of the land obligation is therefore said to be horizontal or vertical.

D.2     This does not present a problem where the land obligation is negative. However many times land burdened by an obligation not to do something is fragmented, all that has to happen is for the various burdened owners not to do the prohibited act. That situation is familiar under the current law relating to restrictive covenants. But where the obligation is positive, questions arise. If the obligation is to pay money, how much does each burdened owner have to pay? If the obligation is to mend a fence, how much of the expenditure and/or the practical task falls to each burdened owner?

D.3     In Part 6 we gave two answers to that question.

D.4     The first is that all the burdened owners must be jointly and severally liable to the benefited owner; we explained why at paragraph 6.122 above.

D.5     The second is that there must be a default rule for the apportionment of liability between the servient owners themselves. We have provided for a default apportionment by area of the burdened land (paragraph 6.126 and following above); but it is open to the servient owners to agree a different apportionment (paragraph 6.128 above), and if they make an apportionment agreement it will take effect as a land obligation (paragraph 6.130 and following above).

D.6     The operation of the default apportionment rules in schedule 1 to the draft Bill can be illustrated by the following examples.

### Example 1

D.7     X sells land to Y, subject to a land obligation upon Y to maintain the boundary fence.

D.8     Y later sells half of his land to Z. Y and Z are jointly and severally liable to X, but as between themselves they share the liability equally. Either one does the work and the other pays half, or they do half the job each.

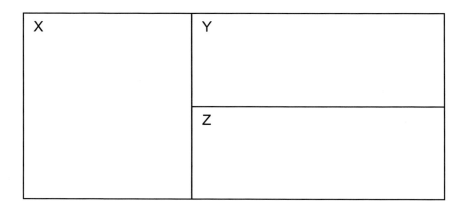

D.9 That example is simplistic, of course, because it uses an easy fraction and involves only one subdivision. A more likely scenario is where Y's land is to be developed; the resulting subdivision of Y's land might look more like this:

| X | Plot 1 | | Plot 5 |
|---|--------|---|--------|
| | Plot 2 | | Plot 6 |
| | Plot 3 | Estate Road | Plot 7 |
| | Plot 4 | | Plot 8 |

D.10 Such an example illustrates, first, the importance of forward planning. Consideration should be given, in drafting the land obligation in the transfer from X to Y, to the possibility of future division; the land burdened by the obligation need not be the whole of the land transferred from X to Y. If what Y buys is a plot for a single dwelling, it will be; if it is a large area which Y is going to develop then the appropriate area would be the land adjoining the boundary, with the intention that eventually (in this example) numbers 1 – 4 would be bound by the obligation but the estate road and numbers 5 – 8 would not. Hence our comments on forward planning at paragraph 6.120 and following above.

D.11 Second, the example and others like it demonstrate the fact that apportionment by area is a starting point only; where it does not yield appropriate results, the burdened owners should make an apportionment agreement – which would be contained in the transfers from Y – so as to set up a more convenient arrangement. Indeed, even where the default apportionment rule appears appropriate, the creation of an express arrangement will prevent future disputes about area.

**Example 2**

D.12 Provided that due care is taken in the drafting of land obligations and the

246

delineation of the benefited and burdened land, instances of complicated apportionment should be few. But in order to illustrate the operation of the default apportionment by area we can imagine a situation where land has been sub-divided a number of times.

D.13 In diagram 3, X sold to Y; X took on a land obligation to maintain the boundary, while Y undertook a reciprocal payment obligation. Y's land was then further subdivided; A and B each own one third of it, C has bought one sixth and Y retains the remaining sixth.

D.14 The owners now pay in proportion to the area of the burdened land that they own. They are jointly and severally liable to X for the whole amount, but to each other they are liable only in proportion to their ownership.

D.15 We can develop that example in order to illustrate the provisions of paragraph 1 (3) of schedule 1 to the draft Bill; suppose that B's land is discharged from the reciprocal payment obligation by an order of the Lands Chamber of the Upper Tribunal.

D.16 The apportionment of liability between A, C and Y now has to be calculated without reference to B's land; so they will pay one half (A) and one quarter (C and Y) respectively. Of course, in deciding whether or not to make such an order in B's favour the Lands Chamber will have regard to all the material circumstances (clause 31(1) of the draft Bill), including the effect upon A, C and Y. If, alternatively, B's land had to be left out of account because it had been the subject of a compulsory purchase (paragraph 1(3)(b) of schedule 1 to the draft Bill), then the compensation for the compulsory purchase will have included compensation for A, C and Y if appropriate.

**Example 3**

D.17 The burdened land may also be subdivided vertically. In Diagram 4, A and B each own one third of the burdened land, and so does Y, but Y has leased his land to C.

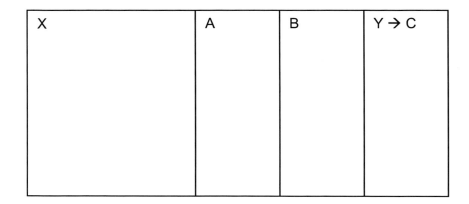

| X | A | B | Y → C |
|---|---|---|---|

D.18   A, B, C and Y are jointly and severally liable to X for the whole of the burden of the obligation. Between themselves, A, B and Y share the burden in thirds. As to C, we have provided that in default of any other arrangement, the landlord bears the burden of the obligation that binds the land. Therefore if C is required to make a payment to X, he can recover not only one third each from A and B but also one third from Y – unless the lease provides otherwise (see paragraph 6.114 above and paragraph 3 of schedule 1 to the draft Bill).

D.19   But what of the case where Y has leased half his land to C?

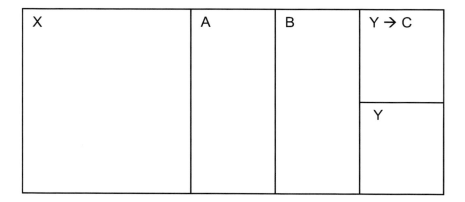

| X | A | B | Y → C |
|---|---|---|---|
| | | | Y |

D.20   The result here is exactly as above, save that C's apportioned liability is for one sixth of the payment. Again, of course, he can recover that sixth from Y unless the lease provides otherwise.

D.21   If Y leases the whole of his land to C and then C assigns the lease in respect of half of the land to D, the position is covered by paragraph 2 of schedule 1 to the draft Bill, which applies the same rules of apportionment as does paragraph 1 but adapts them to the case where a lease that is subject to a positive obligation is divided. Those rules will be of no practical importance in the case where in fact C and D are to be indemnified by their landlord, Y, as above. But if their leases exonerate Y from liability for the burden of the obligation, then as between the three of them the position is that C and D remain liable to X; if, say, C is sued for the whole amount of the obligation, he can recover one third from A and B and one sixth from D.

D.22   Pursuing that example, if the whole payment is £600, and Y is called upon to pay the whole to X, Y can recover £200 from each of A and B, and £100 from each of C and D.

**Conclusion**

D.23   Rules of apportionment are required to meet possibilities. It is not envisaged that all those possibilities will become reality. The examples given here are intended to demonstrate that the rules provided in schedule 1 will meet the possible cases of subdivision of the burdened land. But complex scenarios should be avoided in practice if proper care is taken, first in drafting land obligations and then in making express apportionment arrangements where that is appropriate.

# APPENDIX E
# SECTION 84 OF THE LAW OF PROPERTY ACT 1925

84 Power to discharge or modify restrictive covenants affecting land

(1) The Upper Tribunal shall (without prejudice to any concurrent jurisdiction of the court) have power from time to time, on the application of any person interested in any freehold land affected by any restriction arising under covenant or otherwise as to the user thereof or the building thereon, by order wholly or partially to discharge or modify any such restriction on being satisfied—

> (a) that by reason of changes in the character of the property or the neighbourhood or other circumstances of the case which the Upper Tribunal may deem material, the restriction ought to be deemed obsolete; or

> (aa) that (in a case falling within subsection (1A) below) the continued existence thereof would impede some reasonable user of the land for public or private purposes or, as the case may be, would unless modified so impede such user; or

> (b) that the persons of full age and capacity for the time being or from time to time entitled to the benefit of the restriction, whether in respect of estates in fee simple or any lesser estates or interests in the property to which the benefit of the restriction is annexed, have agreed, either expressly or by implication, by their acts or omissions, to the same being discharged or modified; or

> (c) that the proposed discharge or modification will not injure the persons entitled to the benefit of the restriction;

and an order discharging or modifying a restriction under this subsection may direct the applicant to pay to any person entitled to the benefit of the restriction such sum by way of consideration as the Tribunal may think it just to award under one, but not both, of the following heads, that is to say, either—

> (i) a sum to make up for any loss or disadvantage suffered by that person in consequence of the discharge or modification; or

> (ii) a sum to make up for any effect which the restriction had, at the time when it was imposed, in reducing the consideration then received for the land affected by it.

(1A) Subsection (1)(aa) above authorises the discharge or modification of a restriction by reference to its impeding some reasonable user of land in any case in which the Upper Tribunal is satisfied that the restriction, in impeding that user, either—

(a) does not secure to persons entitled to the benefit of it any practical benefits of substantial value or advantage to them; or

(b) is contrary to the public interest;

and that money will be an adequate compensation for the loss or disadvantage (if any) which any such person will suffer from the discharge or modification.

(1B) In determining whether a case is one falling within subsection (1A) above, and in determining whether (in any such case or otherwise) a restriction ought to be discharged or modified, the Upper Tribunal shall take into account the development plan and any declared or ascertainable pattern for the grant or refusal of planning permissions in the relevant areas, as well as the period at which and context in which the restriction was created or imposed and any other material circumstances.

(1C) It is hereby declared that the power conferred by this section to modify a restriction includes power to add such further provisions restricting the user of or the building on the land affected as appear to the Upper Tribunal to be reasonable in view of the relaxation of the existing provisions, and as may be accepted by the applicant; and the Upper Tribunal may accordingly refuse to modify a restriction without some such addition.

(2) The court shall have power on the application of any person interested—

(a) to declare whether or not in any particular case any freehold land is, or would in any given event be, affected by a restriction imposed by any instrument; or

(b) to declare what, upon the true construction of any instrument purporting to impose a restriction, is the nature and extent of the restriction thereby imposed and whether the same is, or would in any given event be, enforceable and if so by whom.

Neither subsections (7) and (11) of this section nor, unless the contrary is expressed, any later enactment providing for this section not to apply to any restrictions shall affect the operation of this subsection or the operation for purposes of this subsection of any other provisions of this section.

(3) The Upper Tribunal shall, before making any order under this section, direct such enquiries, if any, to be made of any government department or local authority, and such notices, if any, whether by way of advertisement or otherwise, to be given to such of the persons who appear to be entitled to the benefit of the restriction intended to be discharged, modified, or dealt with as, having regard to any enquiries, notices or other proceedings previously made, given or taken, the Upper Tribunal may think fit.

(3A) On an application to the Upper Tribunal under this section the Upper Tribunal shall give any necessary directions as to the persons who are or are not to be admitted (as appearing to be entitled to the benefit of the restriction) to oppose the application, and no appeal shall lie against any such direction; but Tribunal Procedure Rules shall make provision whereby, in cases in which there arises on such an application (whether or not in connection with the admission of persons to oppose) any such question as is referred to in subsection (2)(a) or (b) of this section, the proceedings on the application can and, if the rules so provide, shall be suspended to enable the decision of the court to be obtained on that question by an application under that subsection, or otherwise, as may be provided by those rules or by rules of court.

(5) Any order made under this section shall be binding on all persons, whether ascertained or of full age or capacity or not, then entitled or thereafter capable of becoming entitled to the benefit of any restriction, which is thereby discharged, modified or dealt with, and whether such persons are parties to the proceedings or have been served with notice or not.

(6) An order may be made under this section notwithstanding that any instrument which is alleged to impose the restriction intended to be discharged, modified, or dealt with, may not have been produced to the court or the Upper Tribunal, and the court or the Upper Tribunal may act on such evidence of that instrument as it may think sufficient.

(7) This section applies to restrictions whether subsisting at the commencement of this Act or imposed thereafter, but this section does not apply where the restriction was imposed on the occasion of a disposition made gratuitously or for a nominal consideration for public purposes.

(8) This section applies whether the land affected by the restrictions is registered or not.

(9) Where any proceedings by action or otherwise are taken to enforce a restrictive covenant, any person against whom the proceedings are taken, may in such proceedings apply to the court for an order giving leave to apply to the Upper Tribunal under this section, and staying the proceedings in the meantime.

(11) This section does not apply to restrictions imposed by the Commissioners of Works under any statutory power for the protection of any Royal Park or Garden or to restrictions of a like character imposed upon the occasion of any enfranchisement effected before the commencement of this Act in any manor vested in His Majesty in right of the Crown or the Duchy of Lancaster, nor (subject to subsection (11A) below) to restrictions created or imposed—

> (a) for naval, military or air force purposes,

> (b) for civil aviation purposes under the powers of the Air Navigation Act 1920, of section 19 or 23 of the Civil Aviation Act 1949 or of section 30 or 41 of the Civil Aviation Act 1982.

(11A) Subsection (11) of this section—

> (a) shall exclude the application of this section to a restriction falling within subsection (11)(a), and not created or imposed in connection with the use of any land as an aerodrome, only so long as the restriction is enforceable by or on behalf of the Crown; and

> (b) shall exclude the application of this section to a restriction falling within subsection (11)(b), or created or imposed in connection with the use of any land as an aerodrome, only so long as the restriction is enforceable by or on behalf of the Crown or any public or international authority.

(12) Where a term of more than forty years is created in land (whether before or after the commencement of this Act) this section shall, after the expiration of twenty-five years of the term, apply to restrictions affecting such leasehold land in like manner as it would have applied had the land been freehold:

Provided that this subsection shall not apply to mining leases.

# APPENDIX F
# LIST OF CONSULTEES

Richard Coleman (Clifford Chance LLP)

Jonathan Wragg  (Barrister, Highgate Chambers)

Farrer & Co LLP

Ian Williams (Christ's College, University of Cambridge)

R T Oerton

Peter Gwynne, Tim Brock, Janet Bligh, Sam North

HHJ David Hodge QC (Civil Committee of the Council of Circuit Judges)

Nicola J Coaley

Northumberland County Council

Paul Chiltock

The Legal Office of the National Institutions of the Church of England (on behalf of the Archbishops' Council)

Andrew Francis (Barrister, Serle Court Chambers)

Gerald Moran (Hunters Solicitors)

Martin Pasek

Dr Peter Defoe (calfordseaden LLP)

B S Letitia Crabb (University of Reading)

DLA Piper UK LLP

Ecclesiastical Judges Association

HHJ Ian Leeming QC

G J Wadsworth (University of Newcastle)

Latimer Hinks

Amanda McRae

City of Westminster and Holborn Law Society

Boodle Hatfield

Rohit Radia

Charities' Property Association

Church Commissioners for England

Council for Licensed Conveyancers

Richard Sable

Roger Pickett (Diocese of Southwark)

Jeremy Johnston (Osgoode Hall Law School, Canada)

Jeffrey Shaw (Nether Edge Law)

M I Cunha

National Trust

Dr A L Kaye

Trowers & Hamlins

Wales & West Utilities Ltd

Victor Mishiku (The Covenant Movement)

Country Land and Business Association Ltd

Council of Mortgage Lenders

Creffield Area Residents Association

K Vartanian

Brewster M White and Huguette T M White

Professor Andrea Fusaro (University of Genoa)

Simon Goulding (City Univeristy, London)

Gregory Hill (Barrister, Ten Old Square Chambers)

Network Rail

Addleshaw Goddard LLP

Norton Rose LLP

Agricultural Law Association

Lorraine Boyd

Jeanette Grenby

Professor Alan Gillett

255

Institute of Legal Executives

Wragge & Co LLP

The City of London Law Society

The London Property Support Lawyers Group

Amy Goymour (Downing College, University of Cambridge)

Nicholas Black

Herbert Smith LLP

Mary Curran

David Halpern QC (Barrister, 4 New Square Chambers)

Currey & Co

Valerie Masters

Treasury Solicitor's Bona Vacantia Division

Chorleywood Station Estate Conservation Group

William Shearer (Bidwells)

Nabarro

Churchfields Avenue Residents Association

Mangala Murali

Royal Institution of Chartered Surveyors

Property Litigation Association

National Federation of Property Professionals

Conveyancing and Land Law Committee of the Law Society

The Chancery Bar Association

Peter Bennett (University of Reading)

Kathy Pratt

Mr Justice Lewison

Dr Nicholas Roberts (Oxford Brookes University)

Dr Martin Dixon (Queens' College, University of Cambridge)

Dr Caroline Sawyer (Victoria University of Wellington, New Zealand)

Dr Joshua Getzler (St Hugh's College, University of Oxford)

Land Registry

The Lands Tribunal (now the Lands Chamber of the Upper Tribunal)

Michael Croker, Miriam Brown and Kevin Marsh

Inexus Group (Holdings) Ltd